third edition

MATHEMATICS OF MERCHANDISING

A. P. Kneider

Ryerson Polytechnical Institute
Toronto, Canada

Prentice-Hall, Inc., Englewood Cliffs, New Jersey 07632

Library of Congress Cataloging in Publication Data

Kneider, A. P. (Albert P.), (date)
    Mathematics of merchandising.

    1. Retail trade.   2. Merchandising.   3. Business
mathematics.   I. Title.
HF5429.K58 1986   658.8'001'51   84-26582
ISBN 0-13-563230-7   (pbk.)

Editorial/production supervision and
    interior design: Rick Laveglia and Lisa Halttunen
Cover design: Wanda Lubelska
Manufacturing buyer: Ed O'Dougherty

Printed in the United States of America

10   9   8   7   6   5   4   3   2   1

ISBN 0-13-563230-7   01

Prentice-Hall International (UK) Limited, *London*
Prentice-Hall of Australia Pty. Limited, *Sydney*
Editora Prentice-Hall do Brasil, Ltda., *Rio de Janeiro*
Prentice-Hall Canada Inc., *Toronto*
Prentice-Hall Hispanoamericana, S.A., *Mexico*
Prentice-Hall of India Private Limited, *New Delhi*
Prentice-Hall of Japan, Inc., *Tokyo*
Prentice-Hall of Southeast Asia Pte. Ltd., *Singapore*
Whitehall Books Limited, *Wellington, New Zealand*

Contents

Preface   v

Part I   **TERMS OF PURCHASE**   1

     1   Trade Discounts   3
     2   Cash Discounts and Dating   13
     3   Transportation Terms and Conditions   23

Part II   **CALCULATING MARKUP**   33

     4   Calculating Individual Markup   35
     5   Calculating Average Markup   51
     6   Determining Markup   79

Part III   **INVENTORY VALUATION**   109

     7   The Cost Method of Inventory Valuation   111
     8   The Retail Method of Inventory Valuation   125

9   Planning Turnover   143

10   Sales Planning   163

11   Stock Planning in Dollars   179

12   Planning Purchases—The Merchandise Plan   207

13   Planning Open-to-Buy Controls   227

14   Planning Model Stocks   245

APPENDIXES

285

A   The Operating Statement   287

B   Arithmetic Review   293

C   Mathematical Formulas for Retailers   299

D   Fractional Equivalents   301

E   Answers to Problems   303

Preface

This workbook outlines the basic mathematics involved in the operation of the retail enterprise, and has been designed to supplement the first course in retailing. Through its method of presentation it is also intended to be used by employees and management trainees, who may through self-instruction better understand the principles and techniques of mathematical concepts involved in the operation of retail stores.

After more than two decades of teaching retailing and marketing at the college level, the author has concluded that students are quicker to comprehend concepts when unnecessary and complicated calculations are avoided. With this in mind, the author's primary intention has been to provide the student or trainee with an understanding of the mathematical concepts of retailing without complicated arithmetical calculations. The application of computer technology and electronic calculators has simplified the mechanics of the problem-solving situations presented throughout the book.

These problem situations demonstrate practical decisions that must be made by retailing personnel to arrive at solutions. Merchandise managers, buyers, store managers, merchandise controllers, and independent merchants are faced with decisions that require mathematical computations. It will be readily evident that an understanding of the concepts presented is more important to these decision makers than is the mathematical computation.

The workbook has been designed to facilitate the instructor's presentation of material to achieve maximum understanding of the concepts. The author's classroom experience has revealed that this method of presentation reduces the amount of confusion encountered in solving business problems mathematically.

To accomplish the established objectives, this edition has been divided into four parts. Part I begins with a discussion of the terms of purchase that the merchant or buyer negotiates with suppliers in the acquisition of merchandise. Part II explores the relationships among types of markup that might be encountered by retail personnel in planning and achieving a predetermined profit goal. Part III examines the two methods of inventory valuation encountered by the merchandising operation in establishing its accountability of profit. And finally, the planning and control functions of the retail firm are explained in Part IV to illustrate the coordination of concepts presented throughout the book.

Each of these parts is divided into chapters that discuss aspects of the concepts under study. To facilitate the presentation of material, we have divided each chapter into three areas:

1. Problem types are introduced with sample examples that the instructor can solve with the students. A fully explained solution to the sample problem is given with each example. Students, employees, and management trainees consequently can use the book as a self-instruction manual.

2. After the example a problem is presented for the student to solve in the presence of the instructor or at his or her own pace.

3. At the end of the chapter a group of summary problems is presented to allow students and trainees to examine their understanding of the concepts presented.

To ensure that the student and trainee have grasped the concepts in each part of the workbook, a group of Review Problems is provided. The student is asked to solve these problems without referring to individual chapters and examples; this ensures that the solutions are understood rather than memorized.

Instructors are encouraged to supplement workbook assignments with additional merchandising theory to relate concepts to actual retailing experiences. Various charts and exhibits are provided to help instructors and students understand the concepts presented.

It is hoped that students and trainees will find the appendixes to the workbook useful in tieing together any loose ends. Appendix A briefly explains the retailer's operating statement, representing the results of the store's mathematical merchandising decisions. Appendix B reviews arithmetical calculations. Appendix C provides the reader with a formula summary used in the calculations, and Appendix D charts a table of fractional equivalents for selected percentages. Finally, Appendix E gives the answers to the problems in the workbook to measure the accuracy of the student's completed assignments. (*Students should note that their answers may vary slightly from those presented in the manual. These differences are generally due to the use of different methods for rounding off fractional portions of whole numbers. Students and instructors are asked to use their judgment regarding these variances.*)

The author wishes to express his thanks to his past and present students, who, perhaps unknowingly, have contributed to the most effective means of presenting these mathematical concepts.

A. P. Kneider

Toronto, Canada

part **I**

TERMS OF PURCHASE

Merchandising is said to be the process of acquiring the right merchandise, at the right price, in the right quantity, at the right time, and in the right place. In this process of purchasing merchandise for resale, retailers are constantly in the process of negotiating with suppliers for buying terms that will improve the profitability of the firm.

Consequently, an important aspect of the buying function of retailers involves the terms under which the goods are purchased. Frequently, these terms include a discount or other conditions that will induce the buyers to place orders with specific suppliers. It should be noted that these terms, which are negotiated between buyer and seller, may vary depending upon market conditions and will also vary from one trade to another. The standard terms of purchase that are found in the merchandising of shoes may in fact be significantly different from those negotiated between a hardware merchant and his supplier.

It is possible to combine rates of discount, dating, and other conditions into a wide variety of buying terms, but no attempt will be made here to discuss all the possible combinations. Only those terms and elements of the terms that occur with some frequency will be discussed. In our democratic system, the vendor may offer any terms he or she so wishes to a retailer, provided that such terms do not violate any statute of law and do not prove detrimental to the public's interest.[1]

For purposes of our discussion of the various terms of purchase available to the retailer, Part I of this book has been divided into trade discounts, cash discounts and dating, and shipping terms. The student will observe that all these aspects of the buying function of retail stores are vital in negotiating the profitable acquisition of merchandise.

These terms of purchase that have been negotiated between buyer and seller are defined on the purchase order and subsequently appear on the invoice that is received upon delivery of the

[1]Students who wish to investigate further the legal implications of granting terms of purchase should analyze the Robinson-Patman Act in the United States and the Combines Investigation Act in Canada. Both acts prohibit the seller from offering discriminatory terms to buyers.

goods to the store. The invoice confirms the following three areas of the terms of purchase that need to be negotiated:

1. Trade discount
2. Cash discounts and dating
3. Shipping terms

The remainder of this part explores the variations that may be found in each of these elements.

## chapter 1

Trade Discounts

Some sources of supply prefer to establish the prices at which the retailer may sell the merchandise. In the trade, these prices are referred to as the *suggested list price* (SLP) or suggested retail price (SRP) or *recommended selling price* (RSP). It should be pointed out at this stage that some countries and some sections of certain countries have made it illegal for the supplier to dictate the price at which the goods must be sold by the retailers. The law prohibiting such practices is known as the *resale price maintenance law*. As a result, in countries, states, or provinces where resale price maintenance is illegal, we almost always find the term "suggested" or "recommended" list price on the manufacturer's price list. Although resale price maintenance is illegal in some parts of the country, manufacturers have in some cases, through moral suasion and other techniques, been able to convince retailers that the merchandise should be sold at the retail price suggested.

Consequently, for those suppliers who operate from a suggested selling price, the method of determining the price the retailer will pay for the merchandise requires the establishment of a discount. It should be obvious that this will not be required by suppliers who quote wholesale prices rather than retail selling prices to potential retail buyers.

When the suggested list price is quoted, the price the retailer pays for the merchandise is determined by deducting from the list price a certain percentage called a *trade discount*. The resultant price, or price that the retailer pays for the merchandise, is known as the *net price*. It is this net price that becomes known as the merchant's cost price for the item.

Consider, for example, the merchant's cost for a crystal vase:

	Suggested List Price	$90.00
−	Trade Discount, 60%	54.00
=	Net Price, 40%	$36.00

In this case, the retailer will pay the supplier $36.00 for the crystal vase after receiving the trade discount of 40%.

Trade discounts are used in much of the retail industry. The actual percentage discount offered to the retailer, however, varies among the different trades in the industry and with respect to the quantities purchased. Wholesalers are normally offered larger trade discounts from the manufacturer than are retailers, and, by the same token, large retail chain stores and department store organizations may be offered a larger trade discount than are smaller independent retailers. The legality of this procedure of offering different discounts on the basis of size has been challenged with no clear-cut ruling emerging.

In some cases, the manufacturer may offer the retailer a discount of more than one percentage. For example, a retailer may be offered a discount of 40% off the suggested list price or may be given discounts of 25%, 10%, and 5% off the list price. Although the offering of these three discounts does sum to 40%, the manner in which the three discounts are applied does not give the same net price to the retailer:

EXAMPLE 1:

	Suggested List Price	$100.00
−	Trade Discount Offered, 40%	40.00
=	Net Price, 60%	$ 60.00

EXAMPLE 2: In this example the retailer is offered a trade discount of 25%, 10%, 5%. When a series discount of this nature is offered, each discount in the series is taken from the preceding net amount. Consequently,

Suggested List Price	$100.00
Trade Discount, 25%	25.00
Net Price, First	$ 75.00
Trade Discount, 10%	7.50
Net Price, Second	$ 67.50
Trade Discount, 5%	3.38
Net Price, Third	$ 64.12

Since each discount in the series is taken from the preceding net amount, it can be seen that the resulting net price is not the same in both examples and, consequently, that the series discount of 25%, 10%, 5% is not the same as a trade discount of 40%. This series discount in fact provides for a total discount of only 35.88%: ($25.00 + $7.50 + $3.38)/($100.00).

Manufacturers and other suppliers have attempted to use series discounts with various market conditions or on the basis of the bargaining power of large retailers. The retailer may have been offered a discount of 25% on the first order placed with a supplier and offered the additional discounts as a result of subsequent placings or reordering from the same supplier. Thus, series discounts have been used by suppliers to encourage repeat buying and establish some loyalty among the retail clients.

DEFINITIONS

List Price. This price is referred to as the manufacturer's suggested retail price and is in fact the price or dollar amount to which the trade discount is applied to obtain the retailer's net (cost) price.

Trade Discount. This discount represents the dealer's discount from the suggested list price of the manufacturer or supplier and is offered to both wholesalers and retailers. In cases where the buyer is also offered a cash discount for early payment of the invoice, the trade discount is always taken before the cash discount.

Series Discount. This discount represents the manufacturer's offering of more than one trade discount to a purchaser and is normally quoted as 25%, 10%, 5%. As noted earlier, each discount in the series discount is taken from the preceding net amount before applying the next discount.

Single-Discount Equivalent. This discount represents the equivalent of the series discount that is offered by the manufacturer and is expressed as a single percentage. As noted earlier, the single-discount equivalent of the series discount of 25%, 10%, 5% was calculated to be 35.88%. The purpose of obtaining the single-discount equivalent is to allow the buyer to compare his or her purchasing power within the trade and to allow for the planning of markup and profit.

Net Price. The net price represents the resultant figure after applying the trade discounts to the list price. It represents the retailer's cost price or the price that the buyer must pay for the merchandise that is being acquired for resale to the consumer.

On Percentage. This percentage represents the complement of the single-discount equivalent and is used to determine the net price when a series discount is used. The application of the on percentage to the suggested list price will immediately provide the net price to the buyer.

Quantity Discount. This represents a discount in dollars or in percentage on the basis that the buyer will purchase a given quantity of merchandise. While it is not usual for a buyer to be offered a trade discount and a quantity discount on the same purchase, it should be noted that if such occurs, the trade discount is taken before the quantity discount. Quantity discounts are normally allowed to retailers on the basis of purchases that are concentrated with a supplier over a period of time such as a season or a year.

EXAMPLE 1: Finding the Net Price When a Trade Discount is Offered

The manufacturer of a line of bone china figurines has a suggested list price for each figurine of $145.00. If the buyer is offered a trade discount of 40%, what will be the buyer's net price?

Solution:

By definition, the net price will be 60% of the list price since the buyer is offered a trade discount of 40%.

Therefore,

$$\$145.00 \times 60\%$$
$$\$145.00 \times .60 = \$87.00$$

PROBLEM 1: Determine the net price that a buyer will have to pay for a line of blankets that have a suggested list price of $75 if she is offered a trade discount of $33\frac{1}{3}$%.

$$\$75 \times 66.5\% = \$50.$$

EXAMPLE 2: Finding the Net Price When a Series Discount is Offered

Determine the net price on a line of pillowcases that will retail at $15 per pair if the linen buyer is offered a series discount of 30%, 10%, 5%.

Solution:

The net price for the pillowcases can be determined by applying the complements of the series discounts to the suggested list price of the manufacturer.

Therefore,

$$\$15.00 \times 70\% \times 90\% \times 95\% = \text{net price} = \$8.98$$

or

$$\$15.00 \times \frac{7}{10} \times \frac{9}{10} \times \frac{19}{20} = \text{net price} = \$8.98$$

Thus, the net price of the pillowcases will be $8.98 per pair.

PROBLEM 2: A manufacturer offers a retailer a line of skis that have a suggested list price of $180. In an effort to maintain good relations with the retailer, the buyer is offered a series discount of 30%, 20%, 10%. Find the net price of the skis if the buyer is offered the total series on this purchase.

$$\$180 \times 70\% \times 80\% \times 90\% = \$90.72$$

$$180 \times \frac{7}{10} \times \frac{8}{10} \times \frac{9}{10} =$$

EXAMPLE 3: Finding the Single-Discount Equivalent to a Series Discount

Determine the single-discount equivalent to the series discount of 30%, 10%, 5% that has been offered to the linen buyer.

Solution:

Let the list price equal 100%. Therefore,

$$\text{Net Price} = 100\% \times 70\% \times 90\% \times 95\%$$
$$= 100\% \times \frac{7}{10} \times \frac{9}{10} \times \frac{19}{20}$$
$$= 59.85\%$$

But list price % − net price % = single-discount equivalent. Therefore,

$$100\% - 59.85\% = 40.15\%$$
$$\text{Single-Discount Equivalent} = 40.15\%$$

PROBLEM 3: Calculate the single-discount equivalent of 30%, 20%, 5% offered to the ski buyer.

Net Price = $100% × 70% × 80% × 95% = 46.80

53.2%

100% − 53.2% = 46.80

EXAMPLE 4: Finding the On Percentage of a Series Discount

Find the on percentage of the series discount of 30%, 10%, 5% that was offered to the linen buyer.

Solution:

By definition, the on percentage is the complement of the single-discount equivalent. The calculation is simply the difference between the single-discount equivalent and 100% (list price).

$$\text{On Percentage} = 100\% - 40.15\%$$
$$= 59.85\%$$

PROBLEM 4: Determine the on percentage of the series discount of 30%, 20%, 10% offered to the ski buyer.

100% × 70% × 80% × 90% = 50.4%

100% − 50.4% = $49.60

100% − 49.60 = $50.40

EXAMPLE 5: Finding the List Price When the Net Price and Series Discount Are Given

A furniture buyer is able to purchase a dining room set from a manufacturer for $1,600 as a result of a series discount of 30%, 20%, 10%. Determine the price that the manufacturer would suggest as a retail selling price for this set.

Solution:

If we assume a list price of 100%, then

$$\text{Net Price} = 100\% \times 70\% \times 80\% \times 90\%$$
$$= 50.4\%$$

But

$$\text{Net Price} = \$1,600.00$$

Thus,

$$50.4\% = \$1,600.00$$

and,

$$1\% = \frac{\$1,600.00}{50.4} = \$31.75$$

But

$$\text{List Price} = 100\% = 100 \times \text{value of } 1\%$$
$$= 100 \times \$31.75$$
$$= \$3,175.00$$

PROBLEM 5: The same furniture buyer is able to purchase a less expensive dining room set from a different manufacturer that offers a series discount of 30%, 15%, 5%. After the series discount has been applied, the net price of the set is $819.00. Determine the suggested retail price for this dining room set. $1448.79

$$100\% \times 70\% \times 85\% \times 95\% = \$56.53$$

$$56.53\% = \$819.$$

$$1\% = \frac{819}{56.53} = \$1448.79$$

SUMMARY PROBLEMS

1. The suggested list price of a line of men's attaché cases has been quoted as $115.00 to a buyer of Studio One Men's Apparel, with a series discount of 30%, 20%, 15% being offered. Determine the net price of these cases and the single-discount equivalent of this series discount.

$$\$115 \times 70\% \times 80\% \times 85\% = \$54.74$$

$$\$115 - \$54.74 = \$60.26$$

$$\$115 - 60.26 = \$54.74$$

52.4%

2. A manufacturer of a line of hockey equipment has offered a series discount of 30%, 20% on a quality line of hockey sticks that will retail at $22.50 each. Find the net price of the sticks for the buyer.

$$\$22.50 \times 70\% \times 80\% = \$12.60$$

3. Mattar's Furniture Emporium was able to purchase a line of bedroom sets from a manufacturer at a net price of $803.25 after a series discount of 30%, 15%, 10% has been applied. Determine the suggested list price for one of these bedroom sets. $500

$$100\% \times 70\% \times 85\% \times 90\% = 53.55$$

$$53.55 = \$803.25$$

$$1\% = \frac{803.25}{53.55} =$$

4. Find the on percentage for the two buyers in Summary Problems 1 and 3.

1. 47.6%

$$100 \times 70\% \times 80\% \times 85\% = 47.6\%$$

2. 53.55%

$$100 \times 70\% \times 85\% \times 90\% = 53.55\%$$

5. The buyer of Susan's Fashions purchased an assortment of merchandise for $2,105 from a manufacturer that had offered a series discount of 35%, 15%, 5%. Determine the suggested retail selling price of this merchandise if the series discount has been applied to the purchase.

$4010.29

$$100 \times 65\% \times 85\% \times 95\% = 52.49$$

$$52.49 = \$2105$$

$$1\% = \frac{2105}{52.49} = \$4010.29$$

6. A sporting goods store wishes to celebrate its anniversary by offering special promotional items to its customers. One of the store's suppliers has offered the merchant a line of body-building equipment that will retail at $6,400. To assist in the anniversary promotion, he is allowing a series discount of 55%, 10%. Determine the net price of the equipment to the retailer.

$$\$6400 \times 45\% \times 90\% = \$2,592$$

7. Determine the net price of a 40-piece set of English bone china that a merchant offers at $480.00 if the supplier gives the store a series discount of 30%, 20%, 10%. What is the single-discount equivalent of this series discount? What is the on percentage?

a) 241.92
b) 49.6%
c) 50.4%

a) $480 \times 70\% \times 80\% \times 90\% = $241.92
$480 - $241.92 = 238.08

c) $100\% \times 70\% \times 80\% \times 90\% = 50.4\%$

b) $100\% - 50.4\% = 49.6\%$

8. A supplier of bicycles attempts to encourage retailers to place larger orders by offering an additional 10% discount on orders of more than 12 units. The standard discount offered by the supplier is 40%, 10% on the suggested list price of the $130.00 unit. If a retailer wishes to purchase 20 bicycles, what will be the cost price per unit on the basis of the information given?

9. Calculate the single-discount equivalent of a chain discount of 35%, 15%, 5%. If this discount is being offered to a merchant wishing to purchase an item with a list price of $1,200, calculate the net price of the item.

2
chapter

Cash Discounts and Dating

The usual objective of granting a cash discount is to offer the retailer a premium for paying promptly. When credit terms are extended by the vendors, this premium then is granted for immediate payment or for payment in advance of a specified time. Such discounts are in effect interest payments made by the vendor in exchange for settlement of an obligation in advance of the due date.

The cash discount term consists of three elements and might be expressed as 2/10, n/30:

1. *A percentage discount*, usually varying from 1% upward
2. *A period of time* in which the discount may be taken, often 10 days
3. *A net period*, indicating the date by which the full amount is due and payable

Hence the cash discount of 2/10, n/30 means that the vendor will allow the purchaser a cash discount of 2% from the invoice amount if paid within 10 days, and the net (n) amount is due to the vendor within 30 days.

It is usually advisable for the retailer to take advantage of the cash discount terms offered by the vendor since the savings over a period of time can be quite substantial. Normally, the equivalent annual rates of interest involved in cash discounts are almost always substantially in excess of the cost of borrowing money at a bank for a retailer with a good credit rating.

For example, the terms "2/10, n/30" represent an annual rate of interest of 36.5%. Since the invoice payment is due in 30 days and the 2% cash discount is allowed if payment is made within 10 days, the 2% discount is then being allowed for 20 days' prepayment. With 365 days in the year, the 20-day prepayment in fact represents 1/18.25 (365/20) of the total year. Therefore, the 2% discount represents the equivalent annual interest rate of 36.5%—that is, 18.25 periods multiplied by 2% for each period. It is apparent, therefore, that a merchant can gain by taking advantage of this discount, even though he or she may find it necessary to borrow money to do so.

In the explanation of the cash discount, reference has been made to the fact that a discount will be allowed if the invoice is paid within a certain period of time. However, no mention has been made of the date on which the discount period is to begin. The process by which the manufacturer and the retailer agree with regard to the beginning of the discount date is referred to as dating. Therefore, it is essential that the retailer specify when placing the order and establishing the terms whether the dating will be with regard to the date of invoice, the date of the receipt of goods, or the date represented by the end of the month. As a result, the date on which the discount period begins varies considerably, as does the length of time for which the discount may be taken. The student should note that the physical counting of the days for determining the due date of the cash discount period and the net amount commences on the day following that specified in the buying terms. Consequently, if we negotiate terms of 2/10, n/30 and the dating begins with the date of invoice that might be June 10, the actual counting of the days begins on June 11.

DEFINITIONS

Cash Discount.   A discount allowed to the purchaser for immediate payment or for payment within a specified period of time. The cash discount is calculated on the basis of the invoice cost and, as a result, is applied after the trade discount.

D.O.I. (Date of Invoice, Ordinary Dating).   Terms established with D.O.I. dating indicate that the discount period for the prepayment of the invoice and the due date of the net amount begins with the day following the date of invoice. When dating has not been specified, it is always assumed to be D.O.I. dating.

R.O.G. (Receipt of Goods).   Terms established with R.O.G. dating indicate that all discounts and the net amount of the invoice begins after the date established as the receipt of the merchandise. Such terms allow for delays in the transportation of the merchandise from the source.

E.O.M. (End of Month).   Terms established with E.O.M. dating indicate that the invoice is to be paid within the designated number of days after the end of the month in which the goods were shipped. To allow for goods shipped late in the month, an invoice dated after the twenty-fifth of the month is considered to be dated as the first of the following month. As a result, some firms seek to indicate this dating as "ff," signifying "first of the following" month.

Advance Dating.   Terms that allow for advance dating indicate that the invoice has been postdated to allow for the shipment of merchandise. The purpose of such dating is to allow additional time in which payment can be made and the cash discount taken.

Extra Dating.   Terms that allow for extra dating indicate that the vendor will allow extra or additional time for the purchaser to take the cash discount. In such cases a buyer may be offered 2/10–60X, n/90, which means that he or she is allowed to take the discount for 70 days with the net amount due in 90 days. The terms are written in this manner rather than 2/70, n/90 to show that this is a special bonus rather than standard buying terms.

Anticipation.   With extra or advance dating, an additional discount is allowed to induce merchants to pay the invoice in advance of the expiration date of the discount period. The discount normally allowed for anticipation is the current annual rate of interest and is calculated on the number of days remaining between the date of payment and the last date for which the cash discount is allowed.

Net Period.   This date represents the length of time beyond the cash discount date that the retailer is allowed to make full payment of the invoice. In cases where the net period is not designated, it is normally assumed to be 20 days after the cash discount date. If no cash discount is allowed, the net amount is assumed to be due in 30 days. If payment has not been made by the end of the net period, then the amount owing may be subject to an interest charge by the vendor.

Net Terms. Terms designated as net indicate that the manufacturer is not allowing a cash discount and that the invoice amount will be due at the expiration of the net period.

EXAMPLE 1: Finding the Invoice Payments with a Cash Discount and D.O.I. Dating

A retail merchant of sporting goods has received an invoice of $800 dated June 10 with terms of 2/10, n/30 D.O.I. Indicate the alternative payment dates for this invoice.

Solution:

(a) If paid on or before June 20, the buyer is entitled to take the cash discount and would then pay

$$\$800 - (2\% \text{ of } \$800) = \$800 - \$16 = \$784$$

(b) If paid on or between June 21 and July 10, the net amount of $800 will be due, after which an interest charge may be levied.

PROBLEM 1: Indicate the various alternatives available to a retailer who has received an invoice in the amount of $1,000 with terms of 3/10, n/30 D.O.I. if the invoice is dated January 15.

a) If paid on or before Jan 25 $970 $1000 - (3% of 1000) = $970,   1000 - 30 = $970.

b) If paid on or between Jan 26 and Feb 14, pay full amount $1,000. after which it can be subject to an interest change.

EXAMPLE 2: Finding the Invoice Payments with a Cash Discount and R.O.G. Dating

Indicate the alternatives available to a merchant for payment of an invoice of $875 dated April 4 if the merchandise was received on April 20 and the supplier has offered terms of 2/10, n/30 R.O.G.

Solution:

(a) If the merchant elects to pay the invoice on or before April 30, deduct the cash discount of 2% of $875, which will be $17.50, and pay

$$\$875.00 - \$17.50 = \$857.50$$

(b) If paid on or between May 1 and May 20, the net amount of $875 is due, after which the merchant may be subjected to an interest charge.

PROBLEM 2: An invoice dated November 9 has been received by a hardware merchant for the amount of $500. The merchant observes that the terms of purchase as indicated on the invoice are 3/10, n/30 R.O.G. If the merchandise was received by the store on November 15, indicate the alternatives available to the merchant for paying the invoice.

a) If paid on or before Nov. 25, pay $485
$500 (3% of $500) = $485

b) If paid on or between Nov 26 and Dec. 15, pay full amount of $500 after which it could be subject of a change of interest

EXAMPLE 3: Finding the Invoice Payments with a Cash Discount and E.O.M. Dating

Indicate the alternatives available to a buyer in making payments for an invoice dated November 3 in the amount of $400 with terms of 3/10 E.O.M.

Solution:

(a) If the invoice is paid on or before December 10 (10 days after the end of the month), deduct the amount of the cash discount of $12.00 (3% of 400) and pay

$$\$400.00 - \$12.00 = \$388.00$$

(b) If paid on or between December 11 and December 30, the full amount of $400 is due. While we have not specified n/30 in the buying terms, the net amount is normally due 20 days after the last discount date.

PROBLEM 3: A men's furnishings retailer received an invoice dated April 11 in the amount of $2,700. As a result of previous negotiations with the manufacturer, the retailer was offered terms of 2/10, n/30 E.O.M. Indicate the alternatives available for paying this invoice.

a) If paid on or before May 10 = $2646.
2700 - (2% x 2700) = $2646
$ 54

b) If paid on or between May 11 and May 30, pay full amount of $2700 after which it could be subject of a change of interest

EXAMPLE 4: Finding the Invoice Payments with a Cash Discount and E.O.M. Dating After the Twenty-fifth of the Month

What alternatives are available to a merchant for payment of an invoice dated July 26 in the amount of $900 with terms of 2/10, n/30 E.O.M.?

Solution:

As noted in the definition of E.O.M. dating, invoices dated after the twenty-fifth of the month should be considered as dated at the first of the following month. Consequently, in this example, dating would read August 1:

(a) If paid on or before September 10 (10 days from the end of the month of August), the discount of 2% of $900, or $18.00, can be taken, and the buyer would remit

$$\$900.00 - \$18.00 = \$882.00$$

(b) If paid on or between September 11 and September 30, the net amount of $900 is due and payable, after which the merchant may be subject to an interest charge.

PROBLEM 4: Indicate the alternatives available to a retailer who has received an invoice of $1,500 dated March 27. The terms of payment as specified on the invoice indicate 3/10, n/30 E.O.M.

a) If paid on or before May 10

$$\$1500 \ (3\% \times \$1500) = \$1455.$$
$$- \quad \$45$$

b) If paid on or between May 11 and May 30, Net amount of $1500 is due and payable, after which the merchant may be subject To an interest charge

EXAMPLE 5: **Finding the Invoice Payments with a Cash Discount and Advance Dating**

As a result of advance purchasing by a toy retailer, the vendor has shipped merchandise to him on April 3 but has postdated the invoice 60 days to June 2. If the invoice is in the amount of $1,600, indicate the alternative payment schedule for the retailer, with terms of 2/10, n/30:

Solution:

(a) Since the invoice has been postdated to June 2, the dating begins at this date. Therefore, if paid on or before June 12, the buyer is then allowed the cash discount of $32 and will then remit

$$\$1,600.00 - \$32.00 = \$1,568.00$$

(b) If paid on or between June 13 and July 2, the net amount of $1,600 will be due, after which the merchant may be subject to an interest charge.

PROBLEM 5: On March 7, a merchant received merchandise in the amount of $600. However, because of previous arrangements with the supplier to take possession earlier than required, the supplier postdated the invoice to May 6 and offered terms 3/10, n/30. Indicate the alternatives available to the merchant in the payment of this invoice.

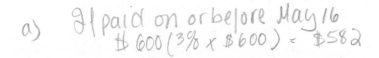

a) If paid on or before May 16
$$\$600 \ (3\% \times \$600) = \$582$$

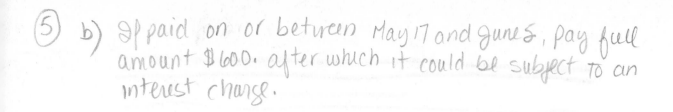

b) If paid on or between May 17 and June 5, pay full amount $600. after which it could be subject to an interest charge.

EXAMPLE 6: **Finding the Invoice Payments with a Cash Discount and Extra Dating**

In an effort to allow a retailer additional time to take advantage of the cash discount, a manufacturer has offered the merchant terms of 2/10–60X, n/90 on an invoice dated September 10 in the amount of $750. Indicate the alternatives available to the merchant in payment of this invoice.

Solution:

(a) If the invoice is paid on or before November 19 (70 days after the invoice date), the discount of $15 can be taken and the merchant will remit $750 – $15 or $735.

(b) If paid on or between November 20 and December 9 (90 days after September 10), the full amount is due, after which the merchant may be subject to an interest charge on the $750.00.

PROBLEM 6: Indicate the alternatives available to a merchant who has received an invoice dated August 12 in the amount of $1,200 with terms of 3/10–30X, n/60.

a) If paid on or before Sept 21
$$\$1200\left(3\% \times \$1200\right) = \$1164$$
$$- \$36$$

b) If paid on or between Sept 2 and Oct 11, pay full amount after which it could be subject to an interest charge.

EXAMPLE 7: **Finding the Invoice Payments with a Cash Discount and an Allowance for Anticipation**

In an effort to capitalize on his ability to pay, a merchant has established with a supplier that he be awarded an additional 10% for anticipation as a result of pre-payment. On May 5, the merchant received an invoice in the amount of $1,200 with terms of 2/10–60X. Indicate the payment to be made by the retailer on May 15 as a result of the anticipation allowed by the manufacturer.

Solution:

The retailer is allowed the 2% cash discount ($24.00) since he will certainly be paying the invoice within the allotted time and only 10 days after the date of invoice.

The net amount then due would be

$$\$1,200.00 - \$24.00 = \$1,176.00$$

However, the retailer is allowed to withhold payment for another 60 days and has been granted an additional 10% discount as a result of anticipation, which is based on an annual rate of interest.

Therefore, since the retailer is paying 60 days in advance, he is allowed to deduct the anticipation for this time period. Since the anticipation discount of 10% is based on the year of 365 days and he is prepaying 60 days in advance, he would find the following payment for May 15:

$$\$1,176.00 \times \frac{10}{100} \times \frac{60}{365} = \$19.33 \text{ (anticipation)}$$

Therefore, the payment on May 15 = \$1,176.00 − \$19.33 = \$1,156.67

PROBLEM 7: Indicate the payment that should be made by a retailer on June 26 for merchandise in the amount of $500 with the invoice dated June 16. The manufacturer has allowed the merchant terms of 2/10–60X and has provided for 11% anticipation.

$$\$500 \underbrace{(2\% \times \$500)}_{\$10} = \$490$$

$$\$490 \times \frac{11}{100} \times \frac{60}{365} = \$8.86$$

$$\$481.14$$

SUMMARY PROBLEMS

1. An invoice in the amount of $2,400 with terms of 2/10–30X, n/60 R.O.G. has been received by Madeline's Gifts. If the merchandise was received on April 21 but the invoice was dated April 16, indicate the choices available to the retailer in paying the invoice.

a) If paid on or before May 31, pay $2352.

$$\$2400 \underbrace{-(2\% \times \$2400)}_{\$48} = \$2352$$

b) If paid on or between June 1 and June 20, pay full amount.

2. Claudette's Cleaning Service has received an invoice dated June 6 in the amount of $675 with terms of 1/10–30X, n/60. Indicate the alternatives available to the merchant for payment of the invoice.

a) If paid on or before July 16
$$\$675 - (1\% \times \$675) = $$
$$6.75 \qquad \$668.25$$

b) If paid on or between July 17 and August 5, pay full amount – – – – .

3. Olga's Lingerie Boutique has received on October 10 an invoice in the amount of $1,600 showing terms of 1/10, n/30 E.O.M. Specify the alternatives that are available to the merchant for paying the invoice.

a) If paid on or before Nov 10
$$\$1600 - (1\% \times \$1600) = \$1584$$
$$\$16$$

b) If paid on or between Nov 11 and Nov 30, pay full amount – – – – –

4. A publisher of children's books has offered terms of 2/10–30X, n/60 with anticipation of 9% to Yolanda's Book Boutique. What payment should be made on an invoice for $1,700 dated October 23 and paid on November 2?

$$\$1700 (2\% \times 1700) = \$1666$$
$$- \$34$$

$$\$1666 \times \frac{9}{100} \times \frac{60}{365} = \$24.64$$

$$\$1666 - \$24.64 = \$1641.36$$

5. Indicate the payment schedule for John's Equipment Rentals for an invoice dated July 27 in the amount of $2,300 with terms of 2/10–30X, n/60 E.O.M.

If paid on or before October 10
$2,300 (2% x 2300) = $2254
$46

If paid on or between Oct 11 and Oct 30, pay full amount.

_____

6. Calculate the payment to be made on February 20 for an invoice received by Camille's Collectibles in the amount of $1,900 with terms of 1/10–30X, n/90 if the invoice is dated February 9 and anticipation of 12% has been negotiated.

$1900 (1% x $1900) = $1881
$19

$1881 x $\frac{12}{100}$ x $\frac{60}{365}$ =

7. Determine the payment that should be made on August 26 by Andrew's Sporting Goods for merchandise in the amount of $2,800 with an invoice dated August 16 and terms of 3/10–60X and 9% anticipation.

8. A buyer of a ladies' sportswear department has received an invoice dated April 23 for merchandise for the spring-summer season. In negotiating the terms of purchase with the manufacturer, a series discount of 35%, 25% and terms of 2/10, n/30 R.O.G. was agreed upon. If the merchandise valued at retail at $1,800 was received by the store on April 28, determine the amount that should be paid to the supplier on May 6.

chapter 3

Transportation Terms and Conditions

An important aspect of the buying function for retail stores that is associated with the negotiating of trade discounts, cash discounts, and dating is also the element of transportation charges and handling responsibilities. In this process of negotiating with the supplier for the best buying terms, the following issues with regard to the transportation terms and conditions must be considered by the retailer.

1. Who will pay for the transportation charges for the merchandise from the supplier to its destination? *The payer.*
2. Who will ultimately be responsible for these transportation charges regardless of who pays? *The bearer.*
3. Where does the transfer of title take place in the transportation of the merchandise? *The owner.*
4. Who is responsible for filing claims in the event of loss or damage to the merchandise in transit? *The insured.*

In this explanation, it should be noted that the party physically paying for the transportation charges (*the payer*) and the party responsible (*the bearer*) for the charges may not be one and the same. The supplier may pay the shipping charges to the carrier but in fact may charge back this amount to the retailer by adding it to the merchandise invoice. In this case, the supplier will pay the transportation charges (*the payer*), but the retailer will in fact be responsible for the charges (*the bearer*).

It is also important to delineate the point at which the title to the merchandise is transferred from the supplier to the retailer. The party that in fact has title to the merchandise while in transit is the party responsible for insuring the merchandise above any coverage provided by the carrier. The title transfer will also determine which party will be responsible for reporting and collecting any claims from the carrier for damage or loss of the merchandise.

The term that is frequently used in shipping merchandise from supplier to retailer is that designated as F.O.B. (free on board). This shipping term signifies that the vendor or shipper retains title and pays all charges to the F.O.B. point. Consequently, the F.O.B. point is critical, since it determines the point of ownership transfer, the responsibility for transportation charges, and damage to merchandise while in transit.

The transportation terms in the definitions that follow outline the basic classification of F.O.B. points that might be available between supplier and retailer. It should be noted that the retailer may wish to be more specific in clarifying the actual F.O.B. point by using terms such as store, plant, factory, and warehouse and, in some cases, using a physical address for the destination point.

DEFINITIONS

F.O.B. Origin, Freight Collect.   In this situation, the retailer bears total responsibility for paying the transportation charges, for taking title to the merchandise while in transit, and consequently for filing any claims against the carrier. Once the merchandise leaves the supplier's shipping point, the retailer assumes no responsibility. The carrier will collect the transportation charges for the shipment on delivery to the merchant.

F.O.B. Origin, Freight Prepaid.   As in the preceding case, the retailer accepts title to the merchandise while it is in transit and consequently bears responsibility for filing claims against the carrier. However, since the freight is prepaid, the supplier will be responsible for paying the transportation charges to the carrier prior to shipment and will not be charging the retailer the freight costs.

F.O.B. Origin, Freight Prepaid and Charged Back.   This situation is identical to F.O.B. origin, freight prepaid, except that the freight is paid by the supplier to the carrier but in fact is charged back to the retailer by adding it to the invoice. Consequently, the supplier physically pays the transportation charges, but all other responsibilities rest with the retailer.

F.O.B. Destination, Freight Collect.   Since destination refers to the point at which the merchandise is being delivered, in this situation, the retailer will pay the freight charges when delivered and will also bear the responsibility for the charges. However, the title will remain with the supplier in transit as will the responsibility for filing claims against the carrier.

F.O.B. Destination, Freight Prepaid.   In this shipping situation, the supplier accepts all responsibility. The supplier will in fact pay the freight charges to the destination and will not be charging these back to the retailer. In addition, the supplier retains title to the merchandise while in transit and is responsible for filing claims against the carrier.

TRANSPORTATION TERMS AND CONDITIONS

	The Payer	The Bearer	The Owner in Transit	The Insured in Transit
F.O.B. origin, freight collect	Retailer	Retailer	Retailer	Retailer
F.O.B. origin, freight prepaid	Supplier	Supplier	Retailer	Retailer
F.O.B. origin, freight prepaid and charged back	Supplier	Retailer	Retailer	Retailer
F.O.B. destination, freight collect	Retailer	Retailer	Supplier	Supplier
F.O.B. destination, freight prepaid	Supplier	Supplier	Supplier	Supplier
F.O.B. destination, freight collect and allowed	Retailer	Supplier	Supplier	Supplier

F.O.B. Destination, Freight Collect and Allowed. Under these terms and conditions, the retailer will physically pay for the transportation when the merchandise is delivered to the destination. However, these charges are then deducted from the invoice amount since the supplier is allowing the retailer the freight charges. Consequently, the supplier then will also retain title to the merchandise while in transit and will also be responsible for filing claims for damage or loss with the carrier.

EXAMPLE 1: The foregoing definitions indicate the various alternatives that are available to the retailer in negotiating transportation terms and conditions. Since each is self-explanatory, the following problems are presented for solution by the student without the benefit of an example.

PROBLEM 1: Jenny's Fashion Boutique in the city of Hamilton has received a shipment of merchandise from Highland Sportswear, Inc., of Ottawa. The transportation charges for the items were $79.90. If the terms negotiated by Jenny's indicate F.O.B. destination, freight collect, outline the responsibilities that the Fashion Boutique and Highland Sportswear each holds.

R- Payer   S -owner
R- bearer   S- Insured

PROBLEM 2: James Sporting Goods in Whitby has received a shipment of ice skates from Bauer's in Oakville with transportation charges of $68.00. The supplier has agreed to terms of F.O.B. origin, freight prepaid. Indicate who—the supplier or the retailer—is responsible for paying the freight charges to the carrier and who is responsible for making any claims to the carrier for two pairs of damaged skates.

R- owner   S-Payer
R- Insured   S bearer

Retailer claimed damages

PROBLEM 3: Lyn's Home Decorating in Shannonville has received a shipment of decorator cushions from Riviera, Inc. of New York. If the buyer has negotiated terms of F.O.B. Shannonville, freight collect, who is responsible for the freight charges of $57.80? Who is responsible for claiming the loss of six of these cushions in transit?   claimed Supplier

S owner   R- Payer
S Insured   R- Bearer

PROBLEM 4: A purchase order shows the following information:

R Buyer: Rosemary Leather Goods, Inc., Cameron, N.J.
S Vendor: Frosty Luggage, Inc., Cookstown, N.Y.
   Shipping terms: F.O.B. Cookstown, freight prepaid → *origin*
   Freight charge: Cookstown to Cameron, $78.80

(a) Who will pay the freight charge of $78.80? *Frosty Luggage Inc.*

(b) Who is responsible for the freight charge? *Frosty Luggage Inc.*

(c) When does Rosemary Leather Goods take title? *At point of origin or shipping - cookstown*

(d) Who claims for damage against the carrier? *Rosemary Leather Goods*

SUMMARY PROBLEMS

1. Jonathan's Hardware in Minden has negotiated terms of 2/10, n/30 D.O.I. with transportation of F.O.B. origin, freight prepaid and charged back with Spectrum Paints, Inc., of Caistorville. Explain to the assistant buyer at Jonathan's what the buying terms and the shipping terms imply with regard to the responsibilities of the store.

a) *2% cash discount is allowed if invoice is paid within 10days from the date of invoice and the net amount is due within 30days from the date of invoice.*

b) *The freight charge from Caistorville to Minden are to be paid by spectrum Paints, Inc., but will be charged back to Jonathan's Hardware. Retailer will have ownership & responsibility for insurance while in transit.*

2. Supplier/Vendor: Andrew's Building Supplies, Inc., Toronto
   Retailer/Buyer: Papp's Home Center, Woodstock
   Shipping Terms: F.O.B. destination, freight collect and allowed
   Buying Terms: 2/10, n/30 R.O.G.
   Freight Charge: $89.90

Explain the implications to Papp's Home Center with regard to the transactions completed with Andrew's Building Supplies, Inc., with regard to the shipping and buying negotiations.

Shipping terms imply Papp's home Centre will pay freight charges $89.90 To the carrier; subsequently deduct this amount from the invoice from the supplier, Andrew Building Supplies, Inc. which retain ownership and insurance responsibility while in transit.

b) 2% is allowed if the invoice is paid within 10 days from receipt of good and net amount is due within 30 days from the receipt of good.

3. A buyer for a chain of retail stores specializing in kitchen accessories has asked its suppliers to ship all merchandise to its central warehouse. The organization subsequently divides the shipment and allocates it to each of the units in the chain. The chain store operates on the policy that the supplier is required to pay all transportation charges to its warehouse while the chain will be responsible for getting the items to all stores in the chain. Indicate the transportation terms and conditions that the buyer must negotiate with all suppliers.

F.O.B warehouse freight Prepaid

4. Supplier/Vendor: Allison Gift Center, Clearwater
   Retailer/Buyer: Samantha's Gifts, Albany
   Freight Charges: $128.00
   Freight Terms: F.O.B. destination, freight collect and allowed
   Invoice Amount: $2,160.00
   Buying Terms: 2/10, n/30 D.O.I.
   Date of Invoice: February 28

(a) Explain the meaning of the freight terms that have been negotiated between Allison Gift Center and Samantha's Gifts.

Samantha's Gifts will pay the transportation charges $128. To the carrier, subsequently deduct this from the amount with the supplier; Allison Gift Center is responsible for insurance and ownership in transit.

(b) What payment should be made by Samantha's Gifts to Allison on March 5 with regard to this invoice and shipment of merchandise?

$2160 (2% x 2160) = 2116.80
*   43.20*

2116.80 - 128 = 1988.80

Review Problems for Chapters 1, 2, and 3

To ensure an understanding of the concepts presented, solve the problems that follow without referring back to the previous chapters. The workspace for each question has purposely been eliminated so that you may review the problems without the solutions being readily available.

1. On March 26, the buyer of a gift department receives an invoice in the amount of $1,800 at the suggested list prices of the manufacturer. The invoice shows terms of 2/10, n/30 E.O.M. In addition, the manufacturer indicates that the buyer has been allowed a trade discount of 45%. Indicate the alternatives available to the buyer for making payments on the invoice.

   If paid on or before May 10

2. The buyer of men's furnishings has negotiated terms of 3/10, n/30 D.O.I. with one of her suppliers. In addition the supplier is offering the buyer a series discount of 30%, 20% and will apply this discount on her present purchase of $1,600 at suggested list prices. If the invoice is dated June 5, indicate the various alternatives the buyer has available in paying this invoice.

3. The shoe department of a large retail establishment has established 11% as its rate of anticipation allowance and instructs all buyers to negotiate this as part of any purchase from suppliers. If a buyer is able to obtain these terms from a manufacturer, indicate what payment should be made on August 4 for an invoice dated July 25 in the amount of $14,000 and bearing terms of 2/10–60X, n/90.

4. A buyer of ladies blouses has contracted with a supplier to purchase 15 dozen of a particular style that lists at $40 each. A series discount of 30%, 20%, 10% is offered by the manufacturer and is to be applied on this purchase. The supplier has also indicated he is prepared to provide transportation terms on this shipment of F.O.B. destination, freight prepaid.

   (a) Find the net price of the invoice.

   (b) Find the single-discount equivalent of the series discount.

   (c) Find the on percentage from the series discount.

   (d) Explain the responsibilities under the transportation terms.

5. A manufacturer offers a buyer merchandise at $3,500 at suggested list prices with a trade discount of 40% and buying terms of 1/10, n/30 E.O.M. If the invoice is dated May 30, indicate the net price of the goods if the merchant wishes to pay the invoice on July 8.

6. On November 26, a buyer of sporting goods received an invoice in the amount of $2,800 at suggested retail prices for merchandise that had been purchased for the Christmas selling season. Information on the invoice shows a trade discount of 45% has been allowed as well as terms of 3/10, n/30 E.O.M. On the basis of this information, determine the alternatives available to the buyer for making payments on this invoice.

7. A buyer of a fashion department has received an invoice dated April 23 for merchandise for the spring-summer season. In negotiating terms of purchase with the supplier, the buyer and supplier agreed to a series discount of 25%, 15%, 5% and terms of 2/10, n/30 R.O.G. If merchandise valued at $1,900 at retail was received by the store on April 28 for which freight charges were paid by the retailer of $69.90, suggest the alternatives that the buyer of the fashion department has for paying the invoice. The invoice also indicates transportation terms of F.O.B. destination, freight collect and allowed.

8. A gift department received merchandise valued at $850 at suggested list prices on December 31 for a special promotion during the month of January. If the invoice is also dated December 31 and shows a trade discount of 30%, 20%, 10% with terms of 3/10, n/30 D.O.I., indicate the alternatives available to the store in payment of the invoice.

9. A departmental supervisor is analyzing the results of her buyers' negotiations with the store's suppliers. On June 24, the buyer of notions received merchandise valued at $1,600 at suggested list prices that carried a trade discount of 37.5%. The date of invoice on this purchase is indicated as June 22. As part of the analysis, you are required to determine the last date possible for taking the cash discount under each of the following conditions and the net amount to be remitted to the supplier:

(a) 2/10, n/30 D.O.I.

(b) 2/10, n/30 R.O.G.

(c) 2/10, n/30 E.O.M.

(d) 2/10-60X, 9% anticipation; 50 days anticipation

10. A Los Angeles retailer received an invoice from a New York manufacturer for merchandise valued at $7,800 at suggested list prices and dated June 10 showing terms of 3/10, n/30 R.O.G., a trade discount of 40%, and transportation terms of F.O.B. origin, freight prepaid. The merchandise was 14 days in transit, and six items were damaged en route.

(a) When does the invoice have to be paid to earn the cash discount?

(b) What is the amount of the remittance if payment was made on the last day of the discount period?

(c) Who will be responsible for filing a claim with the carrier for the six damaged items?

(d) Who is responsible for paying the shipping charges from New York to Los Angeles?

11. On June 10, Morgan Brooke, the buyer of sportswear for the Colony Department Store, wishes to place an order with Jillian-Kate Fashions of 456 Spadina Road in Toronto, Ontario, Canada. As in the past, the supplier offers terms of 2/10, n/30 E.O.M., F.O.B. destination, freight prepaid. The following items will need to be ordered with the size distribution as indicated:

Colony Stock No.	Supplier Stock No.	Description	Quantity Ordered (dozen)	Cost per Dozen
A 530	K 119	J-shirts	10	$144.00
A 415	K 207	T-tops	15	120.00
A 481	K 319	Turtleneck tops	9	180.00
A 3069	K 366	Boatneck tops	12	192.00

The size distribution of the items to be ordered is as follows:

A 530: Small (20%), medium (50%), large (30%)
A 415: Small (25%), medium (50%), large (25%)

COLONY DEPARTMENT STORES.

STREET ADDRESS _____
Ship to above address unless otherwise stated.

CITY & PROVINCE _____

SOURCE NAME & ADDRESS _____

RETAIL SALES TAX PERMIT 96130776

— PURCHASE ORDER —

R 187089

DETACH AT PERFORATION BEFORE MAILING

Write Clearly

| | Store No. | Store Event |
Div. No.

SHOW ALL ABOVE NOS. ON ALL INVOICES, CASES, PACKING SLIPS, BILLS OF LADING AND CORRESPONDENCE

THIS SECTION FOR RETAIL USE ONLY. NOT TO BE SENT TO SUPPLIER

Date of order | Ship on.

Authorized Signature _____

SHIPPING INSTRUCTIONS:

INSURANCE OR DECLARED VALUE

Shipment
Complete ☐ Partial ☐

TERMS: | TRADE-DISCOUNT | F.O.B. | TRANSPORTATION ALLOWANCE

Colony Stock No.	Mfg. Stock No.	Description	Size → Color →								Order Quantity	Buying Unit	Cost Price		Unit Selling	Selling Unit	Markup

CANADIAN SUPPLIERS: –

MAIL INVOICE SAME DAY MERCHANDISE SHIPPED ALONG WITH SHIPPING RECEIPT DIRECT TO RETAIL STORE SHOWN ABOVE'

UNITED STATES SUPPLIERS: –

DO NOT MAIL M.A. INVOICES DIRECT TO RETAIL STORES, REFER TO ATTACHED INSTRUCTION SHEET "HOW TO COMPLETE CANADIAN CUSTOMS FORM M.A."

TOTAL SELLING
$ | ¢

| A 481: | Small (20%), medium (40%), large (30%), X-large (10%) |
| A 3069: | 7-8 (10%), 9-10 (15%), 11-12 (15%), 13-14 (20%), 15-16 (20%), 17-18 (10%), 20 (10%) |

The color assortment is packaged by Jillian-Kate Fashions, and experience reveals that all colors in the assortment are salable.

The department is known as D367 in Division 24. The store is located at 366 Pine Street in Oakville, Ontario, and is referred to as Unit 21 of the chain organization. The merchandise is to be shipped directly to the branch store in Oakville.

(a) Prepare the accompanying purchase order indicating that the merchandise is to be shipped no later than August 10.

(b) Determine the payments that will be required of the accounting department, showing the alternative dates of payment assuming that the date of invoice is August 10.

12. Carol's Fashion Shoppe has placed an order for an assortment of silk scarves at a total list price of $1,850.00. The store is offered a series discount of 35%, 15%, 5% on this purchase with terms of 2/10-30X, n/60 E.O.M., and 10% anticipation. If the invoice is dated June 21, determine the payment to be made to the manufacturer on each of July 10 and July 30.

part **II**

CALCULATING MARKUP

The retail price policies of merchandising operations usually have the result of covering expenses and providing the organization with a margin of profit. There are, however, cases where the prices established for specific items do not generate profit for the firm but merely act as a catalyst in generating traffic and building sales throughout the organization. Such is the role played by special promotional items purchased by the merchant and offered as leader items or loss leader traffic builders. Nevertheless, the retail operation will only succeed if it is able to operate profitably overall. In the retail store, profit is derived only if the selling price is large enough to cover the cost of the merchandise and the operating expenses and still leave a profit for the firm.

Consequently, the basic retail equation that indicates that the difference between the retail selling price and the cost price of the merchandise is known as markup (or markon):

$$\boxed{\text{Markup} = \text{Retail} - \text{Cost}}$$

Although markup appears to be a relatively simple concept as expressed in this equation, it incorporates a number of complex relationships that can be expressed in a variety of ways, as we shall see.

It is obvious from what has been stated that the markup for a retailer may be expressed in dollar amounts or as a percentage. It should be noted that the markup is most useful and valuable to a retailer when expressed as a percentage since it can be then used as a standard of comparison with other items, other departments, other branches, or other retail operations. The percentage figure is not dependent upon the cost and selling prices when used as comparisons as the following situation will illustrate.

Case 1

A buyer has purchased a sweater for $30 and has placed it in her $50 price line. The markup on the item is $20, which represents a markup of 40% on retail ($20/$50 × 100%).

Case 2

The same buyer purchased a pair of slacks for $80 that she retails at $100. With the same dollar markup of $20, the markup percent is only 20% ($20/$100 × 100%).

The student will note that the dollar markup obtains its true meaning only in its relationship to the retail selling price. Consequently, the $20 markups in the two cases have different implications for the buyer, depending on the selling prices of the item.

Obviously, it is unnecessary and impractical to establish prices for merchandise by using the same rate of markup for all classifications of merchandise. In some stores, the markup percentages have been determined by charging to departments or merchandise classifications a proportion of the total store expenses and setting a net profit goal for the classification. In other instances, the markup percentages have been determined from experience without regard to the expenses that should have been charged to the merchandise classification. It must also be recognized that competition and attempted resale price maintenance by manufacturers have a strong bearing on the prices at which the merchandise in a classification can be effectively sold. Therefore, the strict application of markup percentages to all merchandise in a store or retail organization could result in selling prices that are not suitable when other factors are taken into consideration. Of course, items that are in heavy demand can command a higher markup than can those that the retailer can hardly give away. Markup percentages, then, should be used as guides rather than as absolute determinants in establishing selling prices.

As we proceed through this section of the book, the student will be able to understand more readily the various types of markups in use in the retail industry and the complexity encountered by the merchant in establishing the selling prices for the items in inventory.

DEFINITIONS

Individual Markup. This represents the markup that is obtained on an individual item. In the example just given, the individual markup placed on the sweater and the pair of slacks is $20 while the markup percent differs. The individual markup is expressed in both dollars and percent and is expressed as either a percentage of retail or a percentage of cost.

Average Markup. This represents the dollar or percent markup a buyer hopes to achieve for a group of items, for a specific line, for a classification, for an entire department, or for the total store.

Initial Markup. This is the markup that is originally placed on the merchandise when it is offered for sale. This markup, therefore, represents the first markup placed on an item. Obviously, it is not possible for the retailer to obtain this markup on all items offered for sale since this would imply that he or she was able to sell everything without any reductions in retail prices.

Maintained Markup. This is the markup that is finally realized on the sales generated. The maintained markup consequently is what is earned by the merchant after markdowns, stock shortages, and employee discounts have been taken into consideration. Therefore, the maintained markup is the difference between net sales and the gross cost of goods sold.

Gross Margin. The gross margin is the difference between the net sales and the total cost of goods sold. As such, the difference between the gross margin and the maintained markup is the effect of cash discounts and alteration expenses on the firm. In retail operations that have neither cash discounts nor alteration expenses, the gross margin and maintained markup are the same. Students should also note that other industries may use the term gross profit in place of gross margin. They are synonymous.

4

Calculating Individual Markup

We noted earlier that markup could be expressed in dollars or as a percentage. It was also pointed out that markup expressed as a percentage had more meaning to the retailer in determining the effectiveness of the merchandising effort. Obviously, when expressing some figure as a percentage, a base must be established. In expressing markup as a percentage, it is possible to determine the markup percent using cost or selling price as the base. Regardless of which base is used, the same selling price will result.

To simplify the understanding of basing markup on cost or selling price, the explanations will be restricted to calculating the markup on individual items. The student should note that it is possible to calculate the remaining markups explained in this section on both the cost and selling price bases.

MARKUP BASED ON RETAIL

Almost without exception, leading department stores, chain stores, and many other progressive retail operations are basing their calculation of markup percent on the retail selling price. The merit of the markup percent is in its use as a guide in pricing merchandise so that expected expenses will be covered and a profit will be earned. It is customary to show a relationship between expenses and profits and the sales dollar, and, as a result, these are expressed as a percentage of net sales. The net sales represents a summary of the selling prices obtained from all the items that have been sold. Success in retail management depends on the executives' abilities to analyze these expenses carefully when expressed as a percentage of net sales.

Decisions must be made if the executive discovers that salespersons' salaries are using a disproportionate amount of gross margin. On this basis, it now becomes possible for various firms in the industry to compare operating results since all firms will now be operating on the same base. Organizations such as the Retail Hardware Association, National Retail Merchants'

Association, International Council of Shopping Centers, Bureau of Statistics, and others gather and publish these operating results for member retailers to analyze, study, and compare. It is with this analysis and comparison that retailers have been able to gauge their effectiveness in light of new competition and improved profitability.

Further, it will be obvious to the student of retailing that the merchant is unable to earn a profit in his or her operation until the merchandise is sold. As a result, it is reasonable to assume that the markup should be based on retail selling prices, since no markup in fact is achieved until the items have been sold. Once the item has reached the store, the cost of that item to the retailer remains the same in terms of what must be remitted to the manufacturer. However, as a result of markdowns, the selling price frequently changes, which in turn will affect the markup that the retailer can expect on the merchandise.

We will observe later that the markup percentage based on retail is always smaller than the equivalent markup percentage based on cost. This must necessarily be true since retail is the larger base, and subsequently the larger the base, the smaller the percentage, and vice versa. In today's market of consumer awareness and education, a markup of 40% on retail seems more reasonable to the consumer than does the equivalent markup of $66\frac{2}{3}$% based on cost.

Finally, as more and more retailers move to the retail method of inventory, the need for markup based on retail becomes obvious. Simply by reading off the sales tickets of merchandise in inventory and subtracting the markup used on these selling tickets, the retailer is readily able to determine the cost of the inventory. Further discussion of the retail method of inventory will be provided in a later chapter.

It should be noted that retailers are required to calculate the prices and markup from factors that vary among suppliers of the retail store. Some manufacturers quote list prices, while others quote cost prices. As a result, the information given in solving pricing and markup problems varies with each situation. The following problems in establishing markups build on some known and unknown factors.

When the retail price is the base upon which markup is calculated, then the retail price in the basic equation is always equal to 100%. Retail is then the base or unit to which the markup is related.

EXAMPLE 1: Finding Markup Percent Given Cost and Retail Prices

A ladies' wear buyer is able to purchase a line of sweaters that will retail at $75 and for which she must pay the manufacturer $40. Find the markup percent on retail that the buyer will achieve on this item.

Solution: Cost + Markup = Retail.

$$\begin{array}{ll} \text{Cost} & = \$40 \\ + \quad \text{Markup} & = \\ \hline = \quad \text{Retail} & = \$75 \end{array}$$

Therefore the Markup Dollars for the sweater will be $35.

The markup percent based on the retail price is

$$\frac{\$35}{\$75} \times 100\% = 46.67\%$$

PROBLEM 1: A stereo tape system is purchased by a retail merchant for $450 and is to be placed in the store at a selling price of $800. Find the markup percent on retail for the stereo.

Cost $450
+ Markup =
= Retail = $800

$\frac{350}{800} \times 100\% = 43.75\%$

EXAMPLE 2: Finding the Cost Price Given Retail Price and Markup Percent

How much will a men's furnishings buyer have to pay for a sport coat that will retail at $150 and carry a markup of 40% on retail?

Solution:

Since

$$M = R - C$$

then

$$C = R - M$$

And, since retail is the base, then retail equals 100%:

$$
\begin{array}{rlll}
 & C = & ? & = 60\% \\
+ & M = & & = 40\% \\
\hline
= & R = & \$150 & = 100\%
\end{array}
$$

Therefore,

$$\text{Cost} = \frac{\$150}{100\%} \times 60\% = \$90$$

The buyer will have to pay $90 for the sport coat.

PROBLEM 2: A buyer is able to purchase a line of men's ties that she plans to place in her $15 price line that will carry a markup of $33\frac{1}{3}$% on retail. Determine the price she will have to pay for these ties.

$$R = \$15$$
$$+ M = 33.3\%$$
$$\overline{R =}$$

$$\frac{15}{100} \times 66.^2/_3 = \$10.$$

EXAMPLE 3: Finding the Retail Price Given Cost Price and Markup Percent

A buyer is able to purchase a line of dinette sets from a manufacturer for $175 each. The merchant hopes to run a special promotion and place a markup on retail of 37.5% on the suites. What retail price should be placed on the dinette sets?

Solution:

$$
\begin{array}{llll}
& \text{Cost} & = \$175 = & 62.5\% \left(\tfrac{5}{8}\right)^1 \\
+ & \text{Markup} = & = & 37.5\% \left(\tfrac{3}{8}\right) \\
\hline
= & \text{Retail} & = \quad ? & = 100.0\% \left(\tfrac{8}{8}\right)
\end{array}
$$

Since

$$\text{Cost} = \$175 = 62.5\% \left(\tfrac{5}{8}\right)$$

then

$$1\% = \frac{\$175}{62.5\%} = \$2.80$$

and

$$
\begin{aligned}
\text{Retail} = 100\% &= 100 \times \text{value of } 1\% \\
&= 100 \times \$2.80 \\
&= \$280
\end{aligned}
$$

PROBLEM 3: The furniture buyer is also able to purchase a line of rocking chairs that he also wishes to run on a promotion with a markup of 42% on retail. He is able to purchase the chairs for $145 and has asked you to determine the retail price that should be placed on these items.

$$
\begin{array}{ll}
& \text{Cost} = \$145 \\
+ & \text{Markup} = 42\% \\
\hline
= & \text{Retail} = ?\ 100\%
\end{array}
$$

$$\text{Cost} = \$145 = 58\%$$

$$1\% = \frac{145}{58\%} = \$2.5$$

$$\frac{145}{58} \times 100 = \$250$$

$$\text{Retail} = 100\%$$
$$100 \times \text{value of } 1\%$$
$$100 \times 2.5$$
$$\$250$$

EXAMPLE 4: Finding the Cost and Retail Prices Given Markup Dollars and Percent

As an assistant buyer, you have been asked to determine the cost and retail prices on an item that your department has purchased that will carry a markup of $72 or 37.5% on retail.

[1] It is also possible to convert markup percentages to fractions in an effort to facilitate calculations. Students are asked to refer to the fraction equivalent table provided in Appendix D.

Solution:

$$
\begin{array}{llll}
 & \text{Cost} & = \ ? & = \ 62.5\% \ \left(\tfrac{5}{8}\right) \\
+ & \text{Markup} = \$72 & = \ 37.5\% \ \left(\tfrac{3}{8}\right) \\
\hline
= & \text{Retail} & = \ ? & = \ 100.0\% \ \left(\tfrac{8}{8}\right)
\end{array}
$$

Since markup = 37.5% = $\frac{3}{8}$ = $72 then,

$$\frac{1}{8} = \frac{\$72}{3} = \$24$$

and

$$\text{Cost} = \tfrac{5}{8} = 5 \times \text{value of } \tfrac{1}{8} = \$120$$

and

$$\text{Retail} = \tfrac{8}{8} = 8 \times \text{value of } \tfrac{1}{8} = \$192$$

PROBLEM 4: Determine the cost and retail prices for the jewelry buyer on a line of broaches that carry a markup of $135 or 45% on retail.

$$MU = \$135 = 45\%$$
$$RP = \$300 = 100\%$$
$$CP =$$

$$RP = \frac{135}{45} \times 100 = \$300.$$
$$CP = 300 - 135 = 165$$

MARKUP BASED ON COST *will not be on exam*

Although we have pointed out the advantages and growth of basing markup on the retail selling price, some retail organizations continue to use cost as the markup base. When using cost as the base for determining the markup percentage, the exact nature of the cost must be established. The cost of the article may be the invoice cost, but if the store must pay the transportation charges from the supplier, the cost of the merchandise must be the cost of the goods delivered to the store. The cost is then the invoice cost plus the transportation charges, and this figure is to be used as the markup base. When a cash discount is available on the payment of the invoice, it should not be deducted from the invoice price of each item to arrive at the cost, since there is no guarantee that the discount will be taken.

Many retail stores continue to use the cost basis of determining markup percentage, basically because of habit or their familiarity with handling markup problems on this basis. It would appear that such retailers find it extremely difficult to "unlearn" this older method of calculating markup and to comprehend the newer concept of basing markup on retail. However, as the current generation of retail merchants enters the industry with rapidly changing technological tools, markup on retail is likely to gain even more acceptance.

Basing markup on cost appears to be a more common practice among small independent retailers. And since some retailers do in fact utilize this method, the student of retailing must be familiar with the means of calculating markup using cost as the base.

However, before proceeding, the student is asked to observe two principles with regard to the basis of markup calculations in this book:

> 1. Unless otherwise stated, markup is always based on retail.
> 2. Unless otherwise stated, markup is always expressed as a percentage.

In a similar way to assuming a base of 100% when markup is based on retail, so does cost assume a base of 100% when markup is based on cost. However, the change of the base of 100% does not alter the basic retail equation:

$$Cost + Markup = Retail$$

EXAMPLE 5: **Finding the Markup Percent of Cost Given Cost and Retail Prices**

A retail merchant is able to purchase a line of men's shirts to retail at $30 that the manufacturer has offered at a cost of $20. Determine the markup percent of cost that the merchant hopes to obtain on this purchase.

Solution:

$$
\begin{array}{ll}
& \text{Cost} \quad = \$20 \\
+ & \text{Markup} = \\
\hline
& \text{Retail} \quad = \$30
\end{array}
$$

Therefore, markup dollars would be $30 − $20 = $10, and markup percent of cost means cost would become the base:

$$\frac{\$\,Markup}{\$\,Cost} \times 100\% = \frac{\$10}{\$20} \times 100\% = 50\%$$

Therefore, the markup on the men's shirts will be 50% on cost.

PROBLEM 5: If the same men's wear buyer is able to purchase a line of sweater vests at a cost of $35 with a planned retail price of $60, determine the markup percent on cost that will be anticipated.

$$
\begin{array}{ll}
& \text{Cost} = \$35 \\
+ & \text{Markup} = \\
\hline
& \text{Retail} = \$60
\end{array}
$$

$$\$60 - \$35 = \$25$$

$$\frac{\$\,Markup}{\$\,Cost} \times 100\% = \frac{\$25}{\$35} \times 100\% = \$71.42$$

EXAMPLE 6: Finding the Retail Price Given Cost and Markup Percent on Cost

A sporting goods store has purchased a number of golf club sets at a cost of $175 and wishes to place a markup of 60% on cost on these sets. Determine what retail price should be placed on these golf clubs.

Solution:

Since cost is the base, cost must equal 100%:

$$
\begin{array}{lll}
& \text{Cost} & = \$175 = 100\% \\
+ & \text{Markup} = & = 60\% \\
\hline
& \text{Retail} = ? & = 160\%
\end{array}
$$

Therefore,

$$\text{Cost} = 100\% = \$175$$

and

$$1\% = \frac{\$175}{100\%} = \$1.75$$

and

$$
\begin{aligned}
\text{Retail} = 160\% &= 160 \times \text{Value of } 1\% \\
&= 160 \times \$1.75 \\
&= \$280
\end{aligned}
$$

PROBLEM 6: Another special deal is being offered by the same sporting goods manufacturer in the purchase of a line of golf club bags that he is offering to the retailer at a cost of $55. The retailer anticipates that these bags can carry a markup of 37.5% on cost. Find the retail price at which these bags will be sold.

$$
\begin{array}{ll}
\text{Cost} = \$55 = 100\% & \text{Retail} = 137.5\% = 137.5 \times 1\% \overset{value}{} \\
+ \;\; \text{Markup} = = 37.5\% & \phantom{\text{Retail}} = 137.5\% \times .55 \\
\hline
\text{Retail} = \;\; ? \;\; = 137.5\% & \phantom{\text{Retail}} = \$75.63
\end{array}
$$

$$\text{Cost} = 100\% = \$55$$

$$1\% = \frac{\$55}{100\%} = \$.55$$

Students are asked to solve the following two problems without the benefit of an example by applying the principles already established in solving the basic equation:

$$\text{Cost} + \text{Markup} = \text{Retail}$$

PROBLEM 7: A gift department is offering a crystal candy dish to its customers at a retail price of $75. The candy dish carries a markup of 75% of cost. Determine the cost price to the department for this dish.

$$Cost = 100\%$$
$$+ \quad Markup = 75\%$$
$$\overline{\quad\quad Retail = 175\%}$$

Cost = 100%

175% = $75 $\dfrac{75}{175} \times 100 = \$42.86$

PROBLEM 8: A leather goods department is offering a man's wallet for sale to its customers at a markup of $15, which also represents a markup of 40% on the cost price. As an assistant, you are required to determine the cost and retail price of the wallet offered for sale.

Cost ? 100% = 140%

Markup $15 = 40%

Retail = ? = 100%

Markup = 40% = $15

$$\dfrac{15}{40\%} \times 100 = \$37.50$$

CONVERSION OF MARKUP BASE

There are situations in a retail organization requiring that markup percentage be converted from the cost base to the retail base, or vice versa. For example, there are advantages in stating markups on a retail price base when planning and controlling assortments. However, initial pricing of individual lots of merchandise may be simplified with markup percentages based on cost. Further, retailers who are accustomed to expressing markups on cost may wish to compute the equivalent markup on retail to compare their operation with other firms in the trade whose markups are based on retail.

If the retailer is frequently called upon to compute these conversions from one base to another, a chart such as that shown in Table 1 would save much time and effort. In addition, computer technology can easily be programmed to provide calculations at both cost and retail. It should be noted from the table that the markup on cost is always greater than the equivalent markup on retail even though the dollar amount of markup will not change.

TABLE 1

MARKUP (MU) CONVERSION TABLE: SELECTED PERCENTS

MU % of Cost	5.0	5.3	6.4	7.5	8.7	10.0	11.1	12.0	12.4
MU % of Retail	4.8	5.0	6.0	7.0	8.0	9.0	10.0	10.7	11.0
MU % of Cost	12.5	13.6	15.0	16.3	17.7	19.1	20.5	22.0	22.7
MU % of Retail	11.1	12.0	13.0	14.0	15.0	16.0	17.0	18.0	18.5
MU % of Cost	23.5	25.0	26.6	28.2	29.0	29.9	30.0	31.6	33.3
MU % of Retail	19.0	20.0	21.0	22.0	22.5	23.0	23.1	24.0	25.0
MU % of Cost	35.0	37.0	37.5	39.0	40.0	40.9	42.9	45.0	50.0
MU % of Retail	26.0	27.0	27.3	28.0	28.5	29.0	30.0	31.0	33.3
MU % of Cost	53.9	55.0	56.3	58.8	60.0	61.3	64.0	66.7	70.0
MU % of Retail	35.0	35.5	36.0	37.0	37.5	38.0	39.0	40.0	41.0
MU % of Cost	72.4	75.0	80.0	85.0	90.0	95.0	100.0	150.0	300.0
MU % of Retail	42.0	42.8	44.4	46.1	47.5	48.7	50.0	60.0	75.0

EXAMPLE 8: Finding the Equivalent Markup Based on Cost Given Markup on Retail

A retail buyer calculates her markup on the basis of the cost price of the item. If she can obtain a markup of $33\frac{1}{3}\%$ on retail, find the equivalent markup percent on cost.

Solution:

Since markup is based on retail, retail becomes the base of 100%:

$$
\begin{array}{rl}
\text{Cost} & = 66\frac{2}{3}\% \\
+ \quad \text{Markup} & = 33\frac{1}{3}\% \\
\hline
\text{Retail} & = 100\%
\end{array}
$$

To express this markup as a percentage of cost, cost becomes the base.

But

$$\text{Cost} = 66\frac{2}{3}\%$$

and

$$\text{Markup Based on Cost} = \frac{M\%}{C\%} \times 100\% = \frac{33\frac{1}{3}\%}{66\frac{2}{3}\%} \times 100\%$$
$$= 50\%$$

Therefore, the equivalent markup percent would be 50% on cost.

PROBLEM 9: Find the equivalent markup percent of cost of an item that has a markup of 37.5% on retail.

EXAMPLE 10: **Finding the Equivalent Markup on Retail Given Markup on Cost**

Determine the equivalent markup percent on retail of an item that carries a markup of 50% on cost.

Solution: Since markup is based on cost, cost equals 100% and

$$
\begin{array}{ll}
\text{Cost} & = 100\% \\
+\quad \text{Markup} & = \ \ 50\% \\
\hline
\text{Retail} & = 150\%
\end{array}
$$

To convert this markup to retail, retail must become the base.

But

$$\text{Retail} = 150\%$$

and

$$\text{Markup Based on Retail} = \frac{M\ \%}{R\ \%} \times 100\% = \frac{50\%}{150\%} \times 100\%$$
$$= 33\tfrac{1}{3}\%$$

Therefore, the equivalent markup percent would be $33\tfrac{1}{3}\%$ on retail.

PROBLEM 10: Calculate the equivalent markup percent on retail for an item that carries a markup of 45% on cost.

1. If a job lot of sweaters is purchased by a merchant at a cost of $20 each, determine the retail selling price of these sweaters if the retailer wishes to obtain a markup of 37.5%.

2. Determine the equivalent markup percent on cost of an item that carries a markup of 45% on retail.

3. The millinery department offers a ladies' hat to its customers with a markup of $24, which is the equivalent of 60% on cost. As an assistant, you have been asked to determine the cost and retail price of this item, as well as the equivalent markup percent on retail.

4. A marine retailer has decided to carry a line of water skis that can be purchased for $90 per pair. If the buyer wishes to obtain a markup of 40% on cost, determine the retail price of the skis.

5. A men's wear buyer is able to purchase a line of jackets for $65 that he plans to retail at $110. Determine the markup percent at both cost and retail for these jackets.

6. If a sporting goods buyer is able to purchase a line of baseball gloves that will carry a markup of $18, which is the equivalent of 37.5% on retail, determine the cost and selling price for the glove.

7. A ladies' fashion boutique has purchased ladies scarves at a cost of $180 per dozen. If the buyer anticipates a retail price of $27.50, determine the markup percent of both cost and retail that she might expect on these scarves.

8. Answer the following questions in the space provided:
   (a) Calculate the markup on retail of an item that has a markup of 42% on cost.

   (b) Calculate the markup on cost of an item that has a markup of 37.5% on retail.

   (c) Calculate the retail price of an item that has a cost of $36 and carries a markup of $33\frac{1}{3}\%$ on retail.

   (d) Calculate the cost and retail price of a pair of pillowcases that have a markup of $4.50, which is equivalent to a markup of 40% on retail.

   (e) Calculate the cost price of a ladies' purse that retails at $80 and carries a markup of 75% on cost.

9. The paint department is able to purchase paint rollers at a cost of $208 per gross. If the buyer wishes to place a markup of 50% of retail on each of these, determine the retail price of each of these rollers.

10. The men's hosiery buyer purchased 25 dozen men's stretch hose that he plans to retail at $4.50 to provide him with a markup of 37.5% on retail. Determine the price that he paid for the 25 dozen.

11. If summer sandals can be purchased by a buyer at a cost of $17 per pair and will carry a markup of 60% on cost, determine the retail price at which these sandals can be offered to the consumer.

12. Determine the markup percent of retail and cost of placemats that cost the retailer $2.25 each and that are retailed at $4.00 each.

13. A line of ladies' tote bags carries a markup of 42%. The buyer has informed you that the markup per bag is also $8.40. On the basis of this information, determine the cost and retail prices of these tote bags.

14. A buyer of ladies' sportswear is able to purchase a line of swimwear at a clearance price of $15.00 per suit. To induce a quick sale at the store, the buyer is only placing a 32% markup on these swimsuits. At what retail price will these items be offered to the consumer?

15. An independent merchant is able to purchase an item for her store that will retail at $22.00. If the merchant has elected to place a markup of 75% of cost on this item, calculate the cost of this item to the store.

## chapter 5

Calculating Average Markup

It would indeed be simple to calculate the markup percentages for retail stores if, in fact, the retailer applied the same markup percentage to all merchandise. However, for reasons explained earlier, retailers do not apply the same predetermined markup percentages to all items in the store, or department, or even to the same line. Merchandise sold by retail stores must be priced so that it will sell in a competitive environment. Items that normally compete fiercely for market share may offer only a small markup to the retailer. On the other hand, merchandise being sold by the retailer under an exclusive agency may be able to command a much higher markup. In general, the retailer realizes that some items in the store or department can command a better markup than can other goods, but in the final analysis, he or she hopes to obtain a predetermined average markup for the store or for each department in the organization. For this reason, retailers spend much of their efforts in planning the blend of markups the store will obtain on the various merchandise classifications and assortments.

The retailer is faced with four types of problems in attempting to average markup. An understanding of the basic concepts of these problems and the means of solving them will lead to the average markup required by the organization in an attempt to reach a predetermined profit objective.

The types of problems that might be encountered by a retailer in an attempt to average markup are

1. Finding the average markup on a group of purchases
2. Finding the average markup on a line of merchandise that has one cost but two retail prices
3. Finding the average markup on a line of merchandise that has one retail but two cost prices
4. Finding the average markup on the various classifications of a department

The sections that follow illustrate these four problem types. At the beginning of each section, an explanation is given indicating the circumstances under which such a problem might arise in a retail organization.

It should be noted that the problems of averaging markup are found most often in apparel and home furnishings departments of retail organizations as a result of changes in fashion. The cyclical movement of fashion, with its inherent problems, requires that the merchant be constantly aware of changes in the demand for his or her merchandise assortments. In the case of staple merchandise, the buyer usually has less control over markups but tends to increase promotional emphasis on merchandise that carries a higher markup. It has become evident in recent years that fashion has taken on an increasing importance in many merchandise lines, consequently increasing the need for a thorough understanding of average markup.

While many of the problems encountered here by the retailer in planning his or her merchandise assortment could easily be solved with the application of computer technology, an understanding of the selection process must still be thoroughly understood by the buyer-retailer.

AVERAGE MARKUP ON A GROUP OF PURCHASES

In this situation, a buyer may be required to achieve an average markup for the entire store or department during a particular period or season. Therefore, the buyer is required to determine the markup on planned purchases during the period to realize a predetermined average markup. Some retailers have also referred to this as the cumulative markup that is obtained when merchandise is added to an already existing group of items in the store. Consequently, when adding purchases to the opening inventory for a period, the retailer is attempting to reach an average or cumulative markup.

In addition, the buyer may be required to determine the markup on these planned purchases when he or she knows either the cost or retail value of these items and the planned average markup. The method used to calculate the average on two or more purchases will depend upon what information the buyer has available and what decision is required to be made.

EXAMPLE 1: **Finding Average Markup Given Cost and Retail of B.O.M. (Beginning-of-Month) Stock and Purchases**

The B.O.M. stock in a men's clothing department was $46,000 at cost and $70,000 at retail. However, during the month, purchases were received by the department to retail at $90,000 and that cost the department $54,000. Determine the average markup for the month in the men's clothing department.

Solution: The problem may be set up in the following manner:

	Cost	Retail
B.O.M. Stock	$ 46,000	$ 70,000
Purchases	54,000	90,000
Total Available	$100,000	$160,000

Since

$$\text{Markup} = \text{Retail} - \text{Cost}$$
$$= \$160,000 - 100,000$$
$$= \$60,000$$

and

$$\text{Markup \%} = \frac{\$ \text{ Markup}}{\$ \text{ Retail}} \times 100\% = \frac{\$60,000}{\$160,000} \times 100\% = 37.5\%$$

The average markup for this department is 37.5%.

PROBLEM 1: The ladies' swimwear department showed an opening inventory on June 1 of $11,000 at cost and $18,000 at retail. During June, merchandise of $24,000 at cost and $37,000 at retail was received in stock. Determine the buyer's average markup percent for swimwear for the month of June.

$$
\begin{array}{ll}
\text{Cost} & \text{Retail} \\
11,000 & 18,000 \\
24,000 & 37,000 \\
\hline
35,000 & 55,000 \\
\end{array}
$$

$$\frac{20,000}{55,000} \times 100 =$$

$$= 36.36\%$$

$$55,000 - 35,000 = \$20,000$$

EXAMPLE 2: **Finding the Average Markup Given Markup of B.O.M. Stock and Purchases**

A sporting goods department shows an opening inventory of $40,000 at retail on August 1 with a markup of 30%. During August, purchases were received in the amount of $30,000 at cost and were marked up 37.5%. Find the average markup percent for the department for August.

Solution:

	Cost	Retail	Markup
August 1, B.O.M.		$40,000	30.0%
Purchases Received	$30,000	_____	37.5%
Total Available			

To complete this table, we need to calculate the cost of the B.O.M. and the retail value of the purchases received:

(a) Finding B.O.M. at cost,

$$
\begin{array}{lll}
\text{Cost} & = & = 70\% \\
+ \quad \text{Markup} & = & = 30\% \\
\hline
\text{Retail} & = \$40,000 & = 100\% \\
\end{array}
$$

Therefore

$$\text{Cost} = \frac{\$40,000}{100\%} \times 70\% = \$28,000$$

(b) Finding purchases at retail,

$$
\begin{array}{rllll}
 & \text{Cost} & = \$30,000 = & 62.5\% \ (\tfrac{5}{8}) \\
+ & \text{Markup} = & = & 37.5\% \ (\tfrac{3}{8}) \\
\hline
 & \text{Retail} \quad = & = & 100.0\% \ (\tfrac{8}{8})
\end{array}
$$

Therefore, since

$$\text{Cost} = \tfrac{5}{8} = \$30,000$$

then

$$\tfrac{1}{8} = \$6,000$$

and

$$\text{Retail} = \tfrac{8}{8} = \$48,000$$

Therefore, the table now appears as

	Cost	Retail	Markup
B.O.M. August 1	$28,000	$40,000	30.0%
Purchases Received	30,000	48,000	37.5
Total Available	$58,000	$88,000	

$$
\begin{aligned}
\$ \text{ Markup} &= \$ \text{ Retail} - \$ \text{ Cost} \\
&= \$88,000 - \$58,000 = \$30,000 \\
\% \text{ Markup} &= \frac{\$30,000}{\$88,000} \times 100\% = 34.09\%
\end{aligned}
$$

PROBLEM 2: On April 1 a shoe department has $50,000 worth of stock at retail with a markup of 40%. During the month, purchases were received carrying a markup of 37.5% with a retail value of $48,000. The buyer has asked you to calculate the average markup for April in the shoe department.

EXAMPLE 3: Finding the Markup on Planned Purchases Given Retail Value and the Average Markup

A buyer had a budget of $50,000 at retail for the fall-winter season and is expected to realize an average markup of 40% for the period. Midway through the season, the buyer has a cumulative inventory of $18,000 at retail that contains a markup of 45%. The buyer wishes to spend the total budget for the season and wishes to determine the markup required on additional purchases to realized the average of 40%.

Solution:

	Cost	Retail	Markup
Inventory to Date		$18,000	45%
Planned Purchases			
Total Budget Available		$50,000	40%

(a) Find the cost value of the total budget:

$$\begin{array}{rl} \text{Cost} & = \quad = 60\% \\ + \quad \text{Markup} & = \quad = 40\% \\ \hline \text{Retail} & = \$50,000 = 100\% \end{array} \qquad \text{Cost} = \frac{\$50,000}{100\%} \times 60\% = \$30,000$$

(b) Find the cost value of the inventory to date:

$$\begin{array}{rl} \text{Cost} & = \quad = 55\% \\ + \quad \text{Markup} & = \quad = 45\% \\ \hline \text{Retail} & = \$18,000 = 100\% \end{array} \qquad \text{Cost} = \frac{\$18,000}{100\%} \times 55\% = \$9,900$$

(c) Find the cost and retail value of the planned purchases:

	Cost	Retail	Markup
Total Budget Available	$30,000	$50,000	40%
Less: Inventory to Date	9,900	18,000	45
Planned Purchases	$20,100	$32,000	

(d) Find the markup on the planned purchases:

$$\begin{array}{rl} \text{Markup} & = \text{Retail} - \text{Cost} \\ & = \$32,000 - \$20,100 = \$11,900 \end{array}$$

$$\text{Markup \%} = \frac{\$11,900}{\$32,000} \times 100\% = 37.19\%$$

PROBLEM 3: The buyer of a lingerie department is expected to realize an average markup of 40.0%. The inventory to date in her department is priced at $19,200 at retail and carries a markup of 37.5%. If the buyer's purchase limit for the remainder of the period is $8,000 at retail, calculate the markup that will be required on these purchases for the department to realize an average markup of 40.0%.

EXAMPLE 4: **Finding the Markup on Planned Purchases Given Cost Value and Planned Average Markup**

Solve the following problem without the benefit of an example by utilizing the format outline in the preceding example.

PROBLEM 4: The buyer of draperies has a planned average markup of 30%. The budget for the period allows her to spend a cost total of $36,000. To date the buyer has received merchandise valued $21,600 at cost that carries a markup of 32%. Determine the markup she must obtain on the remaining purchases to realize the planned average markup.

EXAMPLE 5: **Finding Additional Purchases Given Planned Average Markup and Retail Value of Past Purchases and Their Markup**

A buyer has a planned average markup of 35% for the period. As a special promotion for the department, the buyer has purchased some merchandise that he retailed at $12,000 but on which he only realized a markup of 30.0%. To achieve an average markup of 35.0%, the buyer wishes to purchase additional merchandise that can be marked up 37.5% without destroying the image of the department. How much additional merchandise will the buyer have to purchase at cost and at retail to meet the average markup?

Solution:

Setting up the markup information, we are given

	Markup to Date	Markup for Remainder
Actual Markup on Purchases	30.0%	37.5%
Average Markup on Purchases	35.0	35.0
Loss or Gain on Average Markup	−5.0%	+2.5%

From this table we can observe that to date the buyer has lost 5.0% from his planned average markup by taking a markup of only 30.0% on his special promotion merchandise. On the other hand, the buyer will gain 2.5% on his average markup on the items he wishes to purchase and mark up 37.5% for the remainder of the period.

Through this analysis we have developed a ratio that can be used by the buyer to determine how much he can sell at each markup and still achieve his desired average markup. In this example, the ratio developed is 5:2.5. To simplify calculations and by virtue of the fact that retailers do not sell fractional portions of items, we eliminate the fractional content of the ratio and arrive at a ratio of 2:1. (We have divided each part of the ratio by 2.5).

From the ratio, we have established that for every *one* item he sold at a markup of 30.0% that produced a loss from the average of 5.0%, he must sell *two* items that will carry a markup of 37.5%, representing a gain of 2.5% on the average markup. At this point, we break even, on average:

$$1 \text{ item} \times (-5.0\%) = -5\%$$
$$2 \text{ items} \times (+2.5\%) = +5\%$$

Therefore, in every group of 3 items (1 + 2) that he sells during the period, he must observe the following to obtain an average markup of 35.0%.

1 @ 30.0% for every 2 @ 37.5%

Students may find it easier to understand the relationship of the ratio to the various markups by applying arrows:

	Markup to Date	Markup for Remainder
Actual Markup on Purchases	30.0%	37.5%
Average Markup on Purchases	35.0	35.0
Loss or Gain on Average	−5.0%	+2.5%
	2	1

Therefore,

2 @ 37.5% and 1 @ 30.0%

From the given factors in the buyer's problem, we also note that he has purchased $12,000 worth of promotional items at retail and has marked these goods up 30%. By virtue of the ratio established, we know that *1 out of every 3 items* can carry a markup of 30% as long as the remaining 2 items will carry a markup of 37.5%. Only in this situation will the buyer be able to obtain the planned average markup. Therefore,

$$\tfrac{1}{3} = \$12,000$$

And we know that for the remainder of the period, *2 out of 3* ($\tfrac{2}{3}$) items will carry the markup of 37.5%. Thus, if

$$\tfrac{1}{3} = \$12,000$$

then

$$\tfrac{2}{3} = \$24,000$$

The retail value of the additional purchases will then be $24,000 and will carry a markup of 37.5%. To find the cost of these purchases,

$$
\begin{array}{rll}
\text{Cost} & = & = 62.5\% \left(\frac{5}{8}\right) \\
+ \quad \text{Markup} & = & = 37.5\% \left(\frac{3}{8}\right) \\
\hline
\text{Retail} & = \$24,000 & = 100.0\% \left(\frac{8}{8}\right)
\end{array}
$$

$$
\text{Retail} = \frac{8}{8} = \$24,000
$$
$$
\frac{1}{8} = \$3,000
$$

and

$$
\text{Cost} = \frac{5}{8} = \$15,000
$$

Therefore, the buyer can purchase additional merchandise at $24,000 at retail and $15,000 at cost and still maintain an average markup of 35%.

PROBLEM 5: A buyer of men's sweaters is expected to obtain an average markup of 42%. On November 1 the buyer realizes that the merchandise has given him a markup of only 39% to date and was valued at $21,000 at retail. How much additional merchandise at cost and at retail will the buyer be required to purchase and mark up 45% to achieve the department's average markup?

[Handwritten notes:]

MU To date

actual = 39%
Average = 42%
‾‾‾‾‾‾
−3%
$21,000 at Retail
$ 11,550

Planned

45% = 100% = 55%
42%
‾‾‾‾‾
+3%
55% × 21,000 = 11,550

EXAMPLE 6: Finding Additional Purchases Given the Planned Average Markup and Cost Value of Past Purchases and Markup

A buyer has purchased $7,500 worth of merchandise at cost that carries a markup of 40.0%. The buyer is required to obtain an average markup of 37.5% in his department for the period. If the buyer anticipates that he can obtain a markup of only 36.0% on additional purchases, determine the cost and retail value of these purchases for the buyer to realize his average markup.

Solution:

The method used here is similar to that illustrated in Example 5, with the very important exception that we are dealing here with the *cost* value of the merchandise purchased to date.

By virtue of the fact that we are dealing with the cost value of the purchases instead of the retail value, this procedure will vary somewhat.

	Markup to Date	Markup for Remainder
Actual Markup on Purchases	40.0%	36.0%
Average Markup on Purchases	37.5	37.5
Loss or Gain on Average (Eliminate the fractional element by muliplying both sides by 2)	+2.5%	−1.5%
	+5	−3

Therefore, as discovered in the previous example, for every 3 he sells at 40%, he must sell 5 at 36%. In this ratio we are dealing with a total of 8 items (3 + 5).

From the factors in the buyer's problem, we also note that he has purchased $7,500 worth of merchandise at cost and marked these goods up 40%. However, since markup percent is based on retail, and the ratios established are based on these markup percents, it is necessary to convert the cost value of these purchases of $7,500 to retail value before aplplying the ratio. It is this portion of the method that differentiates it from Example 5.

Therefore,

$$
\begin{array}{lll}
\text{Cost} & = \$7,500 = & 60\% \\
+ \quad \text{Markup} = & = & 40\% \\
\hline
\text{Retail} \quad = & & = 100\%
\end{array}
$$

Thus

$$
\text{Retail Value of These Purchases} = \frac{\$7,500}{60\%} \times 100\%
$$
$$
= \$12,500
$$

Since we have the retail value of these purchases, we are now able to apply the ratios to determine the cost and retail value of the additional purchases. Thus,

$$
\tfrac{3}{8} = \$12,500
$$

and

$$
\tfrac{1}{8} = \$4,167
$$

But 5 of every 8 items must receive a markup of 36%; therefore,

$$
\tfrac{5}{8} = \$20,835
$$

Thus the retail value of the additional purchases will be $20,835 and will carry a markup of 36%. Therefore, the cost of these purchases will be

$$
\begin{array}{lll}
\text{Cost} \quad = & = & 64\% \\
+ \quad \text{Markup} = & = & 36\% \\
\hline
\text{Retail} \quad = \$20.835 = & 100\%
\end{array}
$$

Thus, the cost of these additional purchases will be

$$
\frac{\$20,835}{100\%} \times 64\% = \$13,334.40
$$

NOTE: In problems of this nature, students should observe that it is essential to convert the committed purchases at cost to a retail value before applying the established ratio.

PROBLEM 6: A buyer has established 37% as the average markup she expects from her department during this season. She has purchased $15,600 worth of merchandise at cost that has been marked up 35%. The buyer feels that she will be able to purchase additional merchandise that she can mark up 40% without loss of sales.

Determine how much merchandise at cost and retail the buyer must purchase and mark up 40% to achieve the desired average markup.

(handwritten work:)

$24000 $16000

Actual   35% ▷   ▷40% $24,000 : 3 = 800(

Average   37%   37%

–2% (2)   :   (3) +3%

                   8000

$15,600 = CP   RP= 100% = 15,600

35% $\frac{15,600}{65}$ ×100=

                                    = $24000

ONE COST, TWO RETAIL PRICES

$CP = \frac{16000}{100} \times 60 = 960

The planning of average markup may result from the ability of the buyer to buy a number of items from a supplier at one cost price but, as a result of item analysis, finds that he is able to retail the items at two different retail pricess. In this way, the buyer is somewhat able to manipulate the average markup for the period.

Such a situation might arise in a retail organization when a manufacturer produces like goods bearing the same wholesale price but differing in value. This may also be true when a buyer is able to purchase like goods from different suppliers at the same price but feels that he or she is able to obtain a larger markup on some of the items as a result of pattern, color, style, or material differences. The smart buyer will detect these differences in the items and operates on the assumption that the observant customer will also detect them. The buyer then marks the more salable merchandise at a higher retail price thus giving a greater markup on the item.

In addition, the buyer may be forced to take a smaller markup on specific merchandise items that have the same cost as other items in the department. Competitive pressures may force the buyer into a smaller markup situation for those items that compete directly with those of another retailer. However, if notable differences in merchandise characteristics can be detected when compared with competitors' merchandise, the buyer will lower the price on some items and maintain or increase the price on others.

EXAMPLE 7: Finding the Proportion with Two Retails Given the Cost and Average Markup

A buyer purchased a line of ladies' sweaters at a cost of $32 each. He is aware of the style and pattern differences of the sweaters and believes that some will fit into the $54 price line while the others will sell at the $46 price point. Determine the proportion of sweaters that should be sold at each price for the buyer to realize an average markup of $33\frac{1}{3}\%$ on these items.

Solution: To achieve his average markup of $33\frac{1}{3}\%$, he must determine what the average retail price should be:

$$
\begin{array}{llll}
& \text{Cost} & = \$32 = & 66\frac{2}{3}\% \ (\frac{2}{3}) \\
+ & \text{Markup} = & = & 33\frac{1}{3}\% \ (\frac{1}{3}) \\
\hline
& \text{Retail} & = & = 100\% \ (\frac{3}{3})
\end{array}
$$

Following the procedure set forth in the previous examples, the average retail price is $48.

Comparing the average retail price with the actual retail prices,

Actual Retail Prices	$46.00	$54.00
Average Retail Price	48.00	48.00
Loss or Gain on Average Retail	-$2.00	+$6.00
	1	3

Therefore, as established in the previous examples, on every sweater he retails at $54, he will gain $6 on his average retail price, and on every sweater he retails at $46, he will lose $2 on his average retail price.

Therefore, if we reduce these to the lowest multiple, we establish a ratio of 3:1; that is, to break even, he will be required to sell 3 sweaters at $46 for every sweater he sells at $54:

$$3 \times (-\$2.00) = -\$6.00$$
$$1 \times (+\$6.00) = +\$6.00$$

Of every 4 sweaters sold, the buyer should have the following proportions to arrive at his average markup of $33\frac{1}{3}\%$:

$$3 @ \$46.00 : 1 @ \$54.00$$

PROBLEM 7: A buyer is able to purchase a job lot of pillowcases at $4.00 per pair. To obtain an average markup of 37.5%, she decides to put some in the $4.50 price line and some in the $7.00 price line. Determine the proportion of pillowcases she may put in each of the two price lines to obtain the average markup of 37.5%.

(handwritten annotations:)

Average MU = 37.5%
CP = 4.00

RP = $\frac{4.00}{62.5} \times 100 = \$6.40$

Actual RP 4.50   7.00
Are RP   6.40   6.40
$-1.90 (×10) $+.60 (×10)
   19   6

of 400 pillows $\frac{400}{25} = 16$ 16×19 = $304
19+6 = 25   16×6 = $96

EXAMPLE 8: Finding the Number of Units at Two Retails Given the Cost and Average Markup

The men's furnishings buyer purchases 12 dozen ties at $8.00 each. To achieve his average markup of 40%, he decides to price some ties at $12.00 while the more salable designs will be priced at $16.00. Determine the number of ties that should be placed in each price line for the buyer to obtain his average markup of 40%.

Solution:

(a) Find the average retail price of the ties:

	Cost	= $8.00 =	60%
+	Markup =		= 40%
	Retail =		= 100%

Therefore, average retail price would be $13.33.

(b) Find the loss or gain from average retail price:

Actual Retail Prices	$12.00	$16.00
Average Retail Price	13.33	13.33
Loss or Gain from Average	−$1.33	+$2.67

Therefore, for every tie that retails at $12.00, he loses $1.33 from average retail, and for every tie that retails at $16.00, he gains $2.67 on the average retail price.

Since portions of ties cannot be sold, $1.33 represents $1\frac{1}{3}$ and $2.67 represents $2\frac{2}{3}$. Using a common multiple that will result in whole numbers, we get a ratio of $1:2$ if we divide both sides by $1\frac{1}{3}$. Thus for every three ties, the proportions will need to be

$$1 @ \$16.00 : 2 @ \$12.00$$

(c) Find the number of ties to be sold at each price:
Since 144 ties were purchases and 1 of 3 are to be at $16.00 while the remaining 2 of 3 are to be at $12.00,

$$\tfrac{1}{3} \text{ of } 144 = 48 \text{ at } \$16.00$$

and

$$\tfrac{2}{3} \text{ of } 144 = 96 \text{ at } \$12.00$$

Therefore, of the 12 dozen ties purchased, 4 dozen will be sold at $16.00 and 8 dozen will be sold at $12.00 for the buyer to realize an average markup of 40% on these purchases.

PROBLEM 8: A ladies' dress buyer has established an average markup of 37.5% on a line of dresses she wishes to purchase for the spring season. The buyer was able to purcase a special assortment of these dresses for $72 and subsequently agreed to purchase 30 dozen. Determine how many of these dresses the buyer may put in her $96 price line and how many in her $120 price line and still realize the average markup planned.

TWO COSTS, ONE RETAIL PRICE

In the previous section we explored the situation under which a buyer would be able to manipulate a markup by pricing merchandise at two different retail prices while the items had the same cost. However, it is a much more common practice in retail organizations to establish one retail price for goods that have different cost prices. The customer shopping in a retail store would become totally confused if the retailer were to carry as many retail price lines as there are wholesale and manufacturer costs.

Retailers who do not find it profitable to place all their orders of merchandise at one time find that the prices they pay for reorders may fluctuate on the same items. Furthermore, manufacturers and wholesalers clear out merchandise in advance of the end of the season, and as a result buyers are able to obtain better cost prices. Retailers of relatively stable merchandise have also found it profitable to purchase some merchandise in anticipation of a price increase by a manufacturer or wholesaler and, as a result, find themselves with the same merchandise at one retail price but different cost prices.

Therefore, retailers have also made use of varying costs of the same merchandise items to achieve the desired average markup for the store or department.

EXAMPLE 9: **Finding the Proportion with Two Costs Given the Retail Price and the Average Markup**

A gift department was able to purchase some cups and saucers for the department at a cost of $11.50. However, midway through the season, the buyer is informed that the reorder cost on these items will be $13.50 as a result of labor costs. The buyer wishes to purchase additional cups and saucers but also realizes that all must be placed in the $20.00 price line. Determine the proportion of cups and saucers the buyer must sell at each retail price to obtain an average markup of 40%.

Solution:

(a) Find the average cost price to obtain the average markup:

$$
\begin{array}{rlcl}
 & \text{Cost} & = & = 60\% \\
+ & \text{Markup} & = & = 40\% \\
\hline
 & \text{Retail} & = \$20.00 & = 100\%
\end{array}
$$

Therefore, the average cost will be $12.00.

(b) Find the loss or gain on average cost of the purchase:

	$11.50	$13.50
Actual Cost		
Average Cost	12.00	12.00
Loss or Gain on Average	+$0.50	-$1.50
	1 :	3

Therefore, for every cup and saucer purchased at $13.50, he loses $1.50 from the average cost, and for every one purchased at $11.50, he gains $0.50 from the average cost. Eliminating the fractional element of the proportions by dividing each side by 0.50, we find that the ratio should be 1:3; that is, for every 4 items purchased, he must purchase

1 @ $13.50   and   3 @ $11.50

PROBLEM 9: A boys' wear buyer is able to purchase a line of boys' shirts at $6.00 from one manufacturer. However, she has not been able to buy enough from this manufacturer and is required to purchase some from another supplier at $7.25. If she wishes to place all the shirts in the $10.00 price line, determine the proportion that should be purchased at each price if she is to attain an average markup of 35%.

EXAMPLE 10: **Finding the Number of Units at Two Costs Given the Retail Price and the Average Markup**

NOTE: The following problem is to be solved without the benefit of an example since it represents the same procedure established in the preceding problems.

PROBLEM 10: A buyer is able to purchase pottery coffee mugs at $25.00 per dozen and $36.00 per dozen. She plans to retail all coffee mugs in her $4.00 collection. If the buyer plans to purchase 44 dozen, determine how many she may purchase at each price to obtain an average markup of $33\frac{1}{3}\%$.

AVERAGE MARKUP ON DIFFERENT CLASSIFICATIONS

It is customary for the departments of retail stores to be composed of different classifications of merchandise. It is also rare to find departments in which all classifications of merchandise contribute equally to the overall sales volume of the department or to obtain the same markup. Consequently, in this section, we become concerned with the buyer's process of planning the average markup on the basis of the various classifications that constitute the department.

Although the buyer of the department is obviously concerned with the markup that he or she obtains in each classification, the buyer is also concerned with achieving a planned average markup for the department. To this point, we have been concerned with the buyer's interest in attempting to reach a predetermined average markup on a line of merchandise that he or she plans to purchase rather than the impact of the department as a whole.

In this section, we now become concerned with decisions that the buyer has to make in deciding on a markup for a classification so that the entire department can achieve the planned average markup. Further, as new developments in merchandise lines and scramble merchandising continue to abound, the buyer must decide what markup he or she must obtain in a new section to be added to the department if the overall average markup is to be reached. These are merely some of the situations a buyer faces in attempting to plan the departmental average markup by the manipulation of the markups anticipated in the various classifications of the department.

Students should note that it is not possible to determine the average markup for the department by adding up the various markups for each classification and then dividing this total by the number of classifications in the department. This situation will result only in the event that each classification represents an equal proportion of total sales or total costs to all other classifications in the department.

EXAMPLE 11: Finding the Department's Average Markup Given the Markups and Relative Retail Values of the Classifications

A gift department is divided into three sections: Section A accounts for three-fifths of the department's sales volume and has a markup of $33\frac{1}{3}$%, Section B accounts for one-fifth of the sales volume and has a markup of 37.5%, and Section C accounts for the remainder of the department sales and carries a markup of 42.0%. As the assistant in the department, you are required to determine the average markup for the department.

Solution:

Since we are dealing in relative figures in terms of the three sections' contributions to departmental sales, we may assume a total sales figure since the ratio remains constant. Therefore, it is advisable to choose a number to represent sales that is easily divisible by all the denominators of the portion of sales and large enough to avoid too many decimal places.

For purposes of this example, we are assuming a sales volume of $1,000, since this is easily divisible by fifths.

Therefore, we set up the problem solution as follows:

Section		Portion of Total Sales		Markup Percent		Markup Dollars
A	=	$\frac{3}{5}$ = $600	@	$33\frac{1}{3}$%	=	$200
B	=	$\frac{1}{5}$ = 200	@	37.5	=	75
C	=	$\frac{1}{5}$ = 200	@	42.0	=	84
Total	=	$\frac{5}{5}$ = $1,000		?	=	$359

The average markup for the department can be determined if it is possible to determine the markup dollars for the department, since

$$\frac{\$ M}{\$ R} \times 100\% = M \% \qquad \frac{359}{1000} \times 100 = 35.9\%$$

The student will note that the portion of sales contributed by Section C is what remains out of a total of five-fifths and, therefore, must be one-fifth.

Since retail values of each section are known and the markup percent of each section is based on retail, markup dollars can easily be determined by multiplying $ R \times M$ %. The dollar markups are then placed in the table and totaled.

Thus,

$$\text{Average Markup} = \frac{\$359}{\$1,000} \times 100\% = 35.9\%$$

Therefore, the average markup for the gift department would be 35.9%.

PROBLEM 11: A department has been divided into four sections for purposes of control. Section A accounts for three-tenths of the department's sales and has a markup of 40%, Section B accounts for two-fifths of the sales and has a markup of 37.5%, Section C accounts for one-fifth of the sales and has a markup of 35%, and Section D accounts for the remainder of the season sales and has a markup of $33\frac{1}{3}\%$. Determine the average markup for the department.

EXAMPLE 12: **Finding the Markup of One Section Given the Markups and Relative Retail Values of the Other Sections and the Average Markup**

A men's apparel shop has been divided into the following sections: Clothing accounts for 30.0% of the sales and has a markup of 40.0%, furnishings account for 40.0% of the sales and have a markup of 37.5%, and shoes account for 15.0% of the sales and show a markup of $33\frac{1}{3}\%$. If the store wishes to add a fourth section that will account for the remainder of the sales, what markup must be obtained in this new accessories section to realize an average markup of 38.0% for the store?

Solution:

Again we assume a sales volume of $1,000, since the distribution is based on percentages.

Section	Portion of Total Sales		Markup Percent		Markup Dollars
Clothing	30% =	$300 @	40.0%	=	$120
Furnishings	40 =	400 @	37.5	=	150
Shoes	15 =	150 @	$33\frac{1}{3}$	=	50
Accessories	15 =	150 @	?	=	—
Total	100% =	$1,000 @	38.0%	=	$380

Multiplying the retail sales in each classification by the markup for each classification, we are able to determine the markup dollars for each section, with the exception of the new accessories department.

$$
\begin{array}{rl}
 & \text{Total Markup Dollars} \qquad\qquad \$380 \\
- & \text{Markup on Clothing, Shoes,} \\
 & \quad \text{and Furnishings} \qquad\qquad\quad \underline{320} \\
= & \text{Markup Dollars - Accessories} \quad \underline{\$60}
\end{array}
$$

$$
\text{Markup Percent in Accessories} = \frac{\$60}{\$150} \times 100\% = 40\%
$$

PROBLEM 12: A shoe department has its merchandise divided into three sections. Men's shoes account for 40.0% of the retail sales in the department and have a markup of 37.5%, ladies' shoes account for 40.0% of the retail sales and have a markup of 35.0%, and the remainder of the sales in the department are generated from the accessory items. Find the markup the buyer requires on these accessory items so that an average markup of 39.0% for the department is realized.

EXAMPLE 13: Finding the Department's Average Markup Given Markups and Relative Cost Values of Sections

A department is divided into four sections: Section A has stock that represents one-fourth of the department's stock at cost and has a markup of $33\frac{1}{3}\%$, Section B represents one-eighth of the stock at cost and has a markup of 37.5%, Section C represents one-half of the stock at cost and has a markup of 37.5%, and Section D represents one-eighth of the stock at cost and has a markup of 25.0%. Find the average markup for the department.

Solution:

Let us assume a total cost figure of $800:

Section		Portion of Total Costs	Markup Percent		Markup Dollars
A	=	$\frac{1}{4}$ = $200	$33\frac{1}{3}\%$	=	$100.00[a]
B	=	$\frac{1}{8}$ = 100	37.5	=	60.00[b]
C	=	$\frac{1}{2}$ = 400	37.5	=	240.00[c]
D	=	$\frac{1}{8}$ = 100	25.0	=	33.33[d]
Total	=	$\frac{8}{8}$ = $800	?	=	$433.33

In solution of the problem, the first step must be in determining the markup dollars in each section. The problem, however, differs from the previous example since we are here dealing with relative cost values, while the markup percent is based on retail. As a result, markup dollars must be calculated by the following means:

(a)

$$C = \$200 = 66\tfrac{2}{3}\% \; (\tfrac{2}{3})$$
$$+ \quad M = \qquad = 33\tfrac{1}{3}\% \; (\tfrac{1}{3})$$
$$R = \qquad = 100\% \quad (\tfrac{3}{3})$$

Markup = $100

(b)

$$C = \$100 = 62.5\% \; (\tfrac{5}{8})$$
$$+ \quad M = \qquad = 37.5\% \; (\tfrac{3}{8})$$
$$R = \qquad = 100.0\% \; (\tfrac{8}{8})$$

Markup = $60

(c)

$$C = \$400 = 62.5\% \; (\tfrac{5}{8})$$
$$+ \quad M = \qquad = 37.5\% \; (\tfrac{3}{8})$$
$$R = \qquad = 100.0\% \; (\tfrac{8}{8})$$

Markup = $240

(d)

$$C = \$100 = 75\% \; (\tfrac{3}{4})$$
$$+ \quad M = \qquad = 25\% \; (\tfrac{1}{4})$$
$$R = \qquad = 100\% \; (\tfrac{4}{4})$$

Markup = $33.33

Therefore, the total markup dollars can be obtained by adding the markup dollars of each section ($433.33):

Total Cost	$800.00
Total Markup	433.33
Total Retail	$1,233,33

and

$$\text{Markup \%} = \frac{\$433.33}{\$1,233.33} \times 100\% = 35.13\%$$

Therefore, the average markup for the department would be 35.13%.

PROBLEM 13: To show a balanced assortment of new spring styles, a buyer of ladies' coats purchased different styles from different suppliers. From the ABC Company she placed 26.0% of her purchases at cost and marked these coats up 35.0%, from the DEF Company she placed 33.0% of her purchases at cost and gave these a markup of 34.0%, from the GHK Company she bought a special promotion that only gave a 30.0% markup, and from the LMN Company she placed the remaining 20.0% of her purchases at cost and gave these a markup of 37.5%. Find the average markup the buyer would obtain on the total purchase of the spring coats.

EXAMPLE 14: Finding the Markup for One Section Given Markups and Relative Cost Values of the Other Sections and Average Markup

NOTE: Since this problem is similar to the preceding examples of departmental classifications, you are asked to solve the following problem without the benefit of an example.

PROBLEM 14: An independent hardware store has decided to add a lawn and garden section to the store. At the present time, one-eighth of the stock at cost is in sporting goods and carries a markup of 50%, one-fourth of the stock at cost is in hand and power tools and carries a markup of $33\frac{1}{3}$%, one-fourth of the stock at cost is in general hardware and carries a markup of 37.5%, one-fourth of the stock at cost is in housewares and carries a markup of 37.5%, and the remaining portion of the stock at cost is to be allocated to the new lawn and garden department. Determine the markup that the merchant will need in this section if he plans to obtain an average markup of 37.5% for all departments.

SUMMARY PROBLEMS

1. While visiting a trade show, a gift buyer places an order for 300 decorator plaques at a cost of $45.00 per dozen. The buyer intends to place some of the items in her $5.25 price line, while the better designs will be placed in the $7.50 price line. Determine the number of plaques that should be placed in each price line if the buyer is to obtain an average markup of 37.5%.

2. This same gift buyer has divided her department into four sections. Linens have a markup of 40.0% and account for one-sixth of the purchases as cost, crystal and glassware has a markup of $33\frac{1}{3}$% and accounts for one-fifth of the purchases at cost, dinnerware earns a markup of 35.0% and accounts for one-third of the purchases at cost, and general gifts account for the remainder of the purchases at cost and are marked up 37.5%. Determine the average markup for the gift department.

3. The buyer of a bed and bath boutique purchased some comforters at a cost of $5,200, which she marked up 42%. The buyer has also determined that she will require some additional items to complete her assortment and wishes to mark these up 47%. Determine the cost and retail value of these purchases if the buyer wishes to obtain an average markup of 45% for the period.

4. A men's apparel store was formerly composed of three sections but now wishes to add shoes to its merchandise assortment. Men's clothing represents 35% of the store's sales and carries a markup of 40.0%, men's furnishings account for 40% of the store's sales with a markup of 37.5%, boys' apparel accounts for 15% of the sales and has a markup of $33\frac{1}{3}$, and the shoe department is expected to account for the remainder of the sales. Determine the markup that will be needed in the shoe section of the store to realize an average markup of 38.0%.

5. The buyer of ladies' swimwear has opted to purchase swimsuits at different times during the season. Her first order accounted for one-half of her budget at cost and had a markup of 37.5%; her second order accounted for one-third of her budget at cost and had a markup of $33\frac{1}{3}$%; and her third order was her final order and accounted for the remainder of her budget allotment at cost. If the buyer wishes to obtain an average markup of 37.5% for this line, determine what the markup should be on her final order of swimsuits.

6. The housewares department is required to obtain an average markup of 39%. At the present time, the department shows an inventory at retail of $12,000 that is marked up 40%. The budget indicates that the total merchandise to be handled by the department for the period is $26,000 at retail. Determine the markup that will be required on the additional purchases for the department if the buyer is to obtain an average markup of 39%.

7. At the beginning of the season, the buyer of ladies' sportswear purchased an assortment of ladies' handbags worth $4,800 at cost that were subsequently marked up 40.0%. The buyer wishes to obtain an average markup of 37.5% in the handbag section of the department. She has been offered a special line of handbags that she can offer as a special promotion to customers at a markup of 36.0%. Determine what the cost and retail value of these additional purchases can be to allow the buyer her average markup.

8. A buyer has a $48.00 price line of blankets that he is offering during the fall-winter season. He needs to refill his stock with 20 dozen in the double bed size and is able to purchase some at $29.00 and some $34.00 from two different manufacturers. How many can he purchase from each manufacturer if he wishes to obtain an average markup of $33\frac{1}{3}\%$ on this line?

9. On September 1 the buyer noted that the B.O.M. stock for the month was $36,000 at cost and was marked up 40%. Upon checking her plan for the season, the buyer notes that she has a budget limit for September of $72,000 at retail and wishes to achieve her average markup of 38% for the month. To achieve these figures, determine the markup she will require on the additional purchases she wishes to make during the month.

10. The buyer of a sporting goods department has a purchase limit of $60,000 at retail for the fall-winter season and is expected to realize an average markup of $33\frac{1}{3}\%$. To date she has a retail inventory of $30,000 that carries a markup of 30%. Determine the markup she will require on her additional purchases to bring her markup to the planned average markup of $33\frac{1}{3}\%$.

11. The drapery department has a retail inventory of $33,500 with a markup of 40%. The buyer has a planned averaged markup of 37% for the period. If the buyer wishes to purchase additional merchandise and mark it up 35%, determine the most she may pay for this merchandise at cost and retail to obtain her average markup of 37%.

12. A ladies' accessories buyer purchased 200 scarves at $12 each. Some of these scarves will be placed in her $18 price line, while the others will be retailed at $24. Determine the number of scarves that should be placed in each retail price line for the buyer to achieve her average markup of 40%.

13. A shoe department is divided into four sections. Men's shoes represent 25% of the purchases at cost and carry a markup of 42.0%, women's shoes represent 40% of the purchases at cost and have a markup of 47.0%, children's shoes represent 20% of the purchases at cost and have a markup of 40.0%, and the accessory section accounts for the balance of the purchases at cost and carries a markup of 37.5%. Determine the average markup for the shoe department.

14. A buyer is able to purchase 35 dozen special promotional items from two different manufacturers: One manufacturer offers her the item at a cost of $9.60, while the other manufacturer requires a cost of $11.00. The buyer wishes to retail all items at $18.00 and has asked you to determine how many she can purchase from each supplier if she is to obtain an average markup of 40%.

15. The buyer in an appliance department purchased some small appliances at $8,000 at cost that he marked up 37.5%. He has spotted some additional merchandise that he can purchase and mark up 42.0%. He has asked you to determine the cost and retail value of these additional purchases if he wishes to obtain an average markup of 40.0%.

16. The home furnishings department is required to obtain an average markup of 36.0% for the spring-summer season. At the opening, the department shows an inventory of $61,000 at cost that is marked up 39.0%. During the season some merchandise was received into stock valued at $40,000 at retail with a markup of 37.5%. Determine the markup that the department will require on additional purchases if the budget limit for the period is $180,000 at retail.

17. Calculate the proportion in which the buyer must purchase merchandise for her department to obtain her average markup, if she has the following information:

Planned Average Markup	38%
Actual Markup to Date	36%
Additional Markup Planned	49%

18. A buyer has a $24.00 price line of polyester sheets. He needs to refill his stock with 30 dozen of the double bed size, plain and fitted. The buyer is able to purchase some at $13.60 each and some at $15.00 each from two different manufacturers. How many can he purchase from each manufacturer if he is to obtain an average markup of 40%?

19. An independent hardware store is divided into five departments: Hardware accounts for 25% of the sales and carries a markup of $33\frac{1}{3}\%$, paints and wallpaper account for 10% of the sales and have a markup of 40%, hand and power tools account for 15% of the sales and have a markup of 35%, and housewares account for 30% of the sales and carry a markup of 42%. Calculate the markup on the sporting goods department, which accounts for the remainder of the sales, if the store is to obtain an average markup of 37.5%.

20. A buyer of men's furnishings has his average markup for a line of men's shirts established at 38%. As a special promotion for Father's Day, the buyer purchased a line of these shirts for $1,800 at cost and placed a markup on these items of 25%. If the buyer anticipates that the largest markup he can obtain on shirts is 40%, calculate the amount of regular merchandise he must sell to obtain his planned markup of 38%.

21. The B.O.M. stock in the housewares department was $26,000 at cost for October and carried a markup of 35%. During October, the buyer received merchandise valued at $38,000 at retail and carried a markup of 42%. Determine the average markup percent in the housewares department during October.

22. A gift department purchased 10 dozen salad bowl sets at a cost of $30 per set. Because of some differences in style and patterns, the buyer wishes to place some in her $40 price line and some in the $60 price line. If she wishes to obtain an average markup of 40%, calculate the number that she must sell at each price line.

23. The buyer of ladies' skirts hopes to achieve an average markup of 41.0% for the fall-winter season. On November 1, the buyer realizes that her merchandise has only produced a markup of 37.5% to date and was valued at $27,000 at retail. With the advent of Christmas buying, the buyer hopes to purchase additional items and mark these up 42.0%, the most she feels she can get. Determine how much additional merchandise the buyer will have to purchase to obtain her average markup.

24. The men's clothing department showed an inventory of $28,000 at cost and $40,000 at retail on November 1. During the month, the department received additional merchandise to take advantage of Christmas selling. The merchandise received during November showed a cost of $30,000 and a markup of 40%. What was the average markup for the clothing department for November?

25. A department has been allocated an average markup figure of 37.5% for the period. The buyer has purchased a select group of items that carries a markup of 40.0% and for which he paid $12,000 at cost. The same buyer wishes to purchase a special promotional assortment that will carry a markup of 36.0%. Determine the cost and retail value of these purchases if the buyer is to meet his predetermined average markup of 37.5%.

chapter 6

Determining Markup

Up to this point, we have been concerned with the process involved in calculating the markup on an individual item and the markups that result from group purchases by retail merchants. What is now required to ensure our understanding of the complexities of markup is to determine the techniques involved in establishing these markups. How does a merchant determine whether the merchandise entering the store should carry a markup of 37.5% or 42.0%? How will the merchant determine whether the average markup figures for this classification should be 39% or 45%?

We have indicated that progressive retail merchants calculate markups on the basis of the retail price, utilizing the basic equation of

$$Cost + Markup = Retail$$

And to determine the markup using retail as the base, we discovered the following relationship:

$$\frac{\$\ Markup}{\$\ Retail} \times 100\% = Markup\ \%\ of\ Retail$$

To understand markup in a retail operation, the true meaning of this retail figure must now be established. If the buyer has purchased a line of gloves for the store and marks these at $35.00 when brought into inventory, and subsequently prices these at $24.00 because they have not sold, which retail price is to be recorded by the merchant? We are, then, faced with two retail prices in a merchandising operation:

1. *Purchase Retail:* This figure represents the retail price we place on an item when it enters the retail store (gloves in the example at $35.00). This in fact is the retail price sug-

gested by the supplier or the price the buyer hopes to realize for the product when the order is placed. Purchase retail is the original or *initial retail price* placed on the item by a merchant.

2. *Sales Retail:* This figure represents the retail price that is received by the merchant when the item is sold (gloves in the example above at $24.00, if they are sold at this price). Hence, the difference between the sale price and the purchase price will be represented by reductions in retail value taken by the merchant. The sales retail consequently represents *the final retail price* of the merchant.

It should then be obvious that the initial retail prices are normally higher than the retail prices at which the goods are ultimately sold, since some reductions in the form of markdowns, stock shortages, or employee discounts may occur. This final retail price or sale retail provides us with what we shall see in our maintained markup. This maintained markup is the difference between the actual price of the sold item and the gross cost of the goods sold, expressed as a percentage of sales.

In this chapter, we are, therefore, concerned with the relationship that exists between our original retail price and the final selling price of the merchandise. Consequently, we need to understand the relationship among initial markup, maintained markup, and gross margin. The student should note that the successful retailer will need to plan all three of these markups to experience growth and profitability of the operation. Since the maintained markup and gross margin represent the retailers' final markups, it is essential that these be planned in relation to the initial or original markup.

In actual practice, retailers soon become aware of the fact that the initial markup placed on the merchandise will be reduced by such factors as markdowns, stock shortages, employee discounts, and alteration expenses. This same initial markup will also be affected by any cash discounts that the retailer has been able to negotiate in the purchase of goods for the store. As a result of these adjustments to markup, the buyer plans the initial markup on the basis of these factors so that the final markup will be large enough to cover operating expenses and still provide a profit.

Planning is required for success in retail management. And the planning of markup is as essential to the operation as the acquisition of the right merchandise. Buying and selling the right merchandise becomes a futile effort if the amount of profit to be obtained in the exercise is not sufficient to allow for continuation of the enterprise. As a result, buyers with their merchandise controllers usually plan the initial markup for the department or store on a seasonal or annual basis. Buyers and department managers are therefore required to plan in advance their estimates of total sales, net profit, operating expenses, markdowns, employee discounts, stock shortages, cash discounts, and, where applicable, alteration expenses for the period. Once this information is obtained, the initial markup is planned to achieve the desired maintained or final markup goal.

The meaning and effect of the following factors are presented here to allow the student a more comprehensive understanding of their impact on the determination of markup.

Reductions :   ## 1º MARKDOWNS

Selling prices do not always remain the same, although the invoice cost does. Markdowns are taken to move merchandise, and these reductions will consequently lessen the amount of the final markup that will be obtained. As a result, the initial markup that is placed on the merchandise must be large enough to cover the amount of the planned markdowns. Very few retail stores have been able to operate without taking markdowns.

2º STOCK SHORTAGES

This amount represents the shrinkage of merchandise inventory through loss or theft. Whether the merchandise is taken by the customer or by the employee, the fact remains that it disappears from inventory. The increasing amount of pilferage and shoplifting in today's society forces the buyer to plan stock shortages carefully in his or her operation. The amount of merchandise shrinkage is a loss that reduces the amount of the final markup; as a result, the initial markup must be planned to include a provision for these shortages.

3º EMPLOYEE DISCOUNTS

Since almost all retail establishments offer their employees special discounts of from 10% to 25% or more off the retail value of their purchases at the store, these discounts affect the final markup that the store receives. Similarly, the amount of the employee discounts is planned so that the initial markup will be large enough to provide for these discounts and still allow the store to obtain a satisfactory maintained markup. Special discounts that are offered to specific customers are treated in the same manner as employee discounts.

REDUCTIONS

These three factors of markdowns, employee discounts, and stock shortages represent the reductions in the retail value of the merchandise sold and will affect the initial and maintained markups of the operation.

1º ALTERATION EXPENSE

Many kinds of merchandise need some adjustments made before the products or services are acceptable to the consumer. Such adjustments are referred to as alteration expenses or workroom costs. It should also be noted that some retailers provide this service free to their customers, as generally found in men's apparel stores. In this type of establishment, the alteration expense may run as high as 5% of net sales. Some retail stores, on the other hand, charge a nominal fee for alterations, and this revenue is set off against the cost of providing the service. In most cases where revenue is received for alterations, the cost of the service will exceed the revenue and the resultant figure will become a net alteration expense. In those cases where alteration revenue outpaces the alteration expense, the result will be a net alteration revenue figure. Again, the initial markup must be planned to be large enough to cover the expenses generated by the service of alterations. It is because alterations may produce some revenue, as we noted, that these are treated separately from operating expenses.

2º CASH DISCOUNTS

As pointed out earlier, cash discounts are offered to retailers by suppliers as an inducement for prompt payment of accounts. The cash discount obtained when invoices are paid reduces the cost of the merchandise and therefore affects the final markup obtained by the store or department. However, it is customary for the buyer to exclude the cash discount in calculating the net profit since, normally, the buyer has no control over the payment of the invoices by the controller's office nor should the buyer consider these as resulting from his or her department's operation. In other words, the buyer will calculate the markup on the billed cost of the merchandise rather than the actual cost.

As we shall now see, these elements become essential ingredients in the planning and determination of the initial and maintained markups for the retail operations. The accompanying exhibit seeks to explain this relationship in establishing markup goals.

THE MARKUP RELATIONSHIP

This chart is designed to explain the relationship that is fundamental among the three markups of gross margin, maintained markup and initial markup and the subsequent relationships that can be derived. The following acronyms are used for each of the elements in explaining the relationships:

G.M. = Gross Margin	O.E. = Operating Expenses	C.D. = Cash Discounts
M.M. = Maintained Markup	N.P. = Net Profit	RED. = Reductions
I.M. = Initial Markup	A.E. = Alteration Expenses	N.S. = Net Sales

Fundamental	Explanations	Derived
G.M. = O.E. + N.P.	G.M. needs to be large enough to cover operating expenses and still provide a profit. Since this is the *final* markup, it is expressed as a percentage of N.S. (100%).	
M.M. = O.E. + N.P. + A.E. - C.D.	M.M. is also the *final* markup but differs from G.M. by the effect of A.E. and C.D. Substituting in this equation, G.M. = O.E. + N.P., we derive	M.M. = G.M. + A.E. - C.D. or G.M. = M.M. - A.E. + C.D.
$I.M. = \dfrac{O.E. + N.P. + A.E. - C.D. + RED.}{N.S.\ (100\%) + RED}$	I.M. is the *original* markup and thus is expressed as a percentage of the original retail price (N.S. + RED.). Consequently, the original markup differs from the final by the effect of RED. And substituting in this equation that M.M. = O.E. + N.P. + A.E. - C.D., we derive	$I.M. = \dfrac{M.M. + RED.}{100\% + RED.}$

Therefore, the relationship is expressed as

$$I.M. = \frac{\overbrace{\underbrace{O.E. + N.P. + A.E. - C.D.}_{G.M.} + RED.}^{M.M.}}{N.S.\ (100\%) + RED.}$$

THE MARKUP RELATIONSHIP

The profit model of the retail store is best expressed in the relationship that is demonstrated from an examination of the retailer's income and expense statement. Students will recall that the fundamental elements of this statement are related in the following manner:

	Net Sales	$100,000
−	Total Cost of Goods Sold	60,000
=	Gross Margin	$ 40,000
−	Operating Expenses	32,000
=	Net Profit	$ 8,000

GROSS MARGIN

From this statement, it should become obvious that the Gross Margin represents the final markup obtained by the merchant. And in planning this figure, we note that the Gross Margin must be large enough to cover our operating expenses and still provide the store with a net profit. Consequently, the final markup as expressed in Gross Margin is noted as

$$Gross\ Margin = Operating\ Expenses + Net\ Profit$$

The student will readily note that Gross Margin can also be expressed in relationship to Net Sales from the foregoing statement. In this case, the Gross Margin equation would appear as

$$Gross\ Margin = Net\ Sales - Total\ Cost\ of\ Goods\ Sold$$

In this equation, the Net Sales figure reported on the profit and loss statement is in fact the total of the final selling prices received by the store as differentiated from the original retail prices placed on the merchandise. To understand the relationship that exists between Gross Margin and Maintained Markup, since both have been classified as the final markup obtained by the merchant, we need to explore the concept of Total Cost of Goods Sold.

The figure referred to as the Total Cost of Goods Sold is made up of the billed invoice cost of the merchandise that has produced the net sales figure. But this figure has been adjusted by the cash discounts earned and the alteration expenses to produce the Gross Cost of Goods Sold. Hence, when retail merchants experience cash discounts and alteration expenses, the Cost of Goods Sold section of the statement now appears as

	Net Sales		$100,000
−	Gross Cost of Goods Sold	$58,000	
+	Alteration Expenses	3,000	
−	Cash Discounts	1,000	
	Total Cost of Goods Sold		60,000
=	Gross Margin		$ 40,000
−	Operating Expenses		32,000
	Net Profit		$ 8,000

On the basis of this information, we are now ready to examine the relationship between Gross Margin and Maintained Markup.

MAINTAINED MARKUP

Since maintained markup and gross margin both represent the final markup obtained by a retail store, it should be noted that this markup is not received until the merchandise is sold. Consequently, both markups will be based on the net sales figure rather than on original retail prices of the merchandise.

Retail stores that are unable to negotiate cash discounts and that offer customers no alteration service will readily find that the maintained markup obtained is equal to the gross margin. However, since many merchants do experience both of these situations, adjustments for cash discounts and alteration expenses will need to be made in planning the differences between Gross Margin and Maintained Markup.

Therefore, the relationship between these two final markups can now be expressed:

	Net Sales	$100,000
−	Gross Cost of Goods Sold	58,000
=	Maintained Markup	$ 42,000
−	Alteration Expenses	$ 3,000
		$ 39,000
+	Cash Discounts	1,000
=	Gross Margin	$ 40,000
−	Operating Expenses	32,000
=	Net Profit	$ 8,000

Therefore, on the basis of this information, the following relationships between Maintained Markup and Gross Margin can be established.

Stores without Cash Discounts and Alteration Expenses find that

> Gross Margin = Maintained Markup
>
> or
>
> Maintained Markup = Operating Expenses + Net Profit

Stores with Cash Discounts and Alteration Expenses find that

> Gross Margin = Maintained Markup − Alteration Expenses + Cash Discounts
> or, transposing terms,
> Maintained Markup = Gross Margin + Alteration Expenses − Cash Discounts

And, since Gross Margin = Operating Expenses + Net Profit,

1st Formula

> $$\text{Maintained Markup} = \frac{\text{Operating}}{\text{Expenses}} + \frac{\text{Net}}{\text{Profit}} + \frac{\text{Alteration}}{\text{Expenses}} - \frac{\text{Cash}}{\text{Discount}}$$

We have now explored the relationship that exists with the final markups that are planned for a retail store. For the merchant to arrive at these planned final figures, it then becomes necessary to establish the beginning markup to arrive at this goal. We now turn to the calculation of initial markup.

INITIAL MARKUP

By definition, the initial markup represents the first markup placed on an item to give us the original retail price that the merchant hopes to receive. However, we have discovered that the original retail price placed on an item differs from the amount that is finally received by the store when the item is sold by the amount of the reductions. These reductions we have said are composed of markdowns, stock shortages, and employee discounts and, consequently, must be planned by the retailer if he or she is to reach the planned maintained markup and gross margin.

The Net Sales figure found on an income and expense statement represents the final retail prices received for items. The original retail price for the merchandise must then be expressed by the sum of net sales and reductions:

$$\text{Original Retail} = \text{Net Sales} + \text{Reductions}$$

Since the final retail price becomes the base upon which all factors of the operation are expressed, the net sales figure always represents 100%. For example, all operating expenses are expressed as a percentage of net sales, gross margin is expressed as a percentage of net sales, and net operating profit is also expressed as a percentage of net sales. Consequently, substituting in the equation, we will also find

$$\text{Original Retail} = 100\% + \text{Reductions}$$

Therefore, since the original retail price placed on an item must be large enough to take care of all reductions and still provide the desired gross margin and maintained markup, initial markup dollars will be expressed as

$$\text{Initial Markup \$} = \text{Maintained Markup \$} + \text{Reduction \$}$$

To express the initial markup as a percentage, it is, therefore, necessary to use the original retail as the base figure. Consequently, combining the two equations of initial markup, we find the following relationship:

$$\text{Initial Markup \%} = \frac{\text{Maintained Markup} + \text{Reductions}}{\text{Net Sales} + \text{Reductions}} \times 100\%$$

The student will note that with this formula, initial markup could be calculated using dollars or percent figures. In addition, by breaking down the maintained markup figure into its components, we could expand the formula to include all the elements in the initial markup figure:

$$\text{Initial Markup \%} = \frac{\begin{array}{c}\text{Operating} + \text{Net} + \text{Alteration} - \text{Cash} + \text{Reductions}\\ \text{Expenses} \quad \text{Profit} \quad \text{Expenses} \quad \text{Discounts}\end{array}}{\text{Net Sales (100\%)} + \text{Reductions}} \times 100\%$$

We have now explored the relationship that exists among the three basic markups (markons) found in the operation of retail stores. It is important for the student to recognize that the successful retail merchant is required to plan the original markup (initial) for the operation based on the final markup (maintained or gross) that has been established as the store's objective.

Thus,

$$\text{I.M.} = \frac{\overbrace{\overbrace{\text{O.E.} + \text{N.P.}}^{\text{G.M.}} + \text{A.E.} - \text{C.D.} + \text{RED.}}^{\text{M.M.}}}{\text{N.S.} + \text{RED.}}$$

CALCULATION OF INITIAL MARKUP

Since the student is now aware of the total meaning of initial markup and the various factors that affect markup, it is now possible to explore the calculation of the planned initial markup for the buyer. Once again, the student is asked to recall that the merchant plans the initial markup in relation to a desired maintained or final markup goal.

The basic formula for calculating initial markup is, therefore, expressed as

$$\text{Initial Markup \%} = \frac{\begin{array}{c}\text{Operating} \\ \text{Expenses}\end{array} + \begin{array}{c}\text{Net} \\ \text{Profit}\end{array} + \begin{array}{c}\text{Alteration} \\ \text{Expenses}\end{array} - \begin{array}{c}\text{Cash} \\ \text{Discounts}\end{array} + \text{Reductions}}{\text{Net Sales (100\%)} + \text{Reductions}} \times 100\%$$

EXAMPLE 1: Finding Initial Markup Given Planned Dollar Figures

Determine the initial markup percent in a department that has the following planned figures for fall-winter:

Net Sales	$144,000	Markdowns	$5,100
Net Profit	4,500	Employee Discounts	300
Operating Expenses	49,000	Stock Shortages	600
Alteration Expenses	2,300	Cash Discounts	1,800

Solution:

$$\text{I.M. \%} = \frac{\begin{array}{c}\text{Operating} \\ \text{Expenses}\end{array} + \begin{array}{c}\text{Net} \\ \text{Profit}\end{array} + \begin{array}{c}\text{Alteration} \\ \text{Expenses}\end{array} - \begin{array}{c}\text{Cash} \\ \text{Discounts}\end{array} + \text{Reductions}}{\text{Net Sales} + \text{Reductions}} \times 100$$

Before substituting in this equation, the total reductions figure is calculated as follows:

Markdowns	$5,100
Employee Discounts	300
Stock Shortages	600
Total Reductions	$6,000

Substituting in the preceding equation,

$$\text{I.M. \%} = \frac{\$49,000 + \$4,500 + \$2,300 - \$1,800 + \$6,000}{\$144,000 + \$6,000} \times 100\%$$

$$= \frac{\$60,000}{\$150,000} \times 100\%$$

$$= 40\%$$

PROBLEM 1: Determine the buyer's initial markup percent using the following planned figures:

Net Sales	$230,000	Alteration Discounts	$3,500
Net Profit	21,000	Stock Shortages	1,800
Operating Expenses	72,000	Employee Discounts	2,200
Markdowns	8,500	Cash Discounts	5,500

EXAMPLE 2: Finding Initial Markup Given Planned Figures as a Percentage of Sales

NOTE: It is a common practice for buyers and merchandise controllers to plan with percentages of net sales rather than specific dollar amounts.

The buyer and merchandise controller have agreed upon the following planned figures for the department for the spring-summer season. Determine the initial markup percent.

Net Profit	5%	Employee Discounts	1%
Operating Expenses	31%	Stock Shortages	1%
Alteration Expenses	2%	Cash Discounts	2%
Markdowns	4%		

Solution:

Since all figures are based on net sales, this figure will be represented by 100% in the equation. The total reductions figure will be calculated to be 6%.

$$I.M.\ \% = \frac{\substack{\text{Operating} \\ \text{Expenses}} + \substack{\text{Net} \\ \text{Profit}} + \substack{\text{Alteration} \\ \text{Expenses}} - \substack{\text{Cash} \\ \text{Discount}} + \text{Reductions}}{\text{Net Sales (100\%) + Reductions}} \times 100\%$$

$$= \frac{31\% + 5\% + 2\% - 2\% + 6\%}{100\% + 6\%}$$

$$= \frac{42\%}{106\%} \times 100\%$$

$$= 39.6\%$$

PROBLEM 2: The following figures have been planned by the buyer for the coming season. As the assistant you have been asked to determine the initial markup percent that is required for the department.

Net Profit	6%	Employee Discounts	1%
Markdowns	5%	Stock Shortages	1%
Alteration Expenses	3%	Operating Expenses	28%
Cash Discounts	2%		

[Handwritten:]

Reductions =
5%
1%
1%
-7%

$$IM\% = \frac{OE + NP + ALT.E - CD + Red}{Net\ sales\ (100\%) + Red} \times 100\%$$

$$\frac{28\% + 6\% + 3\% - 2\% + 7\%}{100\% + 7\%} \times 100\% = 39.25\%$$

CALCULATION OF MAINTAINED MARKUP

There is nothing absolute about the prices that retailers establish for the merchandise they hope to sell. The customer is not concerned with the price that the store paid for the merchandise or whether the store is operated at a profit. The customer is concerned with the price he or she must pay for an item, which may be more or less than the price at which the item is marked.

In fact, the more discriminating the customer becomes in the future, the greater the need for proper markdown planning by the retailer.

If the retailer finds that the merchandise is not selling at the price he or she intended, it will be marked down to a price at which the customer will be induced to buy it. The final price may, in fact, be more or less than the retailer originally paid for the merchandise. Obviously, then, there is a considerable amount of trial and error in the pricing of the merchandise.

Retailers operating on the retail method of inventory control are required to keep records of the markdowns taken for a given period of time. In most cases, the record will indicate the number of items that were marked down, the amount and percentage of the markdown, and the reason for the markdown. For this reason, markdowns are recorded separately from net sales since the latter represents the final dollar amount received for the merchandise from the customer and the markdowns represent the additional markup that should have been received if the merchandise had sold at the original retail price. Retailers who maintain their inventory on a cost basis do not keep records of markdowns and, as a result, are unable to determine effectively the differences in markup obtained on various lines of merchandise.

Earlier, we noted that the relationship between maintained markup and initial markup was expressed in the following equation:

$$\text{Initial Markup \%} = \frac{\text{Maintained Markup} + \text{Reductions}}{100\% + \text{Reductions}} \times 100\%$$

If we transpose the terms in this equation, we find that $MM = IM (100\% + Red) - Red$

$$\text{I.M.} = \frac{\text{M.M.} + \text{RED.}}{100\% + \text{RED.}}$$

and

$$\text{I.M.} (100\% + \text{RED.}) = \text{M.M.} + \text{RED.}$$

And transposing terms,

$$\text{M.M.} = \text{I.M.} (100\% + \text{RED.}) - \text{RED.}$$

Therefore,

$$\text{Maintained Markup} = \text{Initial Markup} (100\% + \text{Reductions}) - \text{Reductions}$$

EXAMPLE 3: Finding the Maintained Markup Given Initial Markup and Markdown Percent

If the buyer of a department plans to take markdowns of 6% during the coming season and plans an initial markup of 42%, determine the maintained markup that is being planned by the buyer.

Solution:

As indicated earlier, the formula for maintained markup is

$$\begin{aligned}
\text{M.M.} &= \text{I.M.} (100\% + \text{RED.}) - \text{RED.} \\
&= 42\% (100\% + 6\%) - 6\% \\
&= [(.42 \times 1.06) - .06]\ 100\% \\
&= 38.52\%
\end{aligned}$$

PROBLEM 3: For the coming fall-winter season, Frank anticipates that markdowns will increase to 7% of his sales. To compensate for this increase, he also plans for an initial markup of 40%. Determine his planned maintained markup for the season.

$$MM = IM \ (100\% + Red) - Red$$
$$= 40\% \ (100\% + 7\%) - 7\%$$
$$= (.40 \times 1.07 \ ) - .07$$
$$= 35.8\%$$

EXAMPLE 4: Finding the Markdown Percent Given the Initial and Maintained Markups

The assistant buyer of ladies' lingerie has been asked by the buyer to determine the maximum markdown percent that may be taken in a department for the coming season. The assistant buyer is informed that a maintained markup is planned at 35% with an initial markup of 42%. Indicate the maximum markdown in the lingerie department that will be allowed for the coming season.

Solution:

Since

$$\text{M.M.} = \text{I.M.} \ (100\% + \text{RED.}) - \text{RED.}$$

then, by transposing terms in the equation, we get

$$\text{RED.} - \text{I.M.} \ (\text{RED.}) = \text{I.M.} - \text{M.M.}$$

Simplifying this equation,

$$\text{RED.} = \frac{\text{I.M.} - \text{M.M.}}{1 - \text{I.M.}}$$

and substituting in the equation, with the figures in the example,

$$\text{RED.} = \left(\frac{.42 - .35}{1 - .42}\right) 100\%$$
$$= 12.07\%$$

Therefore, the maximum reductions allowed in lingerie will be 12.07%.

PROBLEM 4: For the men's furnishings department to realize a maintained markup of 37%, the buyer has decided to place an initial markup of 40% on the merchandise received into the department during the period. Determine the maximum markdown percent that will be allowed under these circumstances in men's furnishings.

EXAMPLE 5: **Finding the Maintained Markup in Dollars Given Sales, Reductions, and Initial Markup**

The housewares department of a major department store has planned sales in one branch of $360,000 with markdowns planned at $22,000 and stock shortages of $2,000. The buyer has planned an initial markup of 37.5% for the period. Determine the maintained markup in dollars for the period being planned.

Solution:

Total reductions being planned are

Markdowns	$22,000
Stock Shortages	2,000
Total Reductions	$24,000

and

Maintained Markup = Initial Markup (100% + Reductions) − Reductions

or, in dollars,

$$\text{M.M. \$} = \text{I.M. \%} (\text{NET SALES \$} + \text{RED. \$}) - \text{RED. \$}$$
$$= .375 (\$360,000 + \$24,000) - \$24,000$$
$$= \$144,000 - \$24,000$$
$$= \$120,000$$

Therefore, the maintained markup in dollars will be $120,000.

PROBLEM 5: The china and giftware department has planned the following figures for the spring-summer season. Susan Smith, the buyer, has asked you to determine the maintained markup dollars that she can expect to realize at the end of the season.

Gross Sales	$200,000	Employee Discounts	$4,000
Sales Returns	10,000	Stock Shortages	1,500
Markdowns	15,000	Initial Markup	37.5%
Markdown Cancellations	3,000		

EXAMPLE 6: **Finding the Maintained Markup Percent Given Initial Markup and Total Reductions as a Percentage of Sales**

NOTE: The same procedure is followed when calculating maintained markup as a percent as that when maintained markup dollars is required. The student is asked to solve the following problem without the benefit of an example.

PROBLEM 6: The buyer of a department has the following planned figures for his department for the coming season. You are asked to determine the maintained markup percent that can be anticipated at the end of the season.

Initial Markup	35%	Employee Discounts	2%
Markdowns	8%	Stock Shortages	2%

EXAMPLE 7: **Finding the Remaining Markdowns Allowable Given Planned Maintained Markup and Activity to Date**

The planned sales for the spring-summer season in the luggage department is $265,000, with a planned initial markup of 40.0% and a planned maintained markup of 37.5%. About midway through the season, the buyer, Jennifer Chalmers, discovers that sales have reached $200,000 with markdowns of $6,000. To maintain control of the department, the buyer has requested that you determine the remaining markdowns in dollars and percent that she will be allowed for the balance of the period.

Solution:

We need to calculate the maximum markdowns allowed for the period based on the Reductions percent:

$$\text{RED.} = \frac{\text{I.M.} - \text{M.M.}}{1 - \text{I.M.}}$$

and, therefore, substituting in the equation from the figures given,

$$\text{RED. \%} = \left(\frac{.40 - .375}{1 - .40} \right) 100\%$$
$$= 4.17\%$$

Thus, the total reductions that will be allowed for the period would be 4.17% of total planned sales.

Since, the department is allowed 4.17% of the sales in reductions,

Markdowns, Allowed for the Season (4.17% of $265,000)	$11,050.50
Markdowns, Taken to Date	6,000.00
Markdowns, Allowed for the Balance	$ 5,050.50

Thus, the markdowns permissible for the balance of the season would be $5,050.50. These markdowns would then be allowed on the remaining sales for the season of $65,000 ($265,000 - $200,000):

$$\frac{\$5,050.50}{\$65,000.00} \times 100\% = 7.77\%$$

Therefore, the markdowns allowed for the balance of the season would be $5,050.50, or 7.77% of the remaining sales.

PROBLEM 7: The lawn and garden department has planned the following figures for spring-summer. Find the markdown percent that may be allowed for the remainder of the period if the department is able to realize its maintained markup.

Planned Sales for Season	$125,000	Planned Initial Markup	37.5%
Actual Sales to Date	$ 50,000	Planned Maintained Markup	32.0%
Actual Markdowns to Date	10%		

EXAMPLE 8: Finding the Markdown per Item Given the Planned Maintained Markup

As a special promotion, the men's furnishings buyer was able to purchase 15 dozen men's sports caps at a cost of $9.00 each to retail at $18.00. The buyer observed that he was able to sell 120 at this price but realized that the remainder would have to be marked down to clear the stock. If the buyer planned a maintained markup of 40% on these caps, determine the amount of the markdown he might take on each cap and still realize his planned figure.

Solution:

$$\text{Buyer's Total Cost} = 180 \ (15 \ \text{dozen}) \times \$9.00 = \$1,620.00$$

and the Planned Maintained Markup is 40%. Therefore, we need to determine the total retail he will require to realize his maintained markup:

	Cost	= $1,620.00 =	60%
+	Markup =	=	40%
	Retail =	? =	100%

Therefore,

$$\text{Total Retail Required} = \frac{\$1,620.00}{60\%} \times 100\% = \$2,700.00$$

Thus,

	Total Planned Sales	$2,700.00
−	Sales to Date (120 × $18.00)	2,160.00
=	Remaining Retail Required	$ 540.00

Thus, the remaining 60 caps (180 − 120) must provide a total retail amount of $540.00, so each cap must retail for

$$\frac{\$540.00}{60} = \$9.00$$

Therefore, each cap may be marked down $9.00, which in this example would mean that the caps would be selling at the cost price. However, the buyer will still realize his maintained markup of 40%.

PROBLEM 8: Melissa Roberts, a coat buyer, was able to purchase 240 all-weather coats for the spring season at a cost of $60.00 and placed these items in her $100.00 price line. After 150 coats were sold, the buyer realized that these coats would have to be reduced to move them off the racks before the end of season. If the buyer wishes to maintain a markup of 34% on these coats at the end of season, determine the markdown per coat that may be allowed at this time.

At the beginning of this chapter, we noted that gross margin represented the final markup that would be obtained by the merchant upon selling the merchandise in inventory. In this context, we observed that the maintained markup and the gross margin differed from each other only by the variances created by cash discounts and alteration expenses. Consequently, we derived the following relationship between Gross Margin and Maintained Markup:

Gross Margin = Maintained Markup − Alteration Expenses + Cash Discounts

In analyzing Gross Margin as it appeared on the statement of income and expense, we noted that the Gross Margin would need to be large enough to cover the merchant's operating expenses and still provide a profit. Consequently,

Gross Margin = Operating Expenses + Net Profit

From the same income statement, we discovered

Gross Margin = Net Sales − Total Cost of Goods Sold

EXAMPLE 9: Finding Maintained Markup and Gross Margin Percentages Given Initial Markup, Reductions, Cash Discounts, and Alteration Expenses

The buyer for a ladies' accessory department has the following planned information and desires to determine her maintained markup and gross margin percentages. Calculate these figures for the buyer:

Net Markdowns	8.0%	Alteration Expenses	1.5%
Cash Discounts	2.0%	Initial Markup	37.5%

Solution:

Maintained Markup = Initial Markup (100% + Reductions) − Reductions
= 37.5% (100% + 8.0%) − 8.0%
= [.375 (1.08) − .08] 100%
= 32.5%

Gross Margin = Maintained Markup + Cash Discounts − Alteration Expenses
= (.325 + .020 − .015) 100%
= 33.0%

Therefore, the buyer can expect to obtain a maintained markup of 32.5% and a gross margin of 33.0%.

PROBLEM 9: In the branch operation of a major department store, the sportswear department has the following planned figures for the spring-summer season: initial markup, 42.0%; net markdowns, 10.0%; cash discounts, 3.0%; alterations expenses, 1.5%. As a management trainee, you are asked to determine the department's maintained markup and gross margin percentages.

EXAMPLE 10: **Finding Markdown Dollars Given Net Sales, Initial Markup, Cash Discounts, Alteration Expenses, and Gross Margin**

If a department shows the following planned figures for the coming season, determine the total markdowns in dollars and percent that might be taken.

Net Sales	$250,000	Cash Discounts	2%
Gross Margin	39%	Alteration Expenses	1%
Initial Markup	45%		

Solution

Since

Gross Margin = Maintained Markup + Cash Discounts – Alteration Expense

Then,

$$\text{Maintained Markup} = \text{G.M.} - \text{C.D.} + \text{A.E.}$$
$$= 39\% - 2\% + 1\%$$
$$= 38\%$$

and substituting in the following equation to find reductions

$$\text{RED.} = \frac{\text{I.M.} - \text{M.M.}}{1 - \text{I.M.}}$$
$$= \frac{45\% - 38\%}{1 - 45\%}$$
$$= \left(\frac{.45 - .38}{1 - .45}\right) 100\%$$
$$= 12.73\%$$

Therefore, the total markdowns allowable would be 12.73%, or $31,825.00 (12.73% of Net Sales of $250,000).

PROBLEM 10: Upon checking his markdowns for the season, the buyer discovers that he has already taken markdowns in the amount of $11,000. If the buyer had planned sales for the season of $145,000 with a planned initial markup of 37.5% and a planned gross margin of 32.0%, determine the total markdowns in dollars that may be allowed for the remainder of the season. The buyer has also informed you that he has planned for cash discounts of 2.5% and alteration expenses of 1.0%.

SUMMARY PROBLEMS

1. Determine the initial markup percent for a department that has the following planned figures:

Planned Sales	$100,000	Stock Shortages	$1,000
Operating Expenses	28%	Alteration Expenses	$3,000
Markdowns	7%	Cash Discounts	2%
Net Profit	$ 5,000		

2. The buyer of a china department featuring imported dinnerware wishes to realize a maintained markup of 39%. To achieve this figure, the buyer has planned an initial markup of 45%. Determine the maximum markdown that may be taken to realize a maintained markup of 39%.

3. Determine the maintained markup in dollars for the suit and coat department that has the following planned figures:

Gross Sales	$195,000	Employee Discounts	2%
Sales Returns	5,000	Stock Shortages	1%
Markdowns	13,000	Initial Markup	40%
Markdown Cancellations	2,000		

4. What should be the initial markup percent in a department that has the following planned figures?

Gross Sales	$280,000	Cash Discounts	2.0%
Sales Returns	$ 5,000	Employee Discounts	$2,500
Markdowns	6.0%	Stock Shortages	$1,000
Markdown Cancellations	$ 1,500	Net Profit	3.5%
Alteration Expenses	1.0%	Operating Expenses	30.0%

5. The buyer and merchandise controller have agreed upon the following figures, from which they request that you determine the initial markup percent.

Net Profits	5.0%	Operating Expenses	32.0%
Markdowns	9.0%	Employee Discounts	1.0%
Markdown Cancellations	2.0%	Cash Discounts	2.0%
Alteration Expenses	4.0%	Stock Shortages	1.5%

6. The children's wear buyer showed the following planned figures to the merchandise controller for the department who has asked you to determine the gross margin and the maintained markup percentages that the buyer expects to realize.

Initial Markup	36%	Cash Discounts	2%
Markdowns	7%	Alteration Expenses	1%

7. What additional markdowns may be taken by a department that has the following information available?

Planned Sales for the Season	$160,000
Actual Markdowns to Date	$ 3,000
Planned Initial Markup, Season	40%
Planned Gross Margin, Season	36%
Planned Cash Discounts	2%
Planned Alteration Expenses	$ 3,200

8. The luggage department purchased 250 men's overnight bags at $16.00 each to retail at $29.95. The department was able to sell 180 of these bags at this price but found it necessary to clear out the remainder by taking a markdown. Determine the markdown in dollars that may be taken on each remaining bag for the department to obtain a desired maintained markup of 42%.

9. What is the maximum markdown percent that may be taken in a department that has a planned initial markup of 41% and a planned maintained markup of 35%?

10. An independent hardware merchant has planned the following figures for the fall-winter season and has asked you to determine the total markdowns in dollars and percent that will be allowed for the season.

Net Sales	$220,000	Cash Discounts	1.5%
Gross Margin	$33\frac{1}{3}\%$	Alteration Expenses	3.0%
Initial Markup	37.5%		

11. Calculate the initial markup percent for a department that has the following planned figures:

Planned Net Sales	$225,000	Employee Discounts	$2,000
Net Profit	4%	Cash Discounts	$4,000
Operating Expenses	32%	Stock Shortages	1%
Alteration Expenses	4%	Markdowns	7%

12. Calculate the amount of additional markdowns that may be taken in a department that has the following planned figures:

Planned Sales, Season	$220,000	Planned Gross Margin, Season	37%
Actual Markdowns to Date	$ 4,000	Planned Cash Discounts	2%
Planned Initial Markup, Season	42%	Planned Alteration Expenses	$2,600

13. Calculate the net profit for a department that has the following figures:

Initial Markup	38%	Markdowns	6%
Operating Expenses	31%	Cash Discounts	2%
Alteration Expenses	1%	Stock Shortages	1%

14. Determine the remaining markdowns that may be taken by a buyer in the infants' wear department if the following planned and actual figures are given:

Markdowns to Date	$ 2,000	Planned Gross Margin	32%
Total Planned Sales	$50,000	Planned Alteration Expenses	2%
Initial Markup	38%	Planned Cash Discounts	2%

15. A department's net sales totaled $265,000 for the season with markdowns of $12,000 and cash discounts of $5,000. Alteration expenses reached $7,500 with employee discounts of $2,000. If the gross cost of goods sold was $175,000, determine the department's maintained markup and gross margin.

16. A ladies' sportswear buyer purchased 3 gross of ladies' belts at a cost of $96.00 per dozen and plans to retail these at $16.00 each. The buyer was able to sell 250 belts at this price, but the remaining belts will have to be reduced because of style and size factors. If the buyer wishes to realize a maintained markup of 42% on these belts, determine the markdowns that may be taken on each of the remaining belts.

17. The housewares department has planned an initial markup of 40% and a planned maintained markup of 34%. To date, sales total $48,000 with markdowns of $2,200. Planned sales for the remainder of the period are $42,000. What markdowns in dollars and percent may be taken for the balance of the period for this department to realize a planned maintained markup of 34%?

18. A giftware buyer purchased 20 dozen sets of creamers and sugar bowls at a cost of $120.00 per dozen and originally retailed these at $21.90 per set. After 120 sets were sold, it become apparent that the remainder would have to be reduced in price to make room for new items. How large a markdown may the buyer take on each remaining set to obtain an average markup of 45% on the entire lot?

19. A department has the following planned and actual figures for the fall-winter season. You are required to determine the markdowns that can be taken for the months of December and January, in both dollars and percent.

Planned Sales, August 1–January 31	$315,000
Actual Sales, August 1–November 30	$195,000
Actual Markdowns, August 1–November 30	$ 10,000
Planned Initial Markup, Season	42%
Planned Gross Margin, Season	36%
Planned Alteration Expenses, Season	1%
Planned Cash Discounts, Season	2%

20. If a department has a planned initial markup of 40.0% and a planned maintained markup of 37.5% on planned sales of $130,000, calculate the maximum amount and percentage of reductions that may be taken.

21. The buyer of a ladies' sportswear department has the following planned figures for the coming season. Determine the initial markup percent being planned by the buyer.

Gross Sales	$320,000	Cash Discounts	2.5%
Sales Returns	$ 10,000	Employee Discounts	3.0%
Operating Expenses	$ 85,000	Stock Shortages	1.0%
Alteration Expenses	$ 8,000	Net Profit	4.5%
Markdowns	8.6%		

22. Find the initial markup percent in a department that has the following planned figures:

Gross Sales	$310,000	Markdown Cancellations	1%
Sales Returns	$ 10,000	Employee Discounts	1%
Net Profit	5%	Alteration Expenses	$4,000
Operating Expenses	31%	Cash Discounts	$3,600
Net Markdowns	8%		

23. Calculate the maintained markup in a department that has the following planned figures:

Initial Markup	42%	Stock Shortages	1%
Markdowns	6%	Employee Discounts	2%

24. The buyer of the toy department purchased 12 dozen dolls at a cost of $144.00 per dozen and originally retailed these at $20.00. After the department recorded sales of 100 of these dolls at the original price, the buyer wished to clear the remainder by taking a markdown. How much of a markdown on each doll will the buyer be permitted to take if she is required to obtain a maintained markup of 37.5% on this purchase?

Review Problems for Chapters 4, 5, 6

To ensure an understanding of the concepts presented, solve the problems that follow without referring back to the previous chapters. The workspace for each question has purposely been eliminated so that you may review the problems without the solutions being readily available.

1. A buyer has purchased merchandise invoiced at $29,000 at cost that carries a markup of 36.0%. The buyer wishes to obtain an average markup of 37.5% for his department for the period. In addition, the buyer feels that he will be able to obtain a markup of 40.0% on subsequent purchases without losing sales. Determine the amount of merchandise at both cost and retail that the buyer must purchase and mark up 40.0% to achieve the desired average markup.

2. A buyer purchased a line of men's golf caps from the Orient at a landed cost of $77.40 per dozen. If the buyer wishes to retail these caps at $10.95, determine the markup percent of both cost and retail on these caps.

3. On July 1, Edward Cizmar noted that his B.O.M. stock for the month was $36,000 at cost and was marked up 40%. Upon checking his plan for the season, he noted that he has established a budget limit for the month of $72,000 at retail and wishes to achieve an average markup of 39% for the month. To realize these figures, determine the markup that the buyer must obtain on the remaining purchases for the month.

4. Vicky's Books and Stationery Shoppe has planned the following figures for the spring-summer season. As the store manager, you are required to find the markdown percent that may be allowed for the remainder of the period if the shop is to realize its maintained markup.

Planned Sales, Season	$140,000
Actual Sales to Date	$ 72,000
Actual Markdowns to Date	7.0%
Planned Initial Markup	37.5%
Planned Maintained Markup	32.5%

5. Sandra's Travel Boutique has purchased a line of canvas bags at a cost of $216 per dozen. If the buyer purchased 15 dozen of these bags, determine how many should be retailed at $26.00 and how many at $34.00 if she is to realize an average markup of 37.5%.

6. Robert Murad operates the suit and clothing department of a men's apparel store with an initial markup of 41%. He is offered a line of 110 coats for $8,000 delivered to the store. After examining the assortment, the buyer estimates that 40 can be sold at $150, 35 at $119.00, and 25 at $99.00. Determine the retail price at which the remaining coats can be sold for the store to reach its markup goal of 41%.

7. Dunnville Hardware has the following planned figures for the fall-winter season. The manager has required that you determine the initial markup, the maintained markup, and the gross margin percents for the period.

Net Sales	$210,000	Markdowns	$12,000
Net Profit	4.0%	Markdown Cancellations	$ 1,500
Operating Expenses	$ 62,000	Employee Discounts	$ 2,000
Alteration Expenses	$ 3,500	Stock Shortages	1.0%
Alteration Revenue	$ 6,000	Cash Discounts	1.2%

8. The linen department of a major department store has planned sales in one of its branches at $125,000 for the season with markdowns planned at $8,500 and stock shortages of $1,000. If the buyer has planned an initial markup of 40% for the period, determine the maintained markup in both dollars and percent for the department.

9. As an assistant buyer in ladies' sportswear, Maureen Bailey has been instructed to apply a 45% initial markup on all purchases. Determine the equivalent markup percent on cost and the cost per dozen of a shirt line that she wishes to retail at $39.95.

10. Given the following information for a department, you are required to determine the planned maintained markup and gross margin in both dollars and percent.

Planned Net Sales	$320,000
Planned Markdowns	15,000
Planned Cash Discounts	4,000
Planned Alteration Expenses	12,000
Planned Alteration Revenue	4,000
Planned Employee Discounts	5,000
Planned Initial Markup	120,000
Planned Stock Shortages	4,500

11. After checking the markdown register for the season, Jessica Cook determines that she has already taken markdowns in the amount of $10,000. If she had planned sales for the season of $170,000 with a planned initial markup of 38% and a planned gross margin of 32%, determine the total markdown in dollars that might be allowed for the remainder of the season. Miss Cook has also informed you that she has planned for cash discounts of 2.5% and alteration expenses of 2.0%.

12. Determine the initial markup percent for Jonathan Cameron, the buyer of the toy department, if he has given you the following information:

Gross Sales	$175,000
Sales Returns and Allowances	$ 5,000
Alteration Expenses	$ 3,000
Employee Discounts	$ 3,400
Net Profit	4%
Operating Expenses	30%
Net Markdowns	8%
Stock Shortages	2%
Cash Discounts	2%

13. Allison's Teen Fashion Boutique is able to purchase a line of casual tops at $108.00 per dozen from one supplier and $126.00 per dozen from another source. If the buyer wishes to purchase 24 dozen, determine how many she may purchase at each price to obtain an average markup of 40% if all tops are to be retailed at $16.00.

14. A gift establishment wishes to show a balanced assortment of gift suggestions for Mother's Day, and consequently the buyer has purchased different items from different manufacturers. From Sito's Gifts, she placed 25% of her purchases at cost and marked these up 45%; from Gido's Creations she placed 35% of her purchases at cost and gave these a 40% markup; a special promotional item was purchased from Ed's Gift Warehouse and received a markup of 25%; and the remaining 20% of her purchases at cost came from Yvette Designs and were given a markup of $37\frac{1}{2}$%. Determine the average markup that the buyer should obtain on the total purchase of Mother's Day gifts.

15. The buyer of home furnishings has the following information available to determine her net profit for the period. As her assistant, you have been asked to make this calculation for the buyer.

Initial Markup	40%	Markdowns	7%
Operating Expenses	29%	Cash Discounts	3%
Alteration Expenses	1%	Stock Shortages	2%

16. Determine the total reductions that may be taken in a department that has planned net sales of $200,000 and an initial markup of 42%, cash discounts of 3%, alteration expenses of 2%, and a planned gross margin of 38%.

17. A department has the following planned figures for the spring-summer season. Determine the markdowns that can be taken for the months of June and July.

Planned Spring-Summer Sales	$180,000
Actual Sales, February 1–May 31	$ 84,000
Actual Markdowns, February 1–May 31	$ 12,000
Planned Initial Markup, Season	40.0%
Planned Gross Margin, Season	35.0%
Planned Alteration Expenses, Season	1.5%
Planned Cash Discounts, Season	3.0%

18. Determine the initial markup percent in a department that has the following planned figures:

Net Profit	4.0%	Employee Discounts	1.5%
Operating Expenses	32.0%	Stock Shortages	.5%
Alteration Expenses	2.5%	Cash Discounts	2.5%
Markdowns	5.0%		

19. A buyer has purchased $58,500 worth of merchandise at cost that she has marked up 35%. In an attempt to reach her desired average markup of 37% for the department, the buyer anticipates purchasing additional items that will carry a markup of 40%. Determine how much merchandise at both cost and retail she must purchase to reach the desired average markup of 37%.

20. Christopher's Stereo Systems has purchased a line of component systems at $1,250 each and $1,800 each and plans to retail all the sets at $2,400 each. If the buyer plans to purchase 36 units, how many will he be able to purchase at each price and still obtain an average markup of $33\frac{1}{3}$%?

21. The buyer in a dinnerware section of the china department purchased English bone china dinnerware place settings at a total cost of $4,000. Since the invoice cost would exceed $3,600, the buyer was entitled to an additional 10% discount. Half of the five-piece settings at cost that she purchased would retail at $65.90 per place setting and would

cost the buyer $40.00; the other half of the dollar purchases at cost represented five-piece place settings that would retail at $30.00 and cost the buyer $20.00 per setting. The merchandise was received into stock on June 10. On July 1, after 10 place settings of $65.90 china and 20 settings of the $30.00 china had been sold, the buyer marked each place setting with a 10% increase as a result of manufacturer's price increases.

a. Determine how many place settings the buyer originally put at each price line.

b. Determine the original markup on each of the $65.90 and $30.00 place settings.

c. Determine the final markup on each of the place settings and for the department as a whole, assuming that all place settings in each price line have been sold.

22. The paint and wallpaper department plans the following figures for the spring-summer season. As a management trainee, you are requested to determine the planned maintained markup for the department and the gross margin.

Planned Initial Markup	40%	Stock Shortages	1%
Planned Markdowns	5%	Cash Discounts	2%
Employee Discounts	2%	Operating Expenses	29%
Customer Discounts	1%		

23. A men's clothing buyer, Paul Kimaid, purchased 175 sport coats at $77.00 each and planned to retail these at $125.00. The buyer realized that he was able to sell 135 of these sport coats at this price, but to clear the stock before the end of the season, he wished to take a markdown on the remainder. What markdown may be allowed on each of the remaining sport coats if the buyer wishes to maintain a markup of 35%?

24. Determine the initial markup, maintained markup, and gross margin in a store that has the following information:

Gross Sales	$350,000
Sales Returns and Allowances	$ 10,000
Net Profit	4%
Operating Expenses	30%
Markdowns	$ 35,000
Markdown Cancellations	$ 7,000
Alteration Expenses	$ 10,000
Alteration Revenue	$ 4,000
Stock Shortages	2%
Cash Discounts	2%
Employee Discounts	$ 6,800

part III

INVENTORY VALUATION

An analysis of the retailer's statement of financial condition will quickly reveal that one of the largest assets on the balance sheet is the stock of merchandise—the inventory. Therefore, it becomes essential in the successful operation of a retail store to manage the inventory investment effectively.

As we have also seen to this point, the planning of gross margin and related markups is vital to the profitability of the enterprise. To determine the gross margin of the firm, the value of the cost of goods sold needs to be determined. Further, it is the cost of the inventory or the merchandise remaining on hand that is fundamental to the determination of the cost of goods sold.

To explain the importance of inventory valuation, the student is asked to recall the basic elements of the retailer's profit and loss statement[1] to understand the impact of the cost of goods sold on the store's profitability:

	Net Sales	$100,000
−	Cost of Goods Sold	60,000
=	Gross Margin	$ 40,000
−	Operating Expenses	32,000
=	Net Profit	$ 8,000

It becomes obvious from the fundamentals of the statement that the proper recording of the "cost of goods sold" figure will affect the gross margin realized by the firm. The value of the inventory on hand, as well as the purchases received during the period being reported, constitutes the composition of this figure, as illustrated here in very simplistic terms:

[1] The student is asked to refer to Appendix A for a further examination and explanation of the store's operating statement.

	Opening Inventory, for the Period	$125,000
+	Purchases, During the Period	45,000
=	Total Merchandise Handled, for the Period	$170,000
-	Closing Inventory, End of the Period	110,000
=	Cost of Goods Sold, for the Period	$ 60,000

It soon becomes apparent that the proper recording and monitoring of the merchandise inventory plays an important role in determining the accuracy of the profit being reported by the firm. The inventory, unlike the other current assets of the firm, does create some difficulties in ensuring its proper valuation. This problem originates from the fact that it is most unlikely that all the items in inventory will actually be worth the amount of money that was originally paid for them. Merchandise deteriorates through handling, becomes perishable through fashion changes, loses customer appeal as new products enter the market, and becomes less valuable as wholesale prices decline. Consequently, the merchant must be especially careful that the merchandise inventory is not overvalued or undervalued.

By examining the basic elements of the cost of goods sold, the student will realize that if the closing inventory is overvalued by indicating that the merchandise on hand is actually worth more than the market indicates, then the cost of goods sold will decrease, the gross margin will increase, and an increase in net profit will increase the tax liability. On the other hand, if the inventory is undervalued, the cost of goods sold will increase, the gross margin will decrease, and the profit will be understated. Consequently, this part of the book explores the principle and techniques available to the merchant in the proper recording and valuation of the inventory.

A proper inventory system implies that the merchant knows what stock he or she started with, how much has been sold, what has been received into stock, how much stock is on order, and what stock is remaining on hand. Therefore, some kind of book inventory system is required for the purposes of recording this data. In this way, the retailer is able to determine the value of the cost of goods sold, so that gross margin and subsequently net profit can be calculated.

The retail method of inventory valuation requires the maintenance of records that indicate all price changes affecting the retail dollar of the stock as well as the recording of all purchases at retail when they are received into stock. Consequently, any activity in the retail operation that affects the inventory position must be recorded at retail. The student is asked to recall the effect that markdowns had on maintained markup in differentiating the original retail price from the final selling price of the merchandise items.

On the other hand, the cost method of inventory valuation requires that all sales be recorded and reduced to a cost figure and subsequently deducted from the previous on-hand position. Since the task of reducing each individual sale to the cost figure is burdensome, retail dollar systems have become much more common.

The discussion that follows examines the principles and techniques employed in both the cost method and retail method of inventory valuation.

## chapter 7

The Cost Method of Inventory Valuation

Simply stated, the cost method of inventory valuation involves recording the actual cost or the current market value (whichever is lower) of each merchandise item at the time the physical inventory is taken. And, as we noted earlier, some retail stores prefer to maintain an inventory control system on this basis of recording the book inventory.

This method requires that the beginning inventory be taken at cost, purchases be taken at cost from the invoices, and all sales be calculated at cost through the coding indicated on the price ticket.

A common method of indicating the cost of an item on the price ticket is through the use of a ten-letter word or expression, with nonrepeating letters, corresponding to the numerals to be employed. An example is

> R E T A I L   S H O P
> 1 2 3 4 5 6   7 8 9 0

Therefore, a retailer using such a cost code would indicate the cost price of $12.47 on the price ticket as REAS.

Other retailers might wish to use a numerical code for the cost of an item and at the same time and with the same code indicate the date at which the merchandise was received into stock. Such a numerical code could be illustrated as

> 6 1 2 7 4 7

In this example, the first and fourth numerals indicate that the merchandise was brought into inventory during June (sixth month) of 1987 (7). The cost price of the item is indicated by the remaining numerals of 1247, that is, the second, third, fifth, and sixth numbers. The retailer may also use a combination of letters and numerals in the code and decide on any sequence that provides him or her with the information desired.

The cost method of inventory valuation is obviously the older of the two methods. As such, it is still used by many independent merchants. But retailers of merchandise of high unit value, where transactions are few, or where the numbers of items carried in stock are limited, have also found this method to be very practical. Consequently, such a method is frequently used by furniture and appliance dealers, automobile dealers, computer merchants, stereo shop operators, furriers, and similar merchants of big-ticket items.

As we shall see, the obvious disadvantage to maintaining a book inventory at cost is that it does not recognize the depreciation of the value of the merchandise in stock; it omits the treatment of cash discounts; it overlooks the results of stock shortages; and it poses special problems in the handling of the transportation charges on the merchandise purchased. Despite these negative elements, it is still frequently employed because it is easy to understand and to implement, and it requires a limited amount of record keeping.

Under the cost method of valuing inventory, different systems are employed to arrive at the appropriate value of the merchandise on hand. Each of the following methods offers certain advantages to the merchant, and the one selected will be governed by the tax consequences outlined by the store's accountant.

THE ORIGINAL COST METHOD

In this method, the cost of the inventory is determined by referring to the cost price as indicated on the price ticket of the merchandise through the cost code described earlier. At the time the inventory is taken, the cost of each article is decoded and entered on an inventory sheet for use in accumulating the total inventory at cost. Consequently, this method is generally used for staple merchandise that depreciates negligibly either in a fashion sense or through physical deterioration. In other words, the merchandise on hand is worth approximately what was originally paid for the items.

COST OR MARKET, WHICHEVER IS LOWER

In this method, the original cost price and the current replacement cost of each item in the inventory are determined. In one column of the inventory sheet, the original cost price is recorded, and the cost at which the supplier will now sell the item to the merchant is recorded in the second column. A third column is prepared that indicates the extension of the total number of an item multiplied by the lower of the cost or market price recorded. Therefore, the total of the extended amounts of all items using this method will give the merchant a conservative valuation of the merchandise inventory, keeping the statement of profits to a minimum.

This method tends to be used primarily by general merchandise stores who watch closely the replacement costs of the merchandise in inventory. If the items are to be replaced at a lower cost, the need for markdowns of existing stock is evident; if the items are to be replaced at a higher cost, careful analysis needs to be undertaken before existing stock is increased in price.

Since this method implies that we must be able to establish the market value of the inventory, it will also indicate that we need to determine the depreciation of the inventory on hand. The three following factors are frequently used by merchants to determine the market value of the inventory.

1. *Comparison Method.* In situations where the market price is different from the initial cost price, the retailer may obtain the market price by checking suppliers' catalogs and

price lists. This may become a burdensome task especially if the store is merchandising a large number of items. In addition, some allowance would have to be made for deterioration of the goods that might be in poor condition. This method is normally restricted to staple merchandise that is handled in large volumes.

2. *Markdown Method.* In this method, the retail price ticket not only carries the initial retail price but also the current selling price. The markup figure is then determined by using the cost code and the original selling price. This initial markup percent is applied to the new selling price to determine the depreciation in the cost of the merchandise. For example, if an item cost the store $6.00, was originally retailed at $10.00, and shows a current selling price of $8.00, the price ticket would appear as follows if the cost code used is RETAIL SHOP:

```
        MORGAN'S

        DEPT. 319          Price Ticket

           LPP

        $10.00

        $ 8.00
```

Therefore, the

$$\text{Original Markup} = \frac{\$4.00}{\$10.00} \times 100\% = 40\%$$

and the

$$\text{Cost Complement} = 100\% - 40\% = 60\%$$

Thus, the derived cost of new selling price of $8.00 would be:

$$\$8.00 \times .60 = \$4.80$$

and

$$\text{Depreciation of Cost Value} = \$6.00 - \$4.80 = \$1.20$$

The obvious problem with this method is the large number of calculations that will be required in establishing market value. All price tickets on merchandise must carry original retail prices, separate percentages must be computed for each item that has been reduced, and each of these is then converted to the market value.

3. *Aging Method.* This method represents an alternative to determing the market valuation of the inventory on hand on the basis of the age of the stock in terms of the length of time it has been in the retailer's possession. On the basis of past experience, a retailer might note that merchandise in stock for less than three months can still be sold at its original retail price. However, stock that is older than three months may be depreciated on the basis of a predetermined rate established by store policy. For example, goods from 6 months to 1 year old may be estimated to be worth only 50% of their original value. The following is an example of how a

retail store may determine the market value of its merchandise by depreciating its cost value at predetermined rates:

Age of Stock	Depreciation Rate
Less than 3 months	0%
3 to 6 months	25
6 to 12 months	50
12 to 24 months	75
Over 2 years	100

It should be noted that this example is only a guide; the depreciation rates will differ for each retail store and for each department within a retail store. Some of the larger department stores might consider that some fashion merchandise 12 months old or more should be depreciated at the 100% rate due to style obsolescence. In other cases such as staple merchandise, merchandise more than 1 year old may still be retailed at the original retail price with no loss of sales.

FIRST IN, FIRST OUT (FIFO)

This and the following method of inventory valuation (LIFO) operate on the premise that retailers are receiving merchandise constantly throughout the season and are subjected to varying prices for the same merchandise from suppliers. Just as retail prices may change through the season, so too do manufacturer or wholesaler prices.

In this method, it is assumed that the first goods purchased are also the first sold. Therefore, when attempting to arrive at a value for the inventory, we assume that the goods that were purchased first are no longer in stock and the merchandise that is on hand is that which was purchased most recently and, consequently, has the most recent cost prices. The following example illustrates, in simple terms, the valuation of the inventory under the FIFO method by observing the movement of goods into and out of stock:

Date	Cost per Unit	Quantity Received	Quantity Sold	Quantity on Hand
August 1	$10.00	150		150
August 5			50	100
August 8			30	70
August 10	11.00	100		170
August 15			70	100
August 22	12.00	50		150
August 26			60	90
August 30	13.00	40		130

Therefore, in this example, we discover that we have 130 units on hand at the end of August. On the basis of the fact that we purchased the item at four different time periods during the month and in fact at four different prices, we must determine the value of these 130 units that remain. Under the FIFO method, we are assuming that the items that were sold came from the inventory that was received first. Consequently, in valuing the 130 items remaining, we derive the cost value on the following basis under FIFO:

Since we need 130 items, from the most recent inventory,

40	Received August 30 @ $13.00 = $	520.00
50	Received August 22 @ $12.00 =	600.00
40	Received August 10 @ $11.00 =	440.00
	(out of total of 100 units)	
130		$1,560.00

It should be obvious then, that under the FIFO method, the inventory on hand is valued at its most current price. In this case, the 130 units that are on hand at the end of the month are in fact valued at $1,560, a figure that is made up of three different prices per unit, as indicated.

A more detailed analysis of the techniques involved in recording merchandise under the FIFO method may be found in any elementary accounting book. Retail firms that wish to determine whether the operation should use the FIFO method for valuing inventory or the LIFO method, which we will discuss now, should seek the advice of the accountant of the firm to determine the tax implications as well as inflationary effects of the economy.

LAST IN, FIRST OUT (LIFO)

In contrast to FIFO, this method assumes that the last merchandise purchased is the first merchandise sold. Hence, the merchandise that is on hand is the oldest by date of purchase. In the example, the 130 units that are on hand at the end of August would receive a different value under LIFO than we discovered under FIFO. These units on hand would need to be valued by accumulating items at the beginning of the month, and in this case all 130 units would come out of our purchase on August 1:

130   Received August 1   @ $10.00 = $1,300.00
             (of the 150 purchased)
             on this date)

Therefore, under LIFO, the 130 units that are remaining on August 30 would be valued at $1,300 at cost rather than at $1,560, as we discovered under FIFO. The student will then note that in using LIFO, the closing inventory will decrease, the cost of goods sold will increase, the gross margin will decrease, and, subsequently, the net profit will be stated at a lower figure. Consequently, the tax liability under LIFO should be less.

Due to the impact of inventory valuation on the statement of profits, LIFO has had its major advantage to merchants during periods of inflation. In this method, it is assumed that we will avoid larger tax liabilities as well as pressures to pay out the larger profits that are actually invested in inventory assortments.

Again, the intricacies of the LIFO method of recording and valuing inventory can be studied further in any basic accounting book.

It should be noted that each of the methods of inventory valuation at cost may produce a different value for a given inventory, and, therefore, the amount of profit will be different depending upon the method of valuation used. As a result, the revenue departments of the various governments usually require that the merchant select one method and consistently report the inventory utilizing this means of evaluation.

THE COST METHOD AND TRANSPORTATION CHARGES

Transportation charges in a retail operation must be considered as part of the purchase price of the goods and not treated just as another expense of doing business. As a result, the transportation charges paid on purchases must be added to the value of the closing inventory. Since it would be extremely difficult and burdensome for the retailer to calculate the transportation charge on each item and record this, the retailer accumulates the total transportation charges and expresses this figure as a percentage of total purchases (*not* as a percent of net sales). The calculation of the gross margin and net profit utilizing this method would then appear as follows:

	Cost	Retail
Opening Inventory	$60,000	
Purchases Received	35,000	
Transportation Charges (2%)	700	
Total Merchandise Handled	$95,700	
Net Sales		$90,000
Ending Inventory, Not		
Including Transportation $40,000		
Transportation in		
Ending Inventory 800	40,800	
Cost of Merchandise Sold	$54,900	
Gross Margin		35,100
Operating Expenses	25,300	
Net Operating Profit		$ 9,800

In this example, we have segregated the transportation charges and have indicated that they are to become part of the purchases received by the organization. In this way, the value of the inventory is more accurately recorded. Some retail operations find it more convenient to allocate the transportation charges as part of the operating expenses, but a more appropriate positioning is including it with the store's purchases.

EXAMPLE 1: **Finding the Market Value of Ending Inventory Given Cost Valuation, Depreciation, and Transportation**

The closing physical inventory for a department for the 6-month season was $50,000 based upon the cost codes on the price tickets. Of the items in inventory, there is a lot of 200 items for which $2.00 each was paid but are now selling for $1.70 each at wholesale. Another group of 800 items bought at $1.00 each are now selling at 80 cents each at wholesale. If the purchases at cost for the 6-month period totaled $125,000 with transportation charges of $625, determine the market value of the closing inventory for the season.

Solution:

(a) Determine the rate of transportation charges on the purchases so that these may be allocated to the closing inventory:

$$\frac{\$625}{\$125,000} \times 100\% = .5\%$$

Therefore, if the closing inventory is $50,000, the transportation charges to be added would be

$$.5 \times \$50,000 = \$250.00$$

(b) Determine the depreciation of the inventory:

$$
\begin{array}{ll}
200 \text{ items} \times \$0.30 \ (\$2.00 - \$1.70) = & \$\ 60.00 \\
800 \text{ items} \times \$0.20 \ (\$1.00 - \$\ .80) = & \underline{\$160.00} \\
\text{Total Depreciation} \qquad\qquad = & \underline{\underline{\$220.00}}
\end{array}
$$

(c) Determine the cost value of the closing inventory at market value:

	Closing Inventory, Billed Cost	$50,000
+	Transportation Charges	250
	Closing Inventory, Transportation in	$50,250
−	Depreciation of Inventory	220
	Closing Inventory, Market Value	$50,030

PROBLEM 1: An independent merchant shows a closing inventory at cost of $75,000 for the 6-month season. The cost code the retailer is using, marked on all tickets is MAKE PROFIT. During the season, the merchant has received purchases of $180,000 with transportation on these purchases of $1,800. Of the items presently in stock, there are 125 items coded APT now selling for $2.10 each wholesale. Another group of 500 items are coded KOP and are now selling for $3.00 each at the wholesale level. Determine the market value of the closing inventory.

EXAMPLE 2: Finding Market Value of Ending Inventory Given Cost Valuation and Depreciation Rates

An independent merchant uses a price code in which he includes the date on which each item is received into stock. Using the numerical code the merchant has established, he has found the following situation with regard to his closing inventory:

Less than 3 months old	$ 60,000
3 to 6 months old	40,000
6 to 12 months old	20,000
More than 1 year old	10,000
Total Physical Inventory (Billed Cost)	$130,000

From past experience and as a basis of store policy, the merchant has established the following depreciation rates:

Less than 3 months old	0%
3 to 6 months old	20%
6 to 12 months old	50%
Over 1 year old	80%

The rate of transportation established is 1.5% of the purchases at billed cost. Determine the market value of the closing inventory at cost.

Solution:

(a) Determine the effect of the depreciation rates on inventory:

Age Groups	Amount	Depreciation	Market Value
Less than 3 months	$ 60,000	0%	$ 60,000
3 to 6 months	40,000	20	32,000
6 to 12 months	20,000	50	10,000
Over 1 year	10,000	80	2,000
Total	$130,000		$104,000

(b) Determine the market value of the closing inventory considering the depreciation and the transportation charges:

Market Value of Closing Inventory (with Depreciation Rates)	$104,000
Transportation in Closing Inventory (1.5% of $130,000)	1,950
Market Value of Closing Inventory at Cost	$105,950

PROBLEM 2: Determine the market value of the closing inventory of the ladies' sportswear department that shows a physical inventory at billed costs of $180,000 and the following information. The rate of transportation in this department is two-fifths of 1% on the purchases at invoice cost.

Age Group	Amount of Stock	Depreciation Rate
Less than 3 months	1/2	0%
3 to 6 months	1/5	30
6 to 12 months	1/5	50
Over 12 months	1/10	75

EXAMPLE 3: Finding Value of Closing Inventory Using First-in, First-out (FIFO) Method

Determine the value of the closing inventory in a retail store that has the following record of items received and sold during the month of June, using First in, First out:

Date	Cost per Unit	Quantity Received	Quantity Sold	Quantity on Hand
June 2	$7.00	40		40
June 5			20	20
June 6	7.50	50		70
June 10			30	40
June 16	8.00	30		70
June 23	8.00	20		90
June 24			40	50
June 30	8.25	15		65

Solution:

Since FIFO implies that the first goods purchased are also the first goods sold and since we have 65 units on hand at June 30, then our on-hand position will be valued as follows:

15	Received June 30 @ $8.25	$123.75
20	Received June 23 @ $8.00	160.00
30	Received June 16 @ $8.00	240.00
65		$523.75

Therefore, the closing inventory of 65 units is valued at $523.75 using the FIFO method.

PROBLEM 3: Find the value of the closing inventory in a retail sporting goods operation, that has the following date on a ski item, using FIFO:

Date	Cost per Unit	Quantity Received	Quantity Sold	Quantity on Hand
January 2	$12.00	40		
January 5			10	
January 9			10	
January 15	12.50	50		
January 17			20	
January 24	12.50	40		
January 26			15	
January 30	13.00	25		

EXAMPLE 4: **Finding the Value of the Closing Inventory Using the Last-in, First-out Method (LIFO)**

Find the closing inventory for a retail merchant using the LIFO method of inventory valuation, given the following information:

Date	Cost per Unit	Quantity Received	Quantity Sold	Quantity on Hand
October 1	$6.00	75		
October 5			30	
October 10			15	
October 12	6.40	40		
October 15	6.40	10		
October 20			25	
October 25	6.60	40		
October 30			30	

Solution:

(a) Determine the quantity on hand as of October 30:

Date	Cost per Unit	Quantity Received	Quantity Sold	Quantity on Hand
October 1	$6.00	75		75
October 5			30	45
October 10			15	30
October 12	6.40	40		70
October 15	6.40	10		80
October 20			25	55
October 25	6.60	40		95
October 30			30	65

(b) Determine the value of the closing inventory of 65 units using LIFO, which implies that the items received last in inventory are sold first. Therefore, our 65 units will come from the October 1 purchase of 75 units:

$$65 \quad \text{Received October 1 @ } \$6.00 = \$390.00$$

The closing inventory of 65 units will have a value at cost of $390 using LIFO.

PROBLEM 4: Using LIFO, calculate the closing inventory of the items on hand for a retailer who has provided you with the following information:

	Transaction	Quantity
July 1	Stock on Hand	0
July 2	Purchases Received at $11.00 each	40
July 5	Purchases Received at $11.00 each	25
July 7	Sold	20
July 12	Sold	10
July 18	Purchases Received at $11.25 each	45
July 25	Sold	30
July 27	Purchases Received at $11.30 each	20
July 30	Purchases Received at $11.00 each	25

SUMMARY PROBLEMS

1. Suzanne's Children's Boutique shows a closing inventory at a cost of $37,500 for the fall-winter season. The cost code being used by the store is PATHFINDER. During the season, the buyer has received purchases at a cost of $60,000 with transportation on these purchases of $720. Of the items presently in stock, there are 110 items coded TFD now selling for $2.75 on the wholesale market. Another group of 200 items are coded AHR and are now selling for

$2.00 each at wholesale. A third group, coded FIR and numbering 310, are now selling at wholesale for $4.00 each. Determine the market value of the closing inventory for the boutique.

2. Determine the market value of the closing inventory in Amelia's Sportswear based on the following information if the department shows a physical inventory at billed cost of $62,000 with the rate of transportation established at 1% of the purchases at invoice cost.

Age Group	Amount of Stock	Depreciation Rate
Less than 3 months	1/2	0%
3 to 6 months	1/4	25
6 to 12 months	1/8	50
Over 12 months	1/8	75

3. Determine the value of the inventory on hand in the perfume department using the First-in, First-out method if the following information from the buyer has been supplied:

Date	Cost per Unit	Quantity Received	Quantity Sold	Quantity on Hand
March 1	$15.00	60		
March 7			15	
March 13	17.00	40		
March 16	16.00	20	25	
March 23			10	
March 30	17.20	30		

4. In the same perfume department, the buyer has also asked you to calculate what the closing inventory would be valued at under the Last-in, First-out method in Problem 3.

5. Michelle's Designs shows a closing inventory for the spring-summer season of $41,500 based on the cost codes indicated on the price tickets of the merchandise. An analysis of the merchandise indicates that some of the items have depreciated in value. If Michelle uses the cost code RETAIL SHOP and indicates purchases of $33,000 with transportation charges of $400 for the season, determine the market value of the closing inventory given the following information:

   275 items coded ETA, wholesale price now, $1.90
   100 items coded SRO, wholesale price now, $6.40
   160 items coded ATE, wholesale price now, $3.80

6. Determine the market value of the closing inventory in a retail store that operates with a transportation rate of one-half of 1% on purchases at billed cost and depreciates merchandise over 6 months of age at the following rates: from 6 months to 12 months, 40%; from 12 months to 24 months, 60%; and over 2 years, 100%. Of the physical inventory at a billed cost of $84,000, one-half is under 6 months of age, one-fourth is from 6 months to a year, one-eighth is from 12 to 24 months in age, and the remainder is over 2 years old.

chapter 8

The Retail Method of Inventory Valuation

The retail method of inventory valuation had its inception in the department store field, but over the years, it has spread to many types of retail organizations. Its growth in almost all areas of retail merchandising continues as computer technology continues its applications throughout the industry. The disadvantages of frequent physical counts and the impracticality of book inventory at cost that are associated with the cost method of inventory valuation has also led to the growth of the retail method of valuing inventory.

The basic premise of the retail method of inventory is that it is designed to maintain a perpetual inventory in terms of retail dollar amounts and at the same time to maintain these records to determine the cost value of the inventory at any time without taking physical inventory. Consequently, the retail method requires that accurate records be kept of any and all activities related to the merchandise inventory in the store. Therefore, records of reducing or increasing retail prices must be maintained, transferring merchandise from one department to another must be noted, and all merchandise received into inventory is noted at retail prices.

The retail method involves the following three-step approach:

1. Determining the physical inventory for each group of merchandise at the current selling price and then extending these to total retail selling prices
2. Determining the markup percent on the total merchandise handled
3. Determining the cost or market value of the closing inventory by applying the cost complement of this markup percentage

As can be observed, this method eliminates the need for cost codes and similar records that are established to determine the amount actually paid for each item in stock and ultimately the determination of the market value of the inventory. It must, however, be noted that although the retail method seems simple in concept, it does require the maintenance of a complete and rather complex system of records.

The adoption of the retail method of inventory control requires that the method be applied to groups of merchandise that are relatively homogeneous. For this reason, the department store was the first to initiate this type of control that requires that a system of departmentalizing be established within the organization. Since the markups and the rates of sale vary greatly among departments and groups of merchandise, each department must be analyzed as a separate unit.

The discussion that follows on the retail method of inventory attempts to explore the procedure required in determining the profitability of the department or a group of merchandise controlled by this means. As might be anticipated from the definition, the retail method utilizes the retail value of the inventory to assist in determining the operation's gross margin and operating profit figures. Consequently, it becomes necessary to maintain accurate records on the upward or downward price changes of the merchandise assortment.

It is not the intention of this chapter to outline the total procedure of the retail method of inventory by illustrating the various records that will need to be kept; rather, it is to explore the method in its ability to define the profit picture of the department or firm.

Consequently, as part of the explanation of the profitability of the operation, it becomes necessary to understand the implications of various price changes on the determination of the value of the inventory. To this point in the book, we have looked at two aspects of changing prices in the retail organization: The effect that markdowns and markdown cancellations have had on initial markup was reflected in the final maintained markup and gross margin. In this chapter, we shall further explore the effect that markdowns, markdown cancellations, and reductions generated by employee and customer discounts will have on the value of the inventory using the retail method.

In addition to reductions in retail value of the merchandise being sold, there are two further types of price changes that can affect the value of the inventory: additional markup and Revision of the Retail Downward.

ADDITIONAL MARKUP

The price change that results from additional markup indicates that the current selling price has been increased above the original retail price, resulting in higher markup to the store since the cost has remained the same for the merchandise in inventory. Such a markup may result if the buyer anticipates a rising market for merchandise, if there has been an increase in the selling price recommended by manufacturers, or if the buyer did not place a large enough markup on the item originally. The recording of additional markups in retail operations can become a rather frequent practice when the demand for a product far exceeds the supply or when, traditionally, staple merchandise sold by the store tends to receive a manufacturer's price increase on a routine basis.

REVISION OF THE RETAIL DOWNWARD

Such a change in retail price indicates that the current selling price is below the original selling price for some reason other than the depreciation in the cost value of the item, considered a markdown. Such a price change may result from a clerical error in original pricing, from a buyer who anticipated that the merchandise would generate a larger retail price originally, or from a rebate offered to the buyer from a manufacturer. Revision of the retail downward represents any decline in the retail price of the merchandise that is not recorded as a markdown caused by physical or fashion depreciation.

As a result of the numerous price changes that take place in retail establishments, the need for adequate record control is essential to the proper functioning of the retail inventory control system. Such a system requires that all invoices are marked correctly, that price tickets are properly marked, and that all price changes are reported on "price change" forms with proper authorization.

EXAMPLE 1: Finding Cost of Merchandise Sold, Gross Margin and Net Profit Given the Retail Method of Inventory Valuation

A sporting goods department has the following information available. As the management trainee, you are asked to determine the operating profit for the department under the retail method of inventory valuation.

	Cost	Retail
Opening Inventory	$38,000	$60,800
Purchases	22,000	39,200
Operating Expenses	18,000	
Net Sales		70,000

Solution: The problem may be set up in the following manner for easy calculation. Footnotes are used to explain the calculations undertaken to arrive at the specific numbers.

	Cost	Retail	Markup Dollars	Markup Percent
Opening Inventory	$38,000	$ 60,800		
Purchases	22,000	39,200		
Total Merchandise Handled	$60,000	$100,000	$40,000	40%[a]
Net Sales		70,000		
Closing Inventory	18,000[b]	30,000		
Cost of Goods Sold	$42,000[c]			
Gross Margin		28,000[d]		
Operating Expenses	18,000			
Operating Profit		$ 10,000[e]		

[a] The total merchandise handled is derived in the same manner as the calculation of average markup. Therefore, the average markup on the total merchandise handled for the period would be $40,000, or 40%.

[b] The closing inventory at retail is calculated as the difference between the total merchandise handled at retail and the amount of the net sales. The closing inventory at cost can then be determined by applying the complement of the initial markup percent to the retail value of the closing inventory. Therefore, the closing inventory at retail is $30,000 ($100,000 – $70,000). The closing inventory at cost then becomes 60% (100% – 40%) of $30,000, which is equal to $18,000.

[c] The cost of merchandise sold then becomes the difference between the closing inventory at cost and the total merchandise handled at cost, that is, $60,000 – $18,000, which is equal to $42,000. This figure then represents the cost of merchandise required to obtain sales of $70,000.

[d] The gross margin, as defined earlier, is the difference between net sales and the cost of merchandise sold ($70,000 – $42,000), which is $28,000.

[e] The operating profit is determined by subtracting the operating expenses from the gross margin ($28,000 – $18,000), which is $10,000.

PROBLEM 1: A shoe buyer has the following information available from which you are required to calculate the operating profit.

	Cost	Retail	Markup
Opening Inventory		$75,000	40%
Purchases Received	$35,000	53,000	
Operating Expenses	25,000		
Gross Sales		86,000	
Sales Returns		6,000	

EXAMPLE 2: Finding Operating Profit Given Transportation Charges, Stock Shortages, and Merchandise Transfers

A department has the following information from the fall-winter season. As a management trainee, you have been asked to determine the following:
(a) Ending book inventory at retail
(b) Stock shortages
(c) Ending physical inventory at cost
(d) Cost of merchandise sold
(e) Gross margin
(f) Operating profit

	Cost	Retail
Inventory August 1	$80,000	$120,000
Purchases, Season	38,380	59,700
Transfers in, Season	500	800
Transfers out, Season	280	500
Transportation Charges	1,400	
Operating Expenses	26,000	
Net Sales		104,000
Physical Inventory, January 31		72,000

Solution:

The problem is set up in the following manner, with the calculations explained by the footnotes:

	Cost	Retail	Markup Dollars	Markup Percent
Opening Inventory, August 1	$ 80,000	$120,000		
Purchases Received	38,380	59,700		
Transportation Charges	1,400[a]			
Net Transfers	220[b]	300[b]		
Total Merchandise Handled	$120,000	$180,000	$60,000	$33\frac{1}{3}\%$[c]
Net Sales		104,000		
Ending Book Inventory		$ 76,000[d]		
Ending Physical Inventory	48,000[e]	72,000		
Stock Shortages		$ 4,000[f]		
Cost of Goods Sold	$ 72,000[g]			
Gross Margin		32,000[h]		
Operating Expenses	26,000			
Operating Profit		$ 6,000[i]		

(a)Note that the transportation charges of $1,400 are added to the purchases and opening inventory as part of the cost of the purchases and, therefore, become part of the original cost of the purchases. Under the retail method, they do not become part of the operating expenses.

(b)A transfer in of merchandise is in fact a purchase from another department or another unit in the chain as opposed to obtaining merchandise from an outside source. A transfer out represents merchandise sent to another department or unit and thus reduces the amount of the total merchandise handled. Consequently, Net Transfers represent the difference between transfers in and transfers out. Thus, in the example, Net Transfers in at Cost would be $220 ($500 − $280), and Net Transfers in at Retail would be $300 ($800 − $500). Students should note that if transfers out exceed transfers in, net transfers then represent a decrease in the total merchandise handled.

(c)As explained earlier, the markup percent on the total merchandise handled is calculated here as $60,000, or $33\frac{1}{3}$%.

(d)The ending book inventory becomes the difference between the total merchandise handled at retail and the net sales for the period. In this case, the ending book inventory would be $76,000 ($180,000 − $104,000).

(e)The cost of the ending physical inventory at cost is calculated by applying the complement of the initial markup of $33\frac{1}{3}$% and, consequently, will be $48,000 ($66\frac{2}{3}$% of $72,000).

(f)Should a discrepancy exist between the actual physical inventory figure and the book inventory figure, the difference is noted as either a stock shortage or a stock overage. In this case, where the physical inventory is less than the book inventory, the difference of $4,000 represents a stock shortage at retail.

(g)The cost of merchandise sold is calculated by subtracting the cost of the physical inventory from the amount of the total merchandise handled at cost: $120,000 − $48,000 = $72,000.

(h)The Gross Margin is calculated by subtracting the cost of the merchandise sold from the net sales figure for the period, that is, $104,000 − $72,000 = $32,000.

(i)Operating profit, then, is the difference between the gross margin and the operating expenses and is, therefore, $32,000 − $26,000 = $6,000.

PROBLEM 2: If the following information is available, determine

    (a) Ending book inventory at retail
    (b) Stock shortages or overages
    (c) Ending physical inventory at cost
    (d) Cost of merchandise sold
    (e) Gross margin
    (f) Operating profit

	Cost	Retail	Markup
Opening Inventory	$57,850	$89,250	
Gross Purchases	32,000	62,000	
Purchase Returns	1,000	1,500	
Transportation Charges	1,000		
Transfers in	300	500	
Transfers out	150	250	
Net Sales		75,000	
Operating Expenses	20,000		
Ending Physical Inventory		72,000	

EXAMPLE 3: Finding Closing Inventory at Retail Given Additional Markups due to Price Changes

Determine the closing inventory at cost and retail in a department that has the following information:

	Cost	Retail
Gross Purchases	$154,800	$260,000
Purchase Returns	13,000	20,000
Transfers in	12,000	18,600
Transfers out	16,000	24,000
Transportation Charges	1,200	
Additional Markups		600
Additional Markup Cancellations		200
Opening Inventory	62,000	100,000
Net Sales		250,000

Solution:

	Cost	Retail	Markup Dollars	Markup Percent
Opening Inventory	$ 62,000	$100,000		
Net Purchases Received	141,800	240,000[a]		
Transportation	1,200			
Net Transfers	(4,000)	(5,400)[b]		
Net Additional Markups		400[c]		
Total Merchandise Handled	$201,000	$335,000	$134,000	40%
Net Sales		250,000		
Closing Inventory	$ 51,000[d]	$ 85,000		

[a]Note that the net purchases have been calculated by subtracting the purchase returns from both gross purchases at cost and retail. Therefore, the net purchases at retail are $240,000 ($260,000 – $20,000) and at cost are $141,800 ($154,800 – $13,000).

[b]Note that transfers out in this example exceed the transfers in, and as a result, the total merchandise handled will be reduced by this amount. Therefore, net transfers at cost are – $4,000 ($12,000 – $16,000) and net transfers at retail are – $5,400 ($18,600 – $24,000). Therefore, the total merchandise handled will be reduced by these amounts.

[c]Additional markups were $600 and additional markup cancellations (revision of the retail downward) totaled $200, leaving net additional markups of $400, which will increase the total merchandise handled at retail by this amount.

[d]The closing inventory at cost is determined by multiplying the closing inventory at retail by the complement of the markup of 40% (60% of $85,000), or $51,000.

PROBLEM 3: The gross purchases in a men's furnishings department totaled $130,000 at cost and $210,000 at retail for the season. During the season, purchase returns totaled $10,000 at cost and $15,000 at retail. The department transferred merchandise into the department worth $9,000 at cost and $14,000 at retail and during the same period transferred merchandise out of the department worth $13,000 at cost and $21,000 at retail. The transportation charges for the department were 1% of the gross purchases at cost. Because of rising demand for certain items, the buyer was able to obtain additional markups on these items of $1,500 but was later required to revise the retail downward because of competition that resulted in additional markup cancellations of $700. The department began the season with an inventory of $80,000 at cost and $130,000 at retail. Gross sales for the period were $215,000 with sales returns of $15,000. The department has operating expenses of $44,000 for the period. The closing physical inventory for the period totaled $115,000 at retail.

As the management trainee in the department, you are required to determine the following:
(a) Closing book inventory at retail
(b) Stock shortages or overages
(c) Closing physical inventory at cost
(d) Cost of merchandise sold
(e) Gross margin
(f) Operating profit

EXAMPLE 4: Finding the Closing Book Inventory at Retail Given Markdowns and Employee and Customer Discounts

Determine the closing book inventory for a buyer who has the following information available.

	Cost	Retail
Opening Inventory	$42,000	$75,000
Net Purchases	27,700	45,000
Transportation Charges	300	
Net Sales		50,000
Markdowns		4,000
Markdown Cancellations		1,000
Discount to Employees and Customers		1,000
Closing Physical Inventory		65,000

Solution:

	Cost	Retail	Markup Dollars	Markup Percent
Opening Inventory	$42,000	$ 75,000		
Net Purchases	27,700	45,000		
Transportation Charges	300			
Total Merchandise Handled	$70,000	$120,000	$50,000	$41\frac{2}{3}\%$
Net Sales		50,000		
Net Markdowns		3,000[a]		
Discounts, Employees and Customers		1,000[b]		
Total Retail Deductions		54,000[c]		
Closing Book Inventory		66,000[d]		
Closing Physical Inventory	$37,915	65,000[e]		
Stock Shortages		1,000		

[a] It should be noted that neither the markdowns nor markdown cancellations can be deducted before determining the total merchandise handled, since these items are not recorded on the purchase records and as such do not affect the average cumulative markup of $41\frac{2}{3}\%$. Markdowns are considered as losses due to the depreciation in the value of the merchandise. Therefore, losses due to markdowns affect gross margin and operating profit, since they are taken in the period in which they occur. Therefore, net markdowns for the period are determined by subtracting the markdown cancellations from gross markdowns ($4,000 – $1,000).

[b] Discounts to employees and customers are a special form of markdowns in that they represent a reduction in the retail price as a special courtesy to employees and some customers.

[c] Total retail deductions represent the total reduction from inventory of merchandise that has been sold or reduced in value. Consequently, this becomes the sum of net sales, net markdowns, and employee and customer discounts ($50,000 + $3,000 + $1,000).

[d] Therefore the buyer is able to calculate the closing book inventory by deducting the total retail deductions from the total merchandise handled at retail: ($120,000 – $54,000 = $66,000).

[e] However, since a physical inventory was taken and amounted to $65,000 at retail, this indicates that there is a stock shortage of $1,000 as deduced from the closing book inventory of $66,000. The cost of the closing inventory is again determined by the complement of the initial markup of $41\frac{2}{3}\%$, or $37,915 (.5833 × $65,000).

NOTE: The initial markup is used to determine the cost value of the closing inventory instead of the maintained markup percent, since good accounting practice requires that the same basis be used to calculate closing inventory as that used for the opening inventory.

PROBLEM 4: In a department that has the following information, the buyer has asked you to determine

    (a) Closing book inventory at retail

    (b) Stock shortages or overages

    (c) Closing physical inventory at cost

    (d) Cost of merchandise sold

    (e) Gross margin

    (f) Net operating profit

	Cost	Retail
Opening Inventory	$ 64,000	$ 96,000
Gross Purchases	108,000	173,200
Purchase Returns	12,000	17,200
Transportation Charges	5,100	
Operating Expenses	32,000	
Additional Markups		9,000
Additional Markup Cancellations		1,000
Gross Sales		168,000
Sales Returns		12,000
Gross Markdowns		10,000
Markdown Cancellations		800
Employee Discounts		2,800
Closing Physical Inventory		92,400

SUMMARY PROBLEMS

1. A gift buyer for a major department store has the following information available for the spring-summer season. As a management trainee in the department, you are required to determine the operating profit for the season.

	Cost	Retail
Opening Inventory	$62,500	$135,000
Purchases Received, Season	45,000	92,000
Operating Expenses, Season	34,000	
Gross Sales, Season		128,000
Sales Returns, Season		4,000

2. Determine the cost of goods sold for a department that has the following information.

	Cost	Retail	Markup
Open Inventory		$125,000	44%
Closing Physical Inventory		100,000	
Net Purchases	$36,000	58,000	
Transportation Charges	400		
Markdowns		7,000	
Markdown Cancellations		1,000	
Net Sales		80,000	
Employee Discounts		1,500	
Customer Discounts		500	

3. The following information is available from the department manager for the fall-winter season. As his assistant, you are asked to calculate the following:
   (a) Ending book inventory at retail
   (b) Stock shortages or overages
   (c) Ending physical inventory at cost
   (d) Cost of merchandise sold
   (e) Gross margin
   (f) Operating profit

	Cost	Retail	Markup
Opening Inventory, August 1		$90,000	$33\frac{1}{3}\%$
Purchases, August 1–January 31	$30,000	46,000	
Transfers in, August 1–January 31	600	1,000	
Transfers out, August 1–January 31	250	500	
Transportation, August 1–January 31	750		
Gross Sales, August 1–January 31		95,000	
Sales Returns, August 1–January 31		4,500	
Physical Inventory, January 31		44,000	
Operating Expenses, August 1–January 31	22,000		

4. As a management trainee, you have been asked to utilize the information that follows to calculate the data required for the operating manager of the department by finding the following:
   (a) Closing book inventory
   (b) Stock shortages and overages
   (c) Closing physical inventory at cost
   (d) Cost of merchandise sold
   (e) Gross margin
   (f) Net operating profit

	Cost	Retail
Opening Inventory	$110,000	$200,000
Gross Purchases	78,000	135,000
Purchase Returns	4,000	6,000
Transportation Charges	1,100	
Operating Expenses	66,000	
Gross Sales		230,000
Sales Returns		5,000
Markdowns, Gross		12,000
Markdown Cancellations		3,000
Additional Markups		8,000
Additional Markup Cancellations		2,500
Employee Discounts		2,000
Customer Discounts		1,000
Closing Physical Inventory		94,000

5. By means of the retail method of inventory, determine the stock shortages and operating profit in a department that has the following information:

	Cost	Retail
Gross Sales		$270,000
Opening Inventory	$ 60,000	95,000
Closing Physical Inventory		75,000
Gross Purchases	150,000	250,000
Transfers in	6,000	10,000
Transfers out	3,000	5,000
Additional Markups		3,000
Transportation Charges	1,000	
Returns from Customers		20,000
Allowances to Customers		5,000
Returns to Suppliers	10,000	20,000
Operating Expenses	73,375	
Gross Markdowns		20,000
Markdown Cancellations		4,000

Review Problems for Chapters 7 and 8

To ensure an understanding of the concepts presented, solve the problems that follow without referring back to the previous chapters. The workspace for each question has purposely been eliminated so that you may review the problems without the solutions being readily available.

1. The following information is available to Matthew Beam, the department manager of men's furnishings. He has asked you to calculate the operating profit for the period under study.

	Cost	Retail
Opening Inventory	$70,000	$112,000
Purchases Received	36,000	60,000
Operating Expenses	25,000	
Net Sales		90,000

2. An independent merchant shows a closing inventory of $85,000 at cost. The cost code used by the merchant is RETAIL SHOP. During the season, the merchant has had purchases of $95,000 with transportation charges of 1% on these purchases. Of the items presently in stock, there are 200 items coded LLP that are now selling at $6.00 wholesale. Another group of 400 items coded OPP are now selling at $8.00 wholesale. A third group of 50 items coded REI are now selling at $1.00 each at wholesale. Determine the market value of the closing inventory using the cost method of inventory valuation.

3. The department buyer, Julie Nicholas, finds through physical inventory counts that she has a closing inventory of $52,000 at cost. The buyer uses a letter and number code to denote age of the merchandise and, through analysis of this code, has found the following: 50% of her stock is less than 3 months old: 20% of the stock is 3 to 6 months old; 20% of the stock is 6 to 12 months old; 5% of her stock is 12 to 24 months old; and 5% is over 2 years old. If the rate of transportation is established as 1% of purchases at billed cost, determine the value of the closing inventory using the following depreciation rates:

Age Group	Depreciation Rate
Less than 3 months old	0%
3 to 6 months old	25%
6 to 12 months old	50%
12 to 24 months old	80%
Over 2 years old	100%

4. The following information is available to the buyer for departmental analysis.

The department had an opening stock of $80,000 at retail that carried a markup of 37.5%. During the period gross purchases of $60,000 at cost were received into stock and marked up 40.0%. However, because of defective items, the department returned to the supplier merchandise valued at $3,000 at cost and $5,000 at retail. Transportation charges for the period amounted to 2% of gross purchases at cost. The department was able to obtain additional markups of $8,000 but was forced to revise the retail downward by the amount of $2,000 during the period. Transfers in were received from another unit in the chain at the agreed cost of $3,000, which the buyer marked up 37.5%. Merchandise that originally retailed at $3,800 was transferred out of the department at an agreed cost of $1,800. Gross sales for the department during the period were $125,000, with customer returns and allowances of $5,000. Gross markdowns were $10,000, but during the period markdown cancellations of $2,000 occurred. Employees and customers were granted discounts that totaled $1,500. The department provided free alterations and, as a result, incurred alteration expenses of 5% of the department's net sales. Cash discounts were earned in the amount of $2,500. The departmental operating expenses were $28,000 for the period. And a physical count revealed a closing inventory of $51,000 at retail.

Determine the following information for the buyer of the department:
(a) Closing book inventory at retail
(b) Closing physical inventory at cost
(c) Stock shortages or overages
(d) Total cost of merchandise sold
(e) Gross margin in dollars and percent
(f) Net operating profile in dollars and percent

5. As an assistant buyer in the department, you are given the following information to determine the requested figures:

	Cost	Retail
Opening Inventory	$54,000	$84,000
Gross Purchases	30,000	50,000
Purchase Returns	1,800	3,000
Transportation Charges	500	
Transfers in	500	800
Transfers out	200	400
Physical Closing Inventory		72,000
Operating Expenses	31,000	
Net Sales		60,400

Determine the following:
(a) Ending book inventory at retail
(b) Stock shortages or overages
(c) Ending physical inventory at cost
(d) Cost of merchandise sold
(e) Gross margin in dollars and percent
(f) Operating profit in dollars and percent

6. A department had an opening inventory of $256,000 at retail with a billed cost of $160,000. Purchases were received during the period at $200,000 at retail and $120,000 at cost, with purchase returns of $6,000 at cost and $10,000 at retail. Transportation charges on these purchases were $2,400. Net additional markups during the period were $12,000. Transfers of merchandise into the department were $3,600 at cost and $7,600 at retail, while transfers out of the department amounted to $6,000 at cost and $9,600 at retail. The gross sales for the department during the period were $260,000, with sales returns of $10,000. Gross markdowns for the period amounted to 8% of net sales with markdown cancellations of 20% of the gross markdowns. Employee and customer discounts amounted to 1% of net sales for the department. Cash discounts earned during the period for the department totaled $5,000, while alteration expenses represented 3% of the net sales. Operating expenses for the period totaled $58,000. At the end of the period, a physical inventory count at retail indicated a closing inventory of $185,000 at retail.

As a management trainee, you are required to determine the following:
(a) Stock shortage or overage
(b) Gross margin amount and percent
(c) Net operating profit amount and percent

7. Determine the gross margin and operating profit in a department that has provided the following information:

Gross Sales, Season	$109,360
Gross Markdowns, Season	7,800
Gross Purchases, at Cost, Season	72,000
Operating Expenses	26,978
Transfers in, at Cost	4,000
Cash Discounts Earned, Season	5,360
Opening Inventory, Season at Cost	16,400
Transportation Charges, Season	7,000
Returns from Customers, Season	8,000
Transfers out, Season at Cost	3,000
Markdown Cancellations, Season	1,800
Gross Purchases at Retail, Season	103,200
Returns to Vendors at Cost, Season	5,000
Transfers in at Retail, Season	6,000
Alteration Expenses	1,400

Closing Physical Inventory, at Retail	19,500
Allowances to Customers, Season	1,560
Transfers out at Retail, Season	4,500
Additional Markups, Season	5,400
Returns to Vendors at Retail, Season	8,000
Opening Inventory, Season at Retail	25,400

8. As a management trainee in the gift department, you have been asked to determine the value of the merchandise on hand using both (a) FIFO and (b) LIFO for the item shown:

Date	Cost per Unit	Quantity Received	Quantity Sold	Quantity on Hand
December 1	$11.50			130
December 5	12.25	50	30	
December 9			60	
December 15	12.25	50		
December 17			130	
December 20	12.75	150		
December 23			110	
December 29	11.00	100		

9. Find the operating profit in a department that has the following information available:

	Cost	Retail
Opening Inventory	$ 32,000	$ 50,000
Net Purchases	100,000	148,000
Net Sales		140,000
Operating Expenses	30,100	
Additional Markups		2,400
Markdowns		5,000
Markdown Cancellations		1,200
Additional Markup Cancellations		400
Discounts to Employees		1,400
Alteration Expenses	2,600	
Cash Discounts Earned	3,000	
Closing Physical Inventory		55,000

10. A department manager using PATHFINDER for his cost code has asked you to determine the value of the inventory on hand for a particular item under both First-in, First-out (FIFO) and Last-in, First-out (LIFO) given the following activity during the period:

Week 1   Bought 50 units at AFR
Week 2   Bought 30 units at AIR
Week 3   Sold 60 units
Week 4   Bought 40 units at ANR
Week 5   Sold 50 units
Week 6   Bought 40 units at TRR
Week 7   Bought 30 units at ANR
Week 8   Sold 25 units

part **IV**

MERCHANDISE PLANNING AND CONTROL

In this part, the student will study the techniques used by retail organizations in the planning and control of the merchandise assortments. Up to this point, we have been concerned with the calculation of the various types of markup, the terms upon which retailers purchase merchandise, and the methods utilized in valuing the inventory of the operation in efforts to determine the firm's profitability.

Perhaps the most difficult task in a retail organization is the ability of the buyer and merchant to decide on the type and quantity of the merchandise presentation. To arrive at such a decision, the retailer must become familiar with the principles and techniques of planning stock turnover and sales. After calculating the desired goals in sales and turnover, the retailer is then able to determine the amount and distribution of the merchandise assortment required. This quantity assortment plan is prepared on a merchandise plan that determines the purchases in dollars that a retailer must make. To control the expenditures of dollars for merchandise, retail operations have instituted a control technique known as the dollar and unit open-to-buy system. Once the open-to-buy figures and the merchandise plan have been obtained, it is then possible to break down the units into a merchandise assortment that will be representative of the demand anticipated by customers of the store or department. Such a breakdown of units is found in the establishment of model stock plans.

Consequently, this planning process is responsible for setting the objectives for sales, inventories, purchases, and other profit factors, whereas control ensures that the plans are reaching the predetermined objectives or subsequently adjusted.

In the management function of any business enterprise, it is obvious that the relationship between planning and control must be a continuous one. In addition to the continuity of these two factors, it is also vital that the execution function be performed to carry out the plans. It soon becomes evident that planning and control are essentially reciprocal functions.

To make planning effective, the control function is essential, for it is the control records that provide the primary source of information for the planning that must be done for future periods. The relationships among sales, inventories, purchases, and model stock plans will be discussed in the following chapters.

The continuity of this management function may best be described by the following circular diagram, which indicates the relationship among the three functions and the importance of the feedback system between planning and control. Obviously, it is this feedback system that allows the retail buyer to make adjustments to merchandise plans, open-to-buy controls, and model stock plans.

The Management Function

chapter 9

Planning Turnover

STOCK TURNOVER

The rate of stock turnover is perhaps the most commonly quoted figure in the retail industry. In essence, it becomes the measure of the degree of balance between a retailer's sales and inventory. Simply, the stock turnover is an index of the velocity with which the merchandise moves into and out of a store or department. Stock turnover is defined as the number of times during a given period (usually a year or season) that the average inventory on hand has been sold and replaced. In other words, if a sporting goods store reports a stock turnover of 2.5, the observer would note that this retail operation has in fact turned over its average stock two and one-half times during the period for which it is reporting.

It should be noted that the rate of stock turnover is not the cause of the merchandising action but, rather, the result of efficient, successful merchandising. The proper selection of merchandise, improved pricing, and promotion will improve the stock turnover for a department or store. Although the rate of stock turnover is in the nature of an operational result rather than a cause, it is, nevertheless, subject to planning and control by department managers and store personnel.

SIGNIFICANCE OF STOCK TURNOVER RATE

Proper buying, pricing, and selling of merchandise can cause markdowns to be a smaller percentage of sales in a store, but the decrease in markdowns does not necessarily mean an increase in the rate of stock turnover. Markdowns can increase while stock turnover is also increasing. For example, large markdowns could occur while sales volume remains the same and the average inventory decreases. The result would be an increase in stock turnover, although this is not necessarily accompanied by an increase in net profit.

Retailers who measure merchandising efficiency of the store by emphasizing the store's turnover rate would do better to put greater emphasis on the turnover of various types of merchandise sold in the store. In other words, a comparison of merchandising efficiency in each department's turnover rate with similar departments in other stores would be more meaningful to the retailer than would a comparison with total store operations.

The best merchandising results are obtained by keeping the inventory adjusted to consumer demand. Therefore, it is vital for the retailer to recognize the concept of consumer demand and to adjust his inventory to this demand. Obviously, then, and only then, will the optimal rate of stock turnover for the store or department be achieved. Therefore, the stock must be continually surveyed to assure the proper balance of the selection factors available in the merchandise line.

CALCULATION OF STOCK TURNOVER RATE

The calculation of the stock turnover rate can be done on either a unit or a dollar basis. On a unit basis, this relationship is expressed as follows:

$$\text{Rate of Stock Turnover} = \frac{\text{Number of Units Sold}}{\text{Average Stock in Units}}$$

Consider the following example. If a men's furnishings department sold 100 dozen pair of men's hosiery during the year, and the department carried an average inventory of 25 dozen pair, the hosiery department would then have a unit turnover rate of 4 times per year (100 dozen/ 25 dozen).

The turnover based on physical units can be useful to the retailer in planning and controlling the breadth and depth of the assortment. However, the method requires that separate calculations take place for each classification of type of merchandise. Obviously, this method would not be feasible for retail stores that handle so many different items.

The rate of stock turnover can also be expressed on a dollar basis as indicated earlier. Further, the calculation of stock turnover on a dollar basis may also be expressed on the basis of retail dollars or cost dollars. Again, it should be obvious to the student of retailing that it is incorrect to mix a cost figure with a retail figure in the same calculation of the turnover using a dollar base. We shall see shortly that this mixture will in fact provide us with the capital turnover rate rather than a stock turnover.

As mentioned earlier, most progressive retail firms maintain their inventory records at retail figures. Therefore, in the calculation of the turnover rate for these stores, we use retail figures:

$$\text{Stock Turnover (Retail)} = \frac{\$ \text{ Net Sales}}{\$ \text{ Average Inventory at Retail}}$$

In a similar fashion, stores that continue to maintain their inventory records on the basis of cost would use the following in the calculation of the stock turnover rate:

$$\text{Stock Turnover (Cost)} = \frac{\$ \text{ Cost of Goods Sold}}{\$ \text{ Average Inventory at Cost}}$$

Once the equations have been developed for determining the stock turnover at retail and at cost, it becomes obvious that we need to explore the means of determining the average inventory.

Computing the average inventory for a month simply becomes the process of taking the store or department opening inventory, adding it to the closing inventory for the month, and dividing the sum total by 2. Consequently, the

$$\text{Average Stock for the Month} = \frac{\$ \text{ B.O.M.} + \$ \text{ E.O.M.}}{2}$$

where B.O.M. means the beginning-of-the-month stock and E.O.M. is the end-of-the-month stock.

Finding the average inventory for the season could then be the opening inventory for the season, added to the ending inventory for the season and then divided by 2. Consequently,

$$\text{Average Stock for Season} = \frac{\$ \text{ B.O.S.} + \$ \text{ E.O.S.}}{2}$$

However, it is more accurate to determine the average inventory for the season by taking the opening inventory for each of the 6 months in the season to arrive at a total sum of these figures. To this sum, we need to add the ending inventory for the last month in the season, which in fact becomes our ending inventory for the season. Consequently, for the spring-summer season, which runs from February 1 to July 31, we would determine the average inventory for the season in the following manner:

$$\text{Average Stock for Season} = \frac{\substack{\text{Feb.}\\\text{B.O.M.}} + \substack{\text{Mar.}\\\text{B.O.M.}} + \substack{\text{Apr.}\\\text{B.O.M.}} + \substack{\text{May}\\\text{B.O.M.}} + \substack{\text{June}\\\text{B.O.M.}} + \substack{\text{July}\\\text{B.O.M.}} + \substack{\text{July}\\\text{E.O.M.}}}{7}$$

This figure represents a truer picture of the average inventory that was available during the spring-summer season than was taking the average of the February B.O.M. and the July E.O.M.

The examples that follow explore the various means of calculating the stock turnover for a department or a total store operation.

EXAMPLE 1: Finding the Monthly Stock Turnover

A sportswear department had a B.O.M. inventory of $36,000 for June and an E.O.M. inventory of $52,000 with both figures quoted at retail. If net sales for the month of June reached $40,000, determine the monthly stock turnover for June in the sportswear department.

Solution:

Since

$$\text{Stock Turnover at Retail} = \frac{\$ \text{ Net Sales}}{\$ \text{ Average Inventory at Retail}}$$

and

$$\text{Average Inventory at Retail} = \frac{\text{B.O.M.} + \text{E.O.M.}}{2} = \frac{\$36,000 + \$52,000}{2}$$

$$= \$44,000$$

$$\text{Stock Turnover for June} = \frac{\$40,000}{\$44,000} = .91$$

Therefore, the stock turnover at retail for June is .91.

PROBLEM 1: Determine the stock turnover for the month of July for the figurine department that shows net sales for the month of $15,000. The buyer has also informed you that the B.O.M. at retail for July was $24,000 while the E.O.M. for the month at retail was $36,000.

EXAMPLE 2: Finding the Monthly Stock Turnover at Cost

NOTE: Solve the following problem without the benefit of an example solution since you need only apply the equation for calculating the stock turnover at cost given earlier.

PROBLEM 2: Determine the stock turnover at cost for a paint department that has the following information:

April 1, Inventory at Cost	$22,000
April 30, Inventory at Cost	36,000
Cost of Sales, April 1-30	29,000

EXAMPLE 3: Finding the Stock Turnover at Cost and Retail

The buyer of ladies' sportswear has the following figures for the 5 months of the spring-summer season. As an assistant buyer, you have been asked to determine the stock turnover at cost and retail for the first five months of the period.

	Inventory		Sales	
	Cost	Retail	Cost	Net
February 1	$22,000	$32,000	$16,000	$28,000
March 1	20,000	36,000	18,000	29,000
April 1	22,000	36,000	18,000	28,000
May 1	28,000	48,000	24,000	33,000
June 1	22,000	38,000	20,000	30,000
July 1	18,000	28,000		

Solution:

(a)

$$\text{Stock Turnover at Retail} = \frac{\$ \text{ Net Sales}}{\$ \text{ Average Inventory at Retail}}$$

Net Sales = $28,000 + $29,000 + $28,000 + $33,000 + $30,000 = $148,000

Average Inventory

$$= \frac{\$32,000 + \$36,000 + \$36,000 + \$48,000 + \$38,000 + \$28,000}{6}$$

$$= \frac{\$218,000}{6} = 36,333$$

The student will note that we have included the July 1 B.O.M. figure since we are attempting to find the average inventory for the period and the July 1 B.O.M. is in fact the same as the E.O.M. for June.
Therefore,

$$\text{Stock Turnover at Retail} = \frac{\$148,000}{\$36,333} = 4.07$$

(b)

$$\text{Stock Turnover at Cost} = \frac{\$ \text{ Cost of Goods Sold}}{\$ \text{ Average Stock at Cost}}$$

Similarly, cost of goods sold for 5 months would equal

$$\$16,000 + \$18,000 + \$18,000 + \$24,000 + \$20,000 = \$96,000$$

and the average stock at cost would also be calculated by including the July 1 B.O.M. at cost since this is the same as the June 30 E.O.M. at cost:

Average Stock at Cost

$$= \frac{\$22,000 + \$20,000 + \$22,000 + \$28,000 + \$22,000 + \$18,000}{6}$$

$$= \frac{\$132,000}{6} = \$22,000$$

And

$$\text{Stock Turnover at Cost} = \frac{\$96,000}{\$22,000} = 4.36$$

Therefore, the Stock Turnover at Cost is 4.36.

PROBLEM 3: As a management trainee, you have been asked to determine the seasonal stock turnover for a section at retail and at cost on the basis of the following information:

	Inventory		Sales	
	Cost	Retail	Cost	Retail
August 1	$ 9,600	$18,000	$ 5,600	$10,000
September 1	20,000	34,000	9,000	14,000
October 1	16,400	30,000	14,000	22,000
November 1	12,000	20,000	9,000	14,000
December 1	9,000	14,000	6,600	12,000
January 1	8,000	14,000	3,000	5,000
January 31	6,000	9,000		

NOTE: The following problems reflect the relationship among the three aspects of the calculation of inventory turnover. The basis of the solution to such problems lies in the substitution of the known factors to obtain the unknown. The substitutions will take place in the basic formula for the calculation of stock turnover. You are asked to solve these problems without the benefit of an example.

$$\text{Stock Turnover} = \frac{\text{Net Sales}}{\text{Average Stock at Retail}}$$

$$\text{Average Stock} = \frac{\text{Net Sales}}{\text{Stock Turnover}}$$

$$\text{Net Sales} = \text{Stock Turnover} \times \text{Average Stock at Retail}$$

PROBLEM 4: A giftware department has an average inventory of $56,000 at retail with a stock turnover of 2. What were the department's sales for the period?

PROBLEM 5: The net sales in a sporting goods department were $240,000 with a stock turnover of 3. Determine the department's average stock at retail.

PROBLEM 6: The misses' dress department had a planned stock turnover of .6 for June. The buyer has also planned for sales for June to be $30,000. If the B.O.M. stock for the month was $30,000, determine the department's E.O.M. stock for June if it is to achieve its stock turnover goal.

EXAMPLE 7: Finding Inventory Reduction to Increase Turnover

As a result of better arrangements with his suppliers, a buyer anticipates that he will be able to increase his turnover from 4.0 to 4.5 for the coming period. The buyer's department was able to obtain sales of $135,000 during the last period and expects to obtain the same sales this period. In dollars and percent, determine the amount of stock reduction that is possible if the buyer is to increase turnover.

Solution: On the basis of the turnover rates, we are able to establish the buyer's previous inventory and his planned inventory:

$$\text{Average Inventory} = \frac{\text{Net Sales}}{\text{Stock Turnover}}$$

Therefore

$$\text{Previous Average Stock} = \frac{\$135,000}{4} = \$33,750$$

and

$$\text{Planned Average Stock} = \frac{\$135,000}{4.5} = \$30,000$$

Therefore, the reduction in average stock will be:

Previous Average Stock	$33,750
Planned Average Stock	30,000
Reduction in Average Stock	$ 3,750

And percentage reduction in average stock will be:

$$\frac{\text{\$ Reduction in Average Stock}}{\text{\$ Previous Average Stock}} \times 100\% = \frac{\$3,750}{\$33,750} \times 100\% = 11.1\%$$

Therefore, the buyer will need to reduce his average stock by 11.1% or $3,750 from the past period to increase stock turnover from 4.0 to 4.5 with the same sales volume of $135,000.

PROBLEM 7: The sales in a department were $250,000 during the fall-winter season. During this season, the department was able to obtain a turnover of 2.5. The buyer anticipates that the sales volume will be the same for the spring-summer season but wishes to increase the departmental turnover to 3.0. If the increase in turnover is to be realized, determine the amount and percentage reduction in average stock, that will have to be obtained to maintain sales at the same level.

EXAMPLE 8: Finding the Increase in Sales to Increase Turnover

NOTE: This is basically the same situation as that in Example 7 except that, as a means of increasing turnover, the buyer wishes to increase sales without decreasing or changing her average inventory. Again, you are asked to solve the problem without the benefit of an example.

PROBLEM 8: The housewares department had an average inventory of $40,000 at retail for the past season and was able to realize a stock turnover of 2. The buyer wishes to maintain this same amount of average stock for the coming period and hopes to increase her stock turnover by increasing sales. If the buyer wishes to increase the turnover to 3 for the period, what dollar and percentage increase in sales will be required?

EXAMPLE 9: Finding the Average Turnover for a Store Given Net Sales and Turnover for Each Department

A men's apparel store is divided into four departments with the following information that is to be utilized to determine the stock turnover for the entire store.

	Net Sales	Stock Turnover
Men's Clothing	$150,000	2.5
Furnishings	120,000	3.0
Boy's Wear	50,000	2.5
Men's Shoes	30,000	2.0

Solution:

Before we are able to determine the stock turnover for the entire store, it is necessary to calculate the average stock for the store as a whole. Since each department accounts for a different portion of total sales, it is not possible simply to add the stock turnovers of the departments and divide the total by 4.

Department	Net Sales	Stock Turnover	Average Stock
Men's Clothing	$150,000	2.5	$ 60,000
Furnishings	120,000	3.0	40,000
Boy's Wear	50,000	2.5	20,000
Men's Shoes	30,000	2.0	15,000
Total	$350,000	?	$135,000

Therefore, with this information, it is now possible to calculate the stock turnover for the total store:

$$\text{Stock Turnover} = \frac{\text{Total Net Sales}}{\text{Total Average Stock}} = \frac{\$350,000}{\$135,000} = 2.6$$

Therefore, the men's apparel store will obtain a stock turnover of 2.6 based on the planned figures.

PROBLEM 9: A ladies' apparel store is divided into six departments with the following figures for the spring-summer season. As a management trainee, you have been asked to determine the stock turnover for the store for the season.

	Net Sales	Stock Turnover
Department A	$ 60,000	3.0
Department B	75,000	3.0
Department C	65,000	4.0
Department D	70,000	2.0
Department E	90,000	5.0
Department F	110,000	2.0

EXAMPLE 10: Finding the Average Turnover Given Proportion of Net Sales and Stock Turnover for Each Department

A hardware store is divided into five departments with the following information provided. The merchant has asked that you determine the average stock turnover for his store.

Department	Portion of Sales	Stock Turnover
Paint and Wallpaper	15%	3.0
Housewares	20	2.0
Hardware	30	3.0
Sporting Goods	25	3.0
Lawn and Garden	10	2.0

Solution:

In a similar manner to that explained in the calculation of average markup, we assume a total retail sales figure of $1,000:

Department	Portion of Sales	Stock Turnover	Average Stock
Paint and Wallpaper	15% = $ 150.00	3.0	$ 50.00
Housewares	20 = 200.00	2.0	100.00
Hardware	30 = 300.00	3.0	100.00
Sporting Goods	25 = 250.00	3.0	83.33
Lawn and Garden	10 = 100.00	2.0	50.00
Total	100% = $1,000.00	?	$383.33

Therefore, the stock turnover for the total store would be:

$$\text{Stock Turnover} = \frac{\text{Total Net Sales}}{\text{Total Average Stock}} = \frac{\$1,000.00}{\$383.33} = 2.6$$

PROBLEM 10: A store is divided into four departments for purposes of control. The store has planned the following figures and has requested that you determine the stock turnover for the entire store:

Department	Portion of Sales	Stock Turnover
A	25.0%	2.0
B	50.0	4.0
C	12.5	4.0
D	12.5	1.0

EXAMPLE 11: Finding the Stock Turnover for a Department Given Average Stock Turnover, Portion of Total Sales, and Turnover for Each Department

> *NOTE:* In a similar manner to the solution of Problem 10, solve this problem without the benefit of an example.

PROBLEM 11: The average stock turnover goal for a retail store was planned at 5 for the year. Department A in the store accounts for 30% of the sales and has a turnover of 4; Department B accounts for 15% of the sales and has a turnover of 3; Department C accounts for 25% of the sales and has a turnover of 5. If Department D is to be added and is to account for the remainder of the sales, calculate the turnover required in this department so that the store may realize its planned turnover goal.

CAPITAL TURNOVER

Capital turnover has become a useful guide for the retailer in determining the efficiency with which the dollars invested in merchandise is used in producing sales volume. Consequently, the capital turnover is the ratio between net sales and the average inventory at cost:

$$\text{Capital Turnover} = \frac{\$ \text{ Net Sales}}{\$ \text{ Average Inventory at Cost}}$$

The student will readily note that the capital turnover measures the number of times the cost of the average inventory investment is in fact converted to sales. This ratio is, therefore, concerned with the capital invested in inventory rather than the total capital commitment of the merchant.

Further, the reader will observe that, while the stock turnover rate has both the numerator and denominator at cost and retail, the capital turnover ratio requires the net sales in the ratio to be at retail while the denominator is at cost.

The capital turnover ratio is always higher than the stock turnover rate. While retailers prefer to utilize the latter ratio, financial analysts tend to find the capital turnover ratio more useful, since retail stock figures are not normally available on published corporate statements.

EXAMPLE 12: Finding Capital Turnover for the Season

> Storie's Sporting Goods had sales for the spring-summer season of $450,000 with the beginning-of-the-season inventory at $75,000 at cost. The stock on hand at the end of the season was $95,000 at cost. Calculate the capital turnover for the store.

Solution:

Since

$$\text{Capital Turnover} = \frac{\text{Net Sales}}{\text{Average Inventory at Cost}}$$

and

$$\text{Average Inventory at Cost} = \frac{\text{B.O.S.} + \text{E.O.S.}}{2} = \frac{\$75,000 + \$95,000}{2}$$
$$= \$85,000$$

substituting, then,

$$\text{Capital Turnover} = \frac{\$450,000}{\$85,000} = 5.3$$

PROBLEM 12: Steve's Building Center has asked you to calculate the capital turnover given the following information:

Net Sales	$330,000
Beginning Inventory, Cost	93,000
Ending Inventory, Cost	76,000

EXAMPLE 13: Finding Capital Turnover Given Stock Turnover

A department has a planned stock turnover of 6 with a markup of $33\frac{1}{3}\%$. As an assistant in the department, you have been asked to calculate the capital turnover rate for the department.

Solution:

Since

$$\text{Stock Turnover} = \frac{\text{Net Sales}}{\text{Average Inventory at Retail}}$$

and since net sales are unknown, we assume a net sales figure of $1,000. Therefore,

$$\text{Average Inventory at Retail} = \frac{\text{Net Sales}}{\text{Stock Turnover}} = \frac{\$1,000}{6}$$
$$= \$166.67$$

But the markup on the inventory is $33\frac{1}{3}\%$; thus average inventory at cost is:

$$
\begin{array}{llll}
& \text{Cost} & = & = & 66\frac{2}{3}\% \ (\frac{2}{3}) \\
+ & \text{Markup} = & & = & 33\frac{1}{3}\% \ (\frac{1}{3}) \\
\hline
& \text{Retail} & = \$166.67 & = 100\% & (\frac{3}{3})
\end{array}
$$

Therefore, average inventory at cost is calculated to be

$$
\frac{\$166.67}{100\%} \times 66\frac{2}{3}\% = \$111.11
$$

And, the capital turnover is

$$
\frac{\text{Net Sales}}{\text{Average Inventory at Cost}} = \frac{\$1,000}{\$111.11} = 9.0
$$

PROBLEM 13: An auto accessory department is able to plan for a stock turnover of 4 for the fall-winter season with a markup of 37.5%. Calculate the capital turnover for the department based on this data.

EXAMPLE 14: **Finding Stock Turnover Given Capital Turnover**

NOTE: Solve the following problem without the benefit of a sample example since this will simply be the reverse of the problem just solved. Recall the relationship between capital turnover and stock turnover.

PROBLEM 14: Determine the stock turnover for a department that has indicated to you that the sales have been planned at $365,000 with a markup of 40.0%. In addition, the buyer has informed you that he has planned for a capital turnover for the department of 8.5.

1. A hardware department wishes to add a fourth section to its merchandise classification. After discussions with the merchandise controller, the planned stock turnover the buyer has established for the total department is 2.5. If this new section, which is to be composed of paint and wallpaper, is to account for 20% of the department sales, calculate the stock turnover that will be required in this section based on the additional information provided: General Hardware accounts for 45% of the department's sales and has a turnover of 3.0; another section, Hand and Power Tools, accounts for 25% of the sales and has a stock turnover of 2.0; and a third section, Seasonal Merchandise, accounts for the balance of the sales in the department and maintains a stock turnover of only 1.5.

2. As a result of pressure from the merchandise controller, a buyer wishes to increase his stock turnover from 3.0 to 3.5. The buyer realizes that he will have to accomplish this by increasing sales and leaving his average stock the same. The buyer has asked you to inform him of the percentage increase needed in sales to affect the planned increase in turnover.

3. A department has the following information available for the 6-month season. You have been asked to calculate the stock turnover at cost and at retail and to determine the capital turnover.

	B.O.M. Inventory		Sales	
Month	Cost	Retail	Cost	Retail
August	$26,000	$40,000	$12,000	$20,000
September	30,000	52,000	24,000	38,000
October	40,000	60,000	24,000	40,000
November	40,000	62,000	30,000	55,000
December	42,000	62,000	33,000	60,000
January	25,000	38,000	12,000	18,000
February	28,000	40,000		

4. During the last period, a department had total sales of $80,000 that yielded a stock turnover of 4. The buyer wishes to increase the stock turnover to 5 by reducing the average inventory but maintaining the same level of sales for the coming period. Determine the amount in dollars and percent that the inventory must be reduced to allow the buyer to increase stock turnover.

5. A ladies' sweater department had planned sales of $240,000 for the season with a planned stock turnover of 3. If the typical markup for the department is 40%, calculate the department's capital turnover.

6. The merchandise controller for the sporting goods department, John Quinn, insisted that the buyer attempt to increase stock turnover from 3.5 to 4.0 for the coming period. To accomplish this, the buyer plans to increase sales without increasing average inventory. Calculate the percentage that the sales must be increased to realize an increase in turnover.

7. A shoe department is divided into four departments. The sales and stock turnover in each department are given. As an assistant store manager, you have been asked to determine the average stock turnover for the total store.

Department	Portion of Sales	Stock Turnover
Men's Shoes	25%	3.0
Ladies' Shoes	30	4.0
Children's Shoes	25	3.5
Accessories	20	4.5

8. A china and gift store is divided into five departments. The dinnerware section accounts for 30% of the store's sales and has a stock turnover of 1.5; the crystal and glassware section accounts for 20% of total sales and has a turnover of 2.0; the silverware department accounts for 15% of sales and has a turnover of 2.0; the figurines section accounts for 15% of sales of the store and has a turnover of 1.5; and the remainder of sales in the store are generated from the general gifts department. If the store anticipates a turnover of 2.0 for the entire store, calculate the turnover required in the general gifts department to obtain the planned inventory.

9. The hosiery department had a B.O.M. inventory of $24,000 at retail that had an initial markup of 40.0%. The department's E.O.M. inventory was valued at $30,000 at retail and carried a markup of 37.5%. During the month, merchandise was sold that cost $12,400, and the department was able to maintain a markup of 38.0% on sales. You are required to calculate the stock turnover for the month at both cost and retail.

10. Calculate the semiannual stock turnover at retail and at cost and the capital turnover for the notions department if the buyer, Yoki Nichol, reports the following figures:

Month	B.O.M. Inventory		Sales	
	Cost	Retail	Cost	Retail
February	$24,000	$36,000	$12,000	$20,000
March	18,000	26,000	18,000	28,000
April	30,000	50,000	16,000	24,000
May	28,000	56,000	20,000	36,000
June	22,000	36,000	24,000	40,000
July	20,000	30,000	16,000	26,000
August	24,000	36,000		

11. Answer the following questions in the space provided:
   (a) The linen department has a planned stock turnover of 2.9 for the year, with a planned average stock of $54,000. Calculate the planned annual sales for the department.

(b) The jewelry department has a planned stock turnover of 1.5 for the season, with planned sales of $150,000. If the buyer's B.O.S. stock for the department is $110,000, calculate the amount of her E.O.S. stock for the season.

(c) The toys and games department has planned sales of $140,000, with a stock turnover of 2.6 for the season. Determine the department's average stock.

12. The men's shoe department had an average stock of $64,000 at retail and a stock turnover of 2.6 during the past year. The buyer planned to maintain the same average stock but to increase sales to the point of increasing stock turnover to 3.0. What increase in sales in both dollars and percent will be required if the buyer is to increase his turnover to 3.0 while maintaining the same average stock? If the buyer operates with a markup of 40%, determine what the capital turnover would be for the coming year.

13. The divisional merchandise manager, Jillian Ashley, has informed a buyer that she will have to increase her division's turnover from 4.0 to 4.5 for the coming season. The buyer realizes that she will have to accomplish this by increasing sales and maintaining the same average stock. You have been asked by the buyer to determine the percentage increase in sales if she is to achieve a turnover of 4.5.

14. An appliance store is divided into four departments and wishes to add a fifth department featuring video recorders. Major appliances as a department is expected to account for 30% of the sales volume and have a stock turnover of 3.6; small appliances are expected to account for 25% of the sales and obtain a turnover of 4.5; radios should account for 15% of the sales and have a turnover of 2.0; television and stereos should account for 20% of the sales and have a turnover of 3.0; the video section is expected to account for the remainder of the sales. If the planned annual stock turnover for the store is 3.0, determine the stock turnover expected in the new video recorder department.

15. A computer store had an opening inventory of $60,000 at retail that carried an initial markup of 37.5%. The store's ending inventory for the month was valued at $75,000 at retail and carried a markup of $33\frac{1}{3}$%. During the month, merchandise was sold that cost $32,000 and the department was able to maintain a markup of 36.0% on these sales. Calculate the stock turnover at cost and at retail as well as the capital turnover for the store.

## chapter 10

Sales Planning

In previous chapters, we have been concerned with the determination and calculation of the various types of markups and the importance of the stock turnover rate and inventory valuation. In this and the following chapters, we become concerned with the actual planning function of the retail buyer and the merchandise planner. The function of merchandise planning is the attempt to set, in advance, goals for each of the major gross margin factors: sales, reductions, inventories, purchases, and markups. The concept of planning forces retailers to set goals and allows the merchant to measure operational performance against the goals established.

Since the estimated sales volume becomes the basis for the merchandise planning function, the first task in preparing a plan is to estimate the sales volume for the period of time for which the plan is made. The inventory level, the volume and selection factors of purchases to be made, and the markups to be achieved will be determined by the sales planning function.

Sales are generally planned for each month of a 6-month period. However, some stores may prefer to plan sales by the week. The length of time for which sales are planned, nevertheless, does not alter the principles involved in sales planning.

We have noted that planning for most retail establishments normally takes place for a 6-month period, classified as a season. For the merchant, the year is usually divided into two seasons: the fall-winter season, from August 1 to January 31; and the spring-summer season, from February 1 to July 31. The division of the calendar year at February 1 and August 1 results from the fact that retail stocks are generally lower at these times and the transition from winter to spring merchandise and from summer to fall merchandise takes place on these respective dates. Each of the 6-month periods is then divided into months or weeks, and the planning is then formulated.

In the calculations of the previous chapter, it was noted that the sales figure could be obtained by substitution in the formula equations for determining stock turnover and capital turnover. It was also noted that the basis for planning sales really becomes the goal of the merchant in light of the planned stock turnover.

However, sales planning must certainly be based on those factors, whether external or internal to the organization, which will influence future forecasts or indicate trends that might be realized at a later date. Some of the internal and external factors that must be considered in planning the sales forecast might be listed as follows:

Internal factors are

1. Actual sales in the corresponding period last year
2. Actual sales realized in the corresponding period over a number of years to develop a trend analysis
3. Any changes in store policy that might affect sales
4. Any changes in departmental space or in-store location that could seriously affect sales positively or negatively.

External factors are

1. The state of the economy, as reflected by business conditions
2. The inflationary spiral and the changes in prices
3. Increases in the quantity and quality of competitive forces
4. Changes in holiday dates, such as Easter Sunday
5. The increased speed of movements in the fashion cycle

Since we have already mentioned some of the factors that are internal and external to the organization, it should also be pointed out that these factors may affect the sales of a retail operation on a short-term or long-term basis. At the same time, some affect the conditions of all retailers, while others affect only the sales of certain types of retail establishments. Therefore, it is obvious that careful planning requires good judgment as well as an understanding of the appropriate mathematical computations required for estimating sales. Sound judgment must be the result of innate ability and experience. In this chapter, therefore, we will be concerned only with the arithmetic calculations required in estimating the planned sales.

The student will recall that the planned sales figure is the quantity of a group of items that are sold by the merchant at a specific retail price. In fact, the net sales figure for the retail establishment is composed of two basic elements: the average dollar sale multiplied by the number of transactions completed.

Net Sales = $ Average Sale × Number of Transactions

On the basis of this relationship in determining the planned sales volume for a retail store, it should be evident that the means of increasing sales volume is by increasing one or both of the sales components. Consequently,

Net Sales increase	if	Average Sale increases and Number of Transactions remains the same
Net Sales increase	if	Number of Transactions increase and Average Sale remains the same
Net Sales increase	if	Number of Transactions increase and Average Sale increases

The successful retailer is constantly attempting to increase volume in the operation by blending the relationship between the average sale and the number of transactions and subsequently relating this to the inventory investment.

EXAMPLE 1: Finding Planned Sales Given Current Activity to Date

The lamp department has the following information available for the spring-summer season. You have been asked to determine the probable sales for April.

| | Sales | |
	Last Year	This Year
February	$12,000	$14,000
March	14,000	16,000
April	16,000	

Solution:

The first step is to determine the trend increase in sales for February and March of this year in comparison with last year:

February increase this year over last year:

$$\frac{\$2,000}{\$12,000} \times 100\% = +16\frac{2}{3}\%$$

March increase this year over last year:

$$\frac{\$2,000}{\$14,000} \times 100\% = +14.3\%$$

It would appear from these figures that the sales increase for April should be somewhat less that 14%, since the increase appears to be diminishing. However, as indicated earlier, a certain amount of judgment is required in planning sales based on previous trends. As a result, we will plan for a 15% increase in sales for April this year over last year, on the basis that we are moving to the height of the spring-summer season.

Therefore,

Planned Sales April, This Year = $16,000 + (15% of $16,000)

= $18,400

The student should note that the selection of the percentage change in this type of situation will depend on the explanation used to defend the position to a merchandise controller.

PROBLEM 1: The merchandise controller is observing the sales in a department during the fall-winter season last year and what the department has achieved to date this year. The controller has asked you to calculate what the sales should be for the remaining two months of the period this year based on the activity to date and last year's sales.

	Sales	
	Last Year	This Year
August	$22,000	$22,000
September	30,000	33,000
October	35,000	38,325
November	45,000	50,400
December	50,000	
January	25,000	

EXAMPLE 2: Finding Seasonal Sales Given Monthly Percentages

Forecast the sales for the remaining months in the season for a department that had sales of $23,000 in February and $29,000 in March. The seasonal distribution of sales by months has been approved by the merchandise controller.

February	10%	May	23%
March	16%	June	16%
April	25%	July	10%

Solution:

On the basis of the sales distribution by months of the season, the sales percent for February and March equals 26% and sales volume for February and March equals $52,000 ($23,000 + $29,000). Thus, 26% = $52,000 and 1% = $2,000. Therefore,

April Sales = 25% = 25 × $2,000 = $50,000

May Sales = 23% = 23 × $2,000 = $46,000

June Sales = 16% = 16 × $2,000 = $32,000

July Sales = 10% = 10 × $2,000 = $20,000

PROBLEM 2: Pegi's Sportswear obtained sales of $90,000 for August and September in the fall-winter season. The seasonal distribution of sales had been planned and are indicated here. You have been asked to determine the planned sales for the remaining months of the season.

August	11%	November	22%
September	14%	December	24%
October	19%	January	10%

EXAMPLE 3: Finding Monthly Sales Given Variance in the Number of Selling Days

In October of last year, the gift department obtained sales of $28,000 with 24 selling days in the month. While the buyer anticipates the same sales volume this year, she realizes that there will only be 23 selling days in October this year. Calculate what the planned sales should be for October this year.

Solution:

Since sales are expected to be the same this year as last year for the month, the variance comes in the number of selling days in October. This year there will be one less (23 not 24) selling day. Therefore, the expected sales for this October would be

$$\frac{23}{24} \times \$28,000 = \$26,833.33$$

PROBLEM 3: In the same department, July sales last year were $42,000 with 25 selling days. The buyer anticipates a 7% increase in sales this year over last year for the month but realizes there will only be 24 selling days. Calculate the planned July sales based on this information.

EXAMPLE 4: Finding March and April Sales Given Variances in the Date of Easter

A ladies' dress department had sales last March of $42,000 and reached a volume of $35,000 last April. Last year Easter fell on April 2, but this year Easter will fall on April 12. The last time Easter fell on April 12 was 10 years ago, at which time the department realized sales of $11,000 in March and $14,000 in April. The rate of sales this year is expected to be similar to that of last year. Calculate the planned sales for March and April for this year, taking into consideration the change in the date of Easter.

Solution:

Since the rate of sale is expected to be similar this year to last year, the combined sales for March and April this year would then be

$$\$42,000 + \$35,000 = \$77,000$$

Ten years ago, the combined sales for March and April were

$$\$11,000 + \$14,000 = \$25,000$$

Thus the portion of sales for each of these two months would be

$$\text{March} = \frac{\$11,000}{\$25,000} \times 100\% = 44.0\% \quad \text{or} \quad 11/25$$

$$\text{April} = \frac{\$14,000}{\$25,000} \times 100\% = 56.0\% \quad \text{or} \quad 14/25$$

Therefore, applying these percentages or fractions to the total planned Easter sales for March and April this year, we get

$$\text{March Sales This Year} = 44\% \text{ of } \$77,000 = \$33,880.00$$
$$\text{April Sales This Year} = 56\% \text{ of } \$77,000 = \$43,120.00$$

PROBLEM 4: In March of last year sales in the coat department were $32,000 and in April were $28,000. The department is planning for a 5% increase in sales this year over last year. However, Easter falls on April 21 this year, the latest it has been in nine years when coat sales were $13,000 in March and $17,000 in April. Calculate the planned sales for March and April of this year based on information given.

EXAMPLE 5: Finding Planned Sales Given Anticipated Price Changes

As a result of economic conditions, price increases are expected to cause the average sale to increase by 10% over last year but also to cause a decrease of 4% in the number of transactions. If the bath boutique had sales last year of $200,000 with an average sale of $10.00, determine the change in planned sales that should be anticipated as a result of the price changes.

Solution:

Last year's average sale was $10.00; last year's total sales were $200,000; therefore, last year's number of transactions were

$$\frac{\$200,000}{\$10.00} = 20,000 \text{ transactions last year}$$

But this year's average sale is to increase 10%; therefore,

This Year's Average Sale = $10.00 + (10% of $10.00) = $11.00

And this year's number of transactions are to decline 4%; therefore,

This Year's Number of Transactions = 20,000 - (4% of 20,000) = 19,200

Therefore,

This Year's Planned Sales = $11.00 × 19,200 = $211,200

and

This Year Planned Dollar Sales	$211,200
Actual Last Year Dollar Sales	200,000
Planned Change in Dollar Sales	+$ 11,200

and

$$\text{Percent Increase in Dollar Sales} = \frac{\$11,200}{\$200,000} \times 100\% = 5.6\%$$

PROBLEM 5: A department was able to realize a sales volume of $160,000 last season. However, during the coming season, there is to be a decrease in prices as a result of new technology that will cause a decrease in the average sale by 5% and an increase in the number of transactions by 8%. In light of these changes, determine the changes in planned sales that should be anticipated. The average sale for last season was $16.00.

EXAMPLE 6: Finding the Change in the Average Sale Given Changes in Dollar Sales and Transactions due to Price Changes

As a result of inflationary pressures, the rising prices for the coming period are expected to increase sales by 10% in total dollar amount. However, the pressures will also result in a decrease in the number of transactions by 5% over the previous period. To plan effectively for these changes, the buyer wishes to determine the change that can be expected in the average sale.

Solution:

Assume that last year's total sales equaled $1,000 and that last year's transactions were 1,000. (Any figures might be assumed.) Therefore, this year's total sales will increase by 10%:

$$\text{Planned Sales} = \$1,000 + (10\% \text{ of } \$1,000) = \$1,100$$

and this year's number of transactions will decrease by 5% over last year's:

$$\text{Number of Transactions, This Year} = 1,000 - (5\% \text{ of } 1,000) = 950$$

Therefore,

$$\text{Last Year's Average Sale} = \frac{\$1,000}{1,000} = \$1.00$$

$$\text{This Year's Average Sale} = \frac{\$1,100}{950} = \$1.158$$

Therefore, the percentage increase in this year's average sale over last year is:

$$\frac{\$.158}{\$1.00} \times 100\% = 15.8\%$$

PROBLEM 6: The merchandise planner of the drapery department anticipates that economic conditions will result in a 7% decrease in total dollar sales and correspondingly will result in a 4% decrease in the number of transactions. On the basis of the decreases, calculate the change that can be anticipated in the average sale for the department.

EXAMPLE 7: Finding Change in Transactions Given Changes in Dollar Sales and the Average Sale due to Price Changes

NOTE: This type of problem is solved in a similar manner to the previous problem. As a result, you are asked to solve this without the benefit of an example.

PROBLEM 7: As a result of new advances in technology, it is expected that there will be a decrease in prices during the coming year. As a result of these price changes, a buyer anticipates that the dollar sales will increase by 8% but that the average sale will decrease by 3%. On this basis, calculate the change that the department might anticipate in the number of transactions for the period.

SUMMARY PROBLEMS

1. The sales in men's furnishings were $50,000 in August and $60,000 in September. If the seasonal distribution of sales for the department is as follows, determine the planned sales for the remainder of the season:

August	10%	November	20%
September	15%	December	24%
October	22%	January	9%

2. In March of last year there were 25 selling days producing sales of $35,000. This year there is expected to be a 6% increase in sales, but there will only be 24 selling days in the month. Calculate the planned March sales.

3. The previous year's sales for March were $38,000 and for April were $50,000. This year Easter falls on March 24 as it did 10 years ago when March sales were $15,000 and April sales were $11,000. It is expected that sales will increase 6% this year over last year. Determine the planned sales for March and April this year.

4. The sales for a retail store reached $275,000 last year. It is anticipated that sales will increase by 10% this year over last year. The number of transactions are also expected to increase, but only by 4%. Calculate the change that will result in the average sale as a result of these changes.

5. Calculate the estimated sales for July in a department that has the following figures:

Month	Sales Last Year	This Year
May	$40,000	$42,000
June	50,000	56,000
July	30,000	

6. As a result of declining prices, a buyer anticipates that his departmental sales will increase by 9% but his average sale will show a decrease of 3% over last year. On this basis, the buyer has asked that you determine the change that he might anticipate in the number of transactions for the period.

7. Determine the probable departmental sales for November given the following information:

Month	Sales Last Year	This Year
August	$12,000	$13,200
September	13,200	14,500
October	15,000	16,600
November	22,000	

8. The hardware department obtained sales of $31,000 last year during April. The department manager expects an increase of 8% in sales for the coming year. However, the manager recognizes that this year April will have 25 selling days instead of the 24 selling days in April last year. As the assistant manager, you have been asked to determine the planned sales for the hardware department for April of this year.

9. The ladies' suit and coat department has its sales influenced by the date of Easter. The buyer has anticipated a 12% increase in sales this year over last year. Last year, March sales were $36,000 and April sales were $24,000. However, this year, Easter falls on April 14. The last time Easter fell on this date, the department realized sales of $16,000 in March and $22,000 in April. Determine the planned sales for March and April for the suit and coat department for the coming year.

10. A department obtained sales of $220,000 last year with an average sale of $11. As a result of the forecasted economic conditions, the buyer anticipates a 6% decrease in the average sale but a 9% increase in the number of transactions. As the management trainee in the department, you have been asked to determine the planned sales for the department for the coming year.

11. As a result of the economic conditions of the city, a department of a retail establishment expects sales to decrease by 5% and the number of transactions also to decrease by 3%. On this basis, determine what the department might anticipate as a change in the average sale.

12. A department expects that the total dollar sales will increase by 10% but that the average sale will decrease by 5%. What anticipated changes can be expected in the number of transactions in the department?

13. August sales in the floor coverings department were $38,000 and September sales reached $42,000. On the basis of the sales to date and the percentage distribution of sales for the season, calculate the probable sales for each of the remaining months in the season.

August	10%	November	20%
September	15%	December	15%
October	30%	January	10%

14. As a result of economic conditions, the buyer, William O'Hara, anticipates that the sales in the TV department will decrease by 10% over last year. If there are 25 selling days in October this year as compared with last October's 24 selling days, determine the planned sales for October this year if last October's sales were $45,000.

15. The ladies' fancy dress department is expected to show an increase in sales of 10% this year over last year. Last year sales during March were $56,000, and during April they were $40,000. This year Easter falls on April 14. The last time Easter fell on this date, the department realized sales of $13,000 in March and $26,000 during April. Calculate the planned sales for March and April this year based on the information given.

16. The average sale is expected to increase 10% and the number of transactions are expected to decrease 5% over last year as a result of the inflationary pressures of the economy. Sales last year for the month of March were $28,000 with 24 selling days, and for April they were $33,000 with 25 selling days. This year March will have 25 selling days and April will have 24 selling days. Calculate the planned sales for March and April this year.

17. If rising prices are expected to increase total sales in a retail store by 12% and to decrease the number of transactions in the store by 6%, calculate what change will result in the average sale for the store.

18. What change in the number of transactions may be anticipated by a retailer who expects total dollar sales to increase by 8% and the average sale to decrease by 3%?

19. Kneider's men's and boys' apparel store reached sales last year of $375,000. It is anticipated that the sales will increase this year by 10% over last year. It is also anticipated that the number of transactions will increase by 5% over last year. Calculate the changes that will result in the average sale as a result of these anticipated changes.

20. A department was able to obtain sales last year of $290,000 with an average sale of $8.00. As a result of forecasted economic conditions, the buyer anticipates a 3% decrease in the average sale but a 10% increase in the number of transactions. As the management trainee in the department, you have been asked to determine the planned sales for the department for the coming year.

## chapter 11

Stock Planning in Dollars

In an earlier chapter, it became apparent that the primary goal of stock planning would be to maintain an inventory that was well balanced with respect to anticipated sales. This means that the breadth of merchandise assortment must be large enough to meet the needs and wants of the customers and that the depth of assortment in the various selection factors must be reasonably in line with the rate of sale of each of these factors. Further, the investment in total inventory should be sufficient to meet all reasonable demand expectancy, yet small enough to assure the advantages inherent in a healthy rate of stock turnover.

In determining the total amount of stock that will be needed at different times of the planning period, retailers are guided basically by their concepts of a satisfactory turnover rate. There are several mathematical approaches to the planning of stocks to achieve the anticipated sales level. However, all these mathematical approaches contain the same basic consideration. The retailer who is planning stock assortment must give consideration not only to the anticipated level of total sales and to variations in the volume by months, but must also allow for differences in individual store experience. These differences in store experience include an analysis of the frequency of stock checking and reordering, the time required to prepare and transmit orders, the delivery time required from the vendors, and the unexpected delays in acquisition.

In this chapter we shall be concerned with four basic methods of stock planning:

1. Basic Stock Method
2. Percentage Variation Method
3. Weeks' Supply Method
4. Stock-Sales Ratio Method

BASIC STOCK METHOD

In this method of stock planning, the retailer determines the basic stock required for the store or department; to this basic stock, the planned monthly sales figure is added to determine the B.O.M. stock. The basic stock method is recommended for use by retail organizations where expected stock turnover is 6 times or less per year. In essence, the basic stock implies that the retailer will begin each month with the amount of the predetermined basic stock for the period. This represents the minimum amount of stock that a retailer will have in the store or department at any time. In fact, if the retailer were to plan no sales at all for a particular month, the stock available in the department would still be the amount of the basic stock. The stock to be carried at the beginning of the month, when the basic stock is used, is equal to the planned sales for that month added to the basic stock. Therefore,

$$\text{B.O.M. Stock} = \text{Basic Stock} + \text{Planned Sales for the Month}$$

By definition, the basic stock is equal to the average stock for the season minus the average monthly sales. Therefore, it represents the minimum amount of stock that should be maintained in the least active month of the period. Therefore,

$$\text{Basic Stock} = \text{Average Stock} - \text{Average Monthly Sales}$$

Graphically, the implication of the basic stock method is shown in the accompanying illustration. The reader will note that the B.O.M. curve is parallel to the planned sales curve and above the sales curve by the amount of the basic stock. In the example, we have assumed the following planned sales with a stock turnover of 3 for the season:

Month	Planned Sales	Planned B.O.M. Stock
February	$ 10,000	$40,000
March	20,000	50,000
April	40,000	70,000
May	30,000	60,000
June	50,000	80,000
July	30,000	60,000
Total	$180,000	

Since total planned sales for the season are $180,000, the average monthly sales would be $30,000 ($180,000 divided by the 6 months in the season). Further, since the planned stock turnover is 3 for the season, the average stock for the season would be $60,000 ($180,000/3). The basic stock is then calculated as $30,000($60,000 - $30,000). As noted earlier in the formula, this basic stock of $30,000 is then added to each of the planned sales figures to determine the planned B.O.M. stock figures.

The student will note in the diagram that the basic stock of $30,000 is the difference between the planned sales curve and the planned B.O.M. curve. Therefore, the department will always have a stock on hand of $30,000 regardless of the planned sales. The calculation of the B.O.M. stock, using the basic stock method, will be discussed further in this chapter.

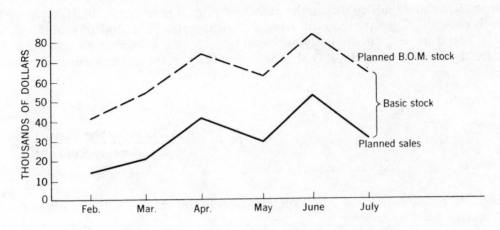

PERCENTAGE VARIATION METHOD

This method of determining the amount of stock required for the beginning of the month differs from the basic stock method in that this technique does not require the provision for a basic amount of stock in the department. On the other hand, the percentage variation method of stock planning requires that the B.O.M. stock be increased or decreased from the average stock by one-half the percentage variation in the planned sales from the average monthly sales. Therefore, if February sales show an increase in 20% over the average monthly sales, the B.O.M. stock for February will be only 10% greater than the average stock for the season. The percentage variation method of determining the amount of stock to be carried is recommended for use in departments that have a stock turnover of more than 6 times per year. Consequently, this method is used with merchandise that experiences a higher turnover rate.

To illustrate the differences that exist with this method, let us assume the same figures as the previous example with the exception of the stock turnover, which we will now assume to be 4 for the season:

Total Planned Sales for Season	$180,000
Stock Turnover for the Season	4
Average Stock for Season	$ 45,000
Average Monthly Sales for Season	$ 30,000

Therefore, if February sales are planned at $10,000 and average monthly sales are planned at $30,000, the planned sales for this month are $20,000 below the average monthly sales or $66\frac{2}{3}$% less ($20,000/$30,000). Applying the principle of the percentage variation, where this variance should be one-half that relation to stock, the B.O.M. stock for February should be $33\frac{1}{3}$% (one-half of $66\frac{2}{3}$%) less than the average stock for the season. Therefore, the B.O.M. stock will be $30,000 for February ($45,000 less one-third of $45,000). And applying the same principles, we would find the remaining B.O.M. stocks as follows:

Month	Planned Sales	Increase or Decrease in Average Monthly Sales	Planned B.O.M. Stock	Increase or Decrease on Average Monthly Stock
February	$ 10,000	$-66\frac{2}{3}$%	$30,000	$-33\frac{1}{3}$%
March	20,000	$-33\frac{1}{3}$%	37,500	$-16\frac{2}{3}$%
April	40,000	$+33\frac{1}{3}$%	52,500	$+16\frac{2}{3}$%
May	30,000	0	45,000	0
June	50,000	$+66\frac{2}{3}$%	60,000	$+33\frac{1}{3}$%
July	30,000	0	45,000	0
Total	$180,000			

The student should notice that in the month of April, for example, the sales planned for that month were $33\frac{1}{3}\%$ greater than the average monthly sales. The student should also note that the B.O.M. stock was subsequently increased by only $16\frac{2}{3}\%$ over the average stock. The formula for the calculation of the B.O.M. stock using the percentage variation method is expressed as follows:

$$\text{B.O.M. Stock} = \text{Average Stock} \times \frac{1}{2} \left(1 + \frac{\text{Planned Sales for the Month}}{\text{Average Monthly Sales}}\right)$$

The application of this formula will be expressed later in this chapter with the solution of various problems encountered by merchants.

WEEKS' SUPPLY METHOD

In this method of stock planning, the amount of stock required to open a month is determined on the basis of a number of weeks' supply of merchandise. The number of weeks' supply that is to be kept on hand during a period is dependent on the rate of stock turnover required for a store or department. The problem inherent in this method of stock planning is that the stock is carried in direct relation to the planned sales. This would mean that too much would be carried in the height of the season and too little during the slower periods. This method also does not provide for a minimum basic assortment for the department and, as a result, is generally unacceptable for general departmental stock. It finds its primary use among the unit control systems of some staple merchandise. Stores or departments using this method of stock planning also plan sales by weeks rather than on a monthly basis. Since we have stated that this method is used primarily by stores that have relatively stable sales volumes, stores that have widely fluctuating seasonal sales find the stock-sales ratio, which follows, a more advantageous method of stock planning.

STOCK-SALES RATIO METHOD

This method of stock planning indicates the relationship that exists between the stock of a department and its sales. This stock-sales relationship can be expressed in either of two ways:

1. The B.O.M. stock-sales ratio represents the relationship of the stock at the beginning of the month to the sales for the month. This ratio implies that a specified amount of stock will be required to achieve the planned sales as indicated by the relationship designated in the ratio;

2. The E.O.M. stock-sales ratio represents the relationship of the stock on hand at the end of the sales month. This ratio implies that a specified amount of stock will remain on hand at the end of the month in relationship to the planned sales for that month. In other words, the stock on hand at the end of the month is there to assist in making sales in the following month.

Of the two ways of expressing the relationship between stock and sales, the student should note that the B.O.M. stock-sales ratio is more useful to the retailer since it indicates a causal relationship to sales. In basic terms, the opening inventory for the month (B.O.M.) is brought into the store to generate sales for that month. The ending inventory, on the other hand, is designed to produce sales during the following month.

The student will recall that the stock turnover rate was also a relationship between sales and stock, but this was between the net sales figure and the average stock for the period under study. The stock-sales ratio on the other hand is a relationship between the opening or closing inventory and the planned net sales. Consequently, the stock-sales ratio differs from the stock turnover rate in the following ways:

1. The period covered for the stock-sales ratio is usually a month, whereas the stock turnover is normally calculated for a period of months, a season, or a year.

2. The stock figure in the stock-sales ratio represents that stock on hand at a specific time, whereas the stock turnover rate utilizes the average stock for the period.

3. The numerators and denominators in the two calculations are reversed since the stock-sales ratio is stock divided by sales, whereas the stock turnover is the sales divided by the stock.

The calculations of the B.O.M. stock using the stock-sales ratio will be explored later in this chapter.

STOCK PLANNING WITH BASIC STOCK

The procedure set forth earlier for determining the B.O.M. stock using the basic stock method is the following (it is recommended for use when the stock turnover is 6 or less per year or 3 or less per season):

1. From the sales figure for the season and the stock turnover, determine the average stock for the season.

2. Since seasonal sales are known and there are 6 months in the season, determine the average monthly sales by dividing total season sales by number of months in the period.

3. Determine the basic stock by subtracting the average monthly sales from the average stock for the period.

4. To the basic stock figure, add the sales planned for the month to determine the B.O.M. stock for that month.

In summary, we therefore have

$$\text{Average Stock} = \frac{\text{Sales for the Period}}{\text{Turnover for the Period}}$$

$$\text{Average Monthly Sales} = \frac{\text{Sales for the Period}}{\text{Months in the Period}}$$

$$\text{Basic Stock} = \text{Average Stock} - \text{Average Monthly Sales}$$

$$\text{B.O.M. Stock} = \text{Sales for the Month} + \text{Basic Stock}$$

EXAMPLE 1: Finding B.O.M. Stock Given Turnover of 6 or Less per Year

A gift department has planned sales of $18,000 for April. The department's planned sales for spring-summer are $90,000 with a planned stock turnover of 2 for the season. Determine the B.O.M. stock for April.

Solution:

Since the stock turnover is 3 or less for the season, the basic stock method is to be employed in finding B.O.M.:

$$\text{Average Stock} = \frac{\$90,000}{2} = \$45,000$$

$$\text{Average Monthly Sales} = \frac{\$90,000}{6} = \$15,000$$

$$\text{Basic Stock} = \$45,000 - \$15,000 = \$30,000$$

$$\text{B.O.M. April} = \$18,000 + \$30,000$$
$$= \$48,000$$

PROBLEM 1: The planned stock turnover in a men's furnishings department is 2.5 for the fall-winter season with planned seasonal sales of $270,000. If the buyer has planned sales for the month of $48,000, calculate the amount of stock he will require to open on September 1.

EXAMPLE 2: Finding B.O.M. Stock Given Turnover of 6 or Less per Year and a Specified Control Period

NOTE: Since some months of the season or year are characterized by 4 weeks while others have 5 weeks, some retailers have seen fit to standardize the number of weeks in each of their control periods rather than take the 6-month or 12-month figures.

If a season is said to consist of 26 weeks (one-half a year), then merchants using a 4-week control period, in fact, have 6.5 control months in a season:

$$\frac{26 \text{ weeks in a season}}{4 \text{ weeks every month}} = 6.5 \text{ "months" or "control periods"}$$

A store that uses 5-week control periods during a season would in fact have 5.2 control months in the season:

$$\frac{26 \text{ weeks in a season}}{5 \text{ weeks every month}} = 5.2 \text{ "months" or "control periods"}$$

The student should note that in the event that the retailer is planning for the year instead of the season, these figures would double: a 4-week control would produce 13.0 control periods per year, and a 5-week control would produce 10.4 control periods per year.

The shoe department operates with the use of a 5-week control period for August. The department has planned sales for the coming season at $160,000 with a stock turnover of 1.6 for the season. Sales have been planned at $24,000 for August. Calculate the B.O.M. stock for August.

Solution:

$$\text{Average Stock} = \frac{\$160,000}{1.6} = \$100,000$$

Since there are 26 weeks in the season and the department uses a 5-week control period for August, then there are 5.2 control periods:

$$\text{Average Monthly Sales} = \frac{\$160,000}{5.2} = \$30,769$$

$$\text{Basic Stock} = \$100,000 - \$30,769 = \$69,231$$

$$\text{August B.O.M. Stock} = \$24,000 + \$69,231$$
$$= \$93,231$$

PROBLEM 2: Calculate the B.O.M. stock for November in a department that has the following planned figures:

Planned Annual Sales	$370,000
Planned November Sales	$ 60,000
Planned Annual Stock Turnover	5
Planned Control Period, November (weeks)	4

EXAMPLE 3: Finding B.O.M. Stock Given Stock Turnover and Variation in Average Sale

Calculate the B.O.M. stock for March in a department that has planned the following figures for the spring-summer season:

Stock Turnover, Season	2
Planned Sales, Season	$220,000
Planned Sales, March	$ 40,000
Average Sale, Season	$ 10.00
Average Sale, March	$ 15.00
Control Period, March (weeks)	4

Solution:

Since the stock turnover is 2 for the season, we can use the basic stock method for determining B.O.M. stock.

NOTE: The average sale for the month of March is greater than the average sale for the season; that is, it is possible to have the same dollar sales for each of two months even though the average sale in each month is different. Consequently, because of this variance in the average sale, we need to find a standardized item that can be used to calculate the inventory with these variances. This standardized unit becomes the complement of the average sale in the calculation of net sales, namely, the number of transactions. Therefore, as we will see, it is necessary to convert the dollar figures to transactions to find the B.O.M. stock and then convert this back to March dollars in this example.

$$\text{Average Stock in Transactions} = \frac{\text{Sales in Transactions for the Season}}{\text{Stock Turnover for the Season}}$$

$$= \frac{\$220,000/\$10.00}{2} = 11,000 \text{ transactions}$$

$$\text{Average Monthly Sales in Transactions} = \frac{\text{Sales in Transactions for the Season}}{\text{Number of Control Periods}}$$

$$= \frac{\$220,000/\$10.00}{26 \text{ weeks}/4} = \frac{22,000}{6.5} = 3,385 \text{ transactions}$$

Therefore,

Basic Stock in Transactions = 11,000 − 3,385 = 7,615 transactions

And since the average sale for March is $15, to convert this basic stock to March dollars to find B.O.M. stock

March B.O.M. Stock = $40,000 + (7,615 transactions × $15)
$40,000 + $114,225
$154,225

PROBLEM 3: Calculate the B.O.M. Stock for November in a department that has the following planned annual figures:

Planned Sales, Annual	$420,000
Planned Sales, November	$ 72,000
Planned Average Sale, Annual	$ 7
Planned Average Sale, November	$ 12
Planned Control Period, November (weeks)	5
Planned Stock Turnover, Annual	6

As established earlier, the percentage variation method of stock planning does not provide for a basic stock but dictates that the B.O.M. stock should vary from the average stock in the ratio of 50% of the variation in the month's sales from the average monthly sales. The procedure for establishing B.O.M. stock using this method is as follows (it is, recommended for use when the stock turnover is more than 6 per year or more than 3 per season):

1. From the sales figure for the season or period and the stock turnover, determine the average stock for the period.

2. From the planned sales figure and the number of months or control periods, determine the average monthly sales.

3. Apply the figures that have been calculated to the formula that has been established to find the B.O.M. stock.

$$\text{B.O.M. Stock} = \text{Average Stock} \times \tfrac{1}{2}\left(1 + \frac{\text{Planned Sales for the Month}}{\text{Average Monthly Sales}}\right)$$

EXAMPLE 4: Finding the B.O.M. Stock Given Stock Turnover of More than 6 per Year

An appliance department had the following planned figures for the spring-summer season. You have been asked to determine the B.O.M. stock for June 1:

Planned Season Sales	$180,000
Planned June Sales	$ 50,000
Planned Stock Turnover, Season	4

Solution: Since the turnover is 4 for the season, the percentage variation method is called for:

$$\text{Average Stock} = \frac{\$180,000}{4} = \$45,000$$

$$\text{Average Monthly Sales} = \frac{\$180,000}{6} = \$30,000$$

Substituting these figures in the formula, we get

$$\text{June B.O.M. Stock} = \$45,000 \times \tfrac{1}{2}\left(1 + \frac{\$50,000}{\$30,000}\right)$$

$$= \$60,000$$

PROBLEM 4: The planned sales for a department for October are $32,500. The total planned sales for the season for this department are $150,000 with a stock turnover of 5 for the period. You are required to determine the stock that should be on hand in the department on October 1.

EXAMPLE 5: **Finding B.O.M. Stock Given Turnover of More than 6 per Year and Variation in the Average Sale**

Calculate the B.O.M. stock for April in a department that has the following planned figures for the year:

Planned Annual Sales	$390,000
Planned Sales, April	$ 40,000
Planned Average Sale, Annual	$ 10.00
Planned Average Sale, April	$ 14.00
Planned Stock Turnover, Annual	8
Planned Control Period, April (weeks)	4

Solution: Following the procedure established in the previous examples, it is necessary to complete the calculations in transactions:

$$\text{Average Stock in Transactions} = \frac{\$390,000/\$10.00}{8} = 4,875$$

$$\text{Average Monthly Sales in Transactions} = \frac{\$390,000/\$10.00}{52 \text{ weeks}/4} = 3,000$$

and since the average sale for April is $14.00, then

Average Stock for April = 4,875 × $14.00 = $68,250
Average Monthly Sales for April = 3,000 × $14.00 = $42,000

And substituting in the formula for percentage variation;

$$\text{B.O.M. Stock, April} = \$68,250 \times \tfrac{1}{2} \left(1 + \frac{\$40,000}{\$42,000}\right)$$
$$= \$66,625$$

PROBLEM 5: As a management trainee, you are asked to determine the stock that should be on hand on June 1 in a department that has the following planned figures:

Planned Sales, Season	$275,000
Planned Sales, June	$ 70,000
Planned Average Sale, Season	$ 8.00
Planned Average Sale, June	$ 11.00
Control Period, June (weeks)	5
Stock Turnover, Season	5

STOCK PLANNING WITH WEEKS' SUPPLY

As explained earlier, this method of stock planning is based on the number of weeks' supply of merchandise established by the desired turnover goal.

EXAMPLE 6: Finding Planned Stock Given Turnover and Weekly Rate of Sale

If a staples department is able to sell $1,800 per week and has a planned stock turnover of 6 for the 6-month period, calculate the amount of stock that should be carried in the department.

Solution: Since

$$\text{Average Stock} = \frac{\text{Sales for the Period}}{\text{Stock Turnover}}$$

the average stock in weeks' supply would be

$$\frac{26 \text{ Weeks in Period}}{\text{Turnover of 6}} = 4\tfrac{1}{3} \text{ Weeks' Supply}$$

Therefore, the stock to be carried will need to be $4\tfrac{1}{3}$ weeks' supply. And since the department is selling at the rate of $1,800 per week, the amount of stock that needs to be carried will be

$$\text{Planned Stock} = 4\tfrac{1}{3} \times 1,800$$
$$= 7,800$$

PROBLEM 6: If a department has an average weekly rate of sale of $5,200 and a planned stock turnover of 8 for the 6-month season, determine the amount of stock that should be kept on hand.

EXAMPLE 7: Finding Planned Stock Given Turnover and Planned Sales for Each Week

The planned annual stock turnover in a department is 10.4. The department has the following information available and has requested that you determine the stock to be carried for the next few weeks.

Weeks of Period	Sales Last Year	This Year
1	$2,200	$2,500
2	2,400	2,680
3	2,800	3,800
4	3,000	3,400
5	3,400	3,600
6	3,600	
7	3,400	
8	3,600	
9	3,600	
10	4,000	
11	4,200	
12	4,400	

Solution:

$$\text{Average Stock in Weeks' Supply} = \frac{52 \text{ weeks}}{10.4} = 5 \text{ Weeks}$$

Since we are already at the end of the fifth week, we are planning the stock that should be on hand at the beginning of the sixth week, this year. And since we have asked for the stock to be carried for the next few weeks, the term "few" means the average stock in weeks' supply—in this case, 5 weeks.

Therefore, from week 6 to week 10 (5 weeks from the end of the fifth week), we had sales last year of $18,200. This would appear to be the amount of stock required at the beginning of the sixth week. However, there appears to be an increase this year over last year as we note in the first five weeks of this year compared with last year's figures.

	Sales First Five Weeks This Year	$15,180
−	Sales First Five Weeks Last Year	13,800
	Increase This Year over Last Year	$ 1,380

$$\text{Percent Increase This Year over Last Year} = \frac{\$1,380}{\$13,800} \times 100\% = 10\%$$

Therefore, the planned stock for the next few weeks should be

$$\text{5 Weeks' Supply, Weeks 6–10} = \$18,200 + (10\% \text{ of } \$18,200)$$
$$= \$20,020$$

PROBLEM 7: The buyer of a department is planning a 5% increase in sales this year over last year and has planned for a stock turnover of 4 for the 6-month season. On the basis of the information given for last year, determine the stock that should be carried for the next few weeks.

Weeks of Period	Sales Last Year
1	$3,000
2	3,500
3	5,000
4	6,200
5	7,800
6	7,000
7	6,500
8	7,000
9	7,200

STOCK PLANNING WITH STOCK-SALES RATIOS

This method of stock planning is used by retail organizations that have been able to establish a relationship between the opening inventory in the department or the store and the planned sales for the operation.

EXAMPLE 8: Finding the B.O.M. and E.O.M. Stock-Sales Ratios

The fabric department had an opening inventory of $32,000 and a closing inventory of $40,000 for the month of April. Sales during the month totaled $15,000. On the basis of this information, you are asked to calculate the B.O.M. and E.O.M. stock-sales ratios.

Solution:

$$\text{B.O.M. Stock-Sales Ratio} = \frac{\text{B.O.M. Stock at Retail}}{\text{Sales}}$$

$$= \frac{\$32,000}{\$15,000} = 2.13$$

$$\text{E.O.M. Stock-Sales Ratio} = \frac{\text{E.O.M. Stock at Retail}}{\text{Sales}}$$

$$= \frac{\$40,000}{\$15,000} = 2.67$$

PROBLEM 8: As an assistant buyer for a department, you have been asked to complete the following chart by determining the B.O.M. and E.O.M. stock-sales ratio for each month in the season.

Month	B.O.M. Stock (Retail)	Planned Sales	B.O.M. Stock-Sales Ratio	E.O.M. Stock-Sales Ratio
August	$25,000	$10,000	_____	_____
September	32,000	8,000	_____	_____
October	35,000	15,000	_____	_____
November	35,000	20,000	_____	_____
December	40,000	25,000	_____	_____
January	30,000	10,000	_____	_____
February	20,000			

EXAMPLE 9: Finding B.O.M. Stock Given Stock-Sales Ratio and Planned Sales

and

EXAMPLE 10: Finding Planned Sales Given Stock-Sales Ratio and Planned B.O.M. Stock

> *NOTE:* These problems are solved by substituting in the basic formula for the B.O.M. stock-sales ratio (no examples are provided).

PROBLEM 9: A department has planned sales of $27,000 for May and has a planned stock-sales ratio of 2 for the beginning of the month. Calculate the beginning-of-the-month stock for May.

PROBLEM 10: The ladies' sweater department has an opening inventory of $54,000 at retail for November. If the buyer operates with a planned B.O.M. stock-sales ratio of 3 for this month, calculate the sales that the buyer is planning for November.

EXAMPLE 11: **Finding Stock Turnover Given Monthly Stock-Sales Ratios**

As a management trainee, you have been asked to determine the B.O.M. stocks for June and July and the stock turnover for June based on the following information:

Month	Planned Sales	B.O.M. Stock-Sales Ratios
June	$26,000	2.0
July	$30,000	2.5

Solution:

$$\text{B.O.M. Stock for June} = \$26,000 \times 2.0 = \$52,000$$
$$\text{B.O.M. Stock for July} = \$30,000 \times 2.5 = \$75,000$$
$$\text{Stock Turnover for June} = \frac{\text{Sales for June}}{\text{Average Stock for June}}$$

and

$$\text{Average Stock for June} = \frac{\text{June B.O.M. Stock} + \text{June E.O.M. Stock}}{2}$$
$$= \frac{\$52,000 + \$75,000}{2} + \$63,500$$

Therefore, the stock turnover for June will be

$$\frac{\$26,000}{\$63,500} = .41$$

PROBLEM 11: In preparation for the Christmas season, the buyer of men's furnishings has planned sales for November of $40,000 with a B.O.M. stock-sales ratio of 2.5. For December, the buyer has planned sales of $45,000 with a B.O.M. stock-sales ratio of 2.0. Determine the B.O.M. stock for both November and December and calculate the stock turnover for November in men's furnishings.

SUMMARY PROBLEMS

1. Calculate the stock that should be on hand on September 1 in a department that has the following planned figures:

Planned Sales, Season	$320,000
Planned Sales, September	$ 60,000
Planned Average Sale, Season	$ 16.00
Planned Average Sale, September	$ 12.00
Planned Stock Turnover, Season	2
Planned Control Period, September (weeks)	4

2. Calculate the stock that should be on hand in a department on March 1 if the following information is available:

Planned Annual Sales	$312,000
Planned March Sales	$ 45,000
Planned Control Period (weeks), March	5
Planned Annual Stock Turnover	8

3. A millinery department has a planned stock-sales ratio of 1.5 for April 1. Determine the B.O.M. stock for April if the department has planned sales for that month of $16,000.

4. If the annual stock turnover in a department is planned at 8, calculate the amount of stock that should be carried for the next few weeks.

Weeks of Period	Sales	
	Last Year	This Year
1	$10,000	$12,000
2	11,000	13,200
3	12,000	14,400
4	15,000	18,000
5	17,000	
6	19,000	
7	20,000	
8	22,000	
9	18,000	
10	20,000	
11	21,000	
12	20,000	

5. A department has planned sales of $130,000 for the spring-summer season with a planned stock turnover of 2.6 for the season. The department operates with a 5-week control period. Calculate the B.O.M. stock for May if the planned sales for May represent 30% of the total seasonal sales.

6. Calculate the B.O.M. stock for September in a department that has the following planned figures for the fall-winter season.

Planned Sales, Season	$180,000
Planned Sales, September	$ 36,000
Planned Average Sale, Season	$ 8
Planned Average Sale, September	$ 10
Planned Stock Turnover, Season	4

7. If a ladies' hosiery department sells ladies' pantyhose at the rate of 36 dozen per week at a retail of $1.50 per pair, calculate the amount of stock that should be carried to allow the department a turnover of 6 for the 6-month season on this line.

8. Calculate the stock to be carried for the next few weeks in a department that has the following information and a planned annual stock turnover of 8.

Weeks of Period	Sales	
	Last Year	This Year
1	$3,300	$3,600
2	3,600	4,000
3	3,900	
4	4,400	
5	4,900	
6	5,800	
7	6,200	
8	7,000	
9	6,300	

9. The lingerie department has a planned stock turnover of 2 for the fall-winter season with sales planned at $190,000. Planned sales for the 4-week control period are $39,000. On the basis of this information, calculate the planned B.O.M. stock for the 4-week control period.

10. The boys' clothing department uses a 5-week control period for June. The planned sales for the month are $38,000. For the entire spring-summer season, the buyer has planned sales of $198,000 with a seasonal stock turnover of 1.5. As the assistant buyer in the boys' department, determine the B.O.M. stock for June.

11. Suzanne Cizmar, the buyer of the leather goods department, has planned the following figures for her department for the fall-winter season:

Planned Seasonal Turnover	2
Planned Sales, Season	$102,000
Average Sale, Season	$ 8.50
Planned Sales November	$ 26,000
Planned Average Sale, November	$ 10.00
November Control Period (weeks)	4

Calculate the B.O.M. for November for the leather goods department.

12. The small appliance department of a large department store has a planned stock turnover of 8 for the year with planned annual sales of $450,000. If the buyer has planned sales of $45,000 for March and the month has a 4-week control period, calculate the amount of stock that will be required on March 1.

13. The planned figures for a department for the spring-summer season are indicated as follows. On the basis of these figures, the buyer has asked that you determine the stock that will be required on July 1.

Planned Sales, Season	$208,000
Average Sale, Season	$ 4
Planned Sales, July	$ 40,000
Average Sale, July	$ 5
Control Period (weeks), July	5
Planned Stock Turnover, Season	5

14. A department is anticipating a 10% increase in the average sale and a 4% decrease in the number of transactions as a result of price increases. The planned stock turnover for the department is 4 for the 6-month season. Based upon last year's sales for the first 12 weeks of the period, as listed, calculate the stock that should be carried for the next few weeks.

Weeks of Period	Sales Last Year
1	$2,800
2	2,600
3	3,000
4	3,200
5	3,300
6	3,000
7	3,200
8	3,500
9	3,600
10	3,400
11	3,600
12	3,800

15. The planned annual stock turnover in a department is 10. If the department plans to sell merchandise on an average of $2,500 per week, calculate the amount of stock that needs to be carried in the department for the next few weeks.

16. Calculate the stock to be carried in a department on April 1 if the planned sales for April are $14,000 and the department has a stock-sales ratio of 3.5 for the month.

17. Calculate the stock that should be on hand in a department on November 1 if the department has the following planned figures:

Planned Sales, August 1–January 31	$260,000.00
Planned Sales, November 1–30	$ 50,000.00
Planned Average Sale, August 1–January 31	$ 6.50
Planned Average Sale, November 1–30	$ 5.00
Planned Stock Turnover, August 1–January 31	2
Planned Control Period (weeks), November	4

18. What stock should be on hand in a department on May 1 if the department has the following information available?

Planned Annual Sales	$325,000
Planned May Sales	$ 31,000
Planned Control Period (weeks), May	4
Planned Annual Stock Turnover	8

19. If a sporting goods store is able to sell golf balls at the rate of 12 dozen per week, calculate the amount of stock that should be carried to allow the store to obtain a turnover of 6 for the 6-month season in this item.

20. Calculate the amount of stock that should be on hand on June 1 in a department that has the following planned figures:

Planned Sales, Season	$170,000.00
Average Sale, Season	$ 8.50
Planned Sales, June	$ 35,000.00
Average Sale, June	$ 7.00
Control Period (weeks), June	4
Planned Stock Turnover, Season	5

21. The sporting goods department had planned sales of $35,000 for October and a B.O.M. stock-sales ratio of 3.0 for the month. For November, the department had planned sales of $45,000 with a stock-sales ratio of 2.5. On the basis of this information, calculate the stock turnover for October.

22. As an assistant buyer for a department, you have been asked to determine the B.O.M. and E.O.M. stock-sales ratios for each month in the season by completing the following chart:

Month	B.O.M. Stock (Retail)	Sales	B.O.M. Stock-Sales Ratio	E.O.M. Stock-Sales Ratio
August	$30,000	$ 8,000	—————	—————
September	34,000	10,000	—————	—————
October	42,000	25,000	—————	—————
November	40,000	20,000	—————	—————
December	35,000	25,000	—————	—————
January	30,000	12,000	—————	—————
February	24,000			

23. Calculate the stock turnover for July in the sporting goods department if the B.O.M. stock-sales ratio is 3.0 and the E.O.M. stock-sales ratio is 2.5.

24. The B.O.M. stock in the gift department was planned at $36,000 for October. If the B.O.M. stock-sales ratio for October is planned at 3.2, calculate the planned sales for the month.

## chapter 12

Planning Purchases—The Merchandise Plan

The planning functions of the various merchandising activities are now brought together in the form of a dollar plan or budget for a department or the store in total. The culmination of all these factors is illustrated in a plan, known as the *merchandise plan*. As will be seen, the merchandise plan is a budget in dollars for a certain period of time, usually for a season. The plan attempts to coordinate the various factors that we have discussed in previous chapters: sales, reductions, opening and closing inventories, retail and cost purchases, and planned markups.

The primary purpose of the merchandise plan is to integrate the various merchandising activities involved in determining the purchases required by the retail operation to achieve its planned sales estimates. Obviously, if the merchandise is not on hand, sales will not be made. On the other hand, if more merchandise is brought into stock than can be sold at current prices, the amount and percentage of markdowns will be greater than anticipated. If the merchandise plan is to be effective, orders must be placed somewhat in advance of the selling date of the merchandise. The amount of the merchandise ordered in advance of the selling season depends upon the speed at which delivery can be affected and the stability of the wholesale prices. If delivery can be made quickly and wholesale prices are not expected to change, orders can be placed closer to the selling date of the merchandise. It should be noted that the retailer, on one hand, wishes to place orders as close to the selling date as possible to reduce the element of risk, whereas the suppliers, on the other hand, strive to obtain orders far in advance of the selling date for the same reason. For example, toys for Christmas sales may be placed as much as a year in advance, fashion merchandise is normally placed at least four months in advance, and staple hardware items may be ordered only a few weeks in advance of the selling date.

The preparation of the merchandise plan is normally the result of the combined efforts of the divisional merchandise manager, the merchandise controller, and the buyer. As pointed out earlier, the plan is normally for a period of 6 months, a season of spring-summer or fall-winter. As a result, the dates of the plan are normally from February 1 to July 31 for the spring-summer season and from August 1 to January 31 for the fall-winter season.

Although some stores plan a markup goal for each month, most stores plan an initial markup for the season. In addition, to obtain a predetermined maintained markup, retailers are required to plan markdowns, cash discounts, alteration expenses, and all retail reductions. Moreover, the store and department are required to plan an anticipated stock turnover rate for the season or period under study. All these control figures are placed on the left-hand side of the merchandise plan being illustrated in this chapter.

After these calculations have been made, the monthly figures of sales, stocks, reductions, and purchases are determined and inserted on the merchandise plan. It is possible for the merchandise plan to provide space for other expenses, such as newspaper advertising, if such expenses remain under the buyer's control.

Although the format of the merchandise plan may vary from one retail organization to another, the contents and means of preparation remain essentially the same. The student will note the accompanying example of a merchandise plan designed to facilitate the calculation of retail and cost purchases for a department. Throughout this workbook the same format for the merchandise plan is used, as in Exhibit 1.

PREPARATION OF THE MERCHANDISE PLAN

The procedure that should be followed in the preparation of the merchandise plan for a department should be as follows:

1. Complete the left-hand portion of the plan by determining the required percentages that must be planned, based on the information given.
2. On the basis of the total planned sales and the seasonal distribution of sales, determine the sales for each month of the season.
3. From the planned stock turnover, determine the method to be used in the calculation of the B.O.M. stock.
4. With the turnover figure and the total planned sales, determine the average stock for the period, and from the total planned sales and the number of control periods, determine the average monthly sales.
5. Depending on the method used for determining B.O.M. stock, calculate the B.O.M. stock for each month in the season.
6. Since each month's E.O.M. stock is the same as the following month's B.O.M. stock, determine the E.O.M. stock for each of the months; the last month's E.O.M. stock, since the B.O.M. stock for the seventh month is not known, is determined by utilizing the average stock, as we shall see.
7. On the basis of the planned reductions figure given in the control section and the planned sales, determine the total reductions, and then, with the percentage distribution of reductions, determine the reductions planned for each month in the season.
8. With the foregoing information, it is now possible to determine the purchases by month at retail by determining the merchandise needed in each month and subtracting the merchandise available in each month:

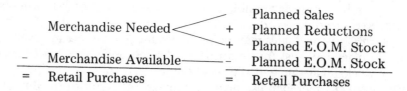

This relationship is expressed on the plan by the column indicating the category to which each horizontal line applies. By reading down on the plan immediately to the right of the left margin, (see arrow), one is reminded of the following:

Planned Sales + Planned E.O.M. + Planned Reductions - Planned B.O.M. = Retail Purchases

The 6-Month Merchandise Plan

SIX-MONTH MERCHANDISE PLAN	Spring / Fall	Feb. / Aug.	Mar. / Sept.	Apr. / Oct.	May / Nov.	June / Dec.	July / Jan.	Total
Sales — Last Year								
Plan								
Actual								
Retail E.O.M. + — Last Year								
Plan								
Actual								
Reductions + — Last Year								
Plan								
Actual								
Retail B.O.M. − — Last Year								
Plan								
Actual								
Retail Purchases = — Last Year								
Plan								
Actual								
Cost Purchases — Last Year								
Plan								
Actual								

DEPARTMENT _____

DEPARTMENT NO. _____

FROM _____ 19 _____

TO _____ 19 _____

Department Control Data

	L.Y.	T.Y.
% Initial Markup		
% Reductions		
% Maintained Markup		
% Alteration Expense		
% Cash Discount		
% Gross Margin		
% Operating Expense		
% Net Profit		
Season Turnover		
Control Period		

Planning and Authorization

Buyer _____

Merchandise Controller _____

Date Prepared _____

Date Authorized _____

9. Since the initial markup is known on the basis of the calculations undertaken in the first step, the cost of these planned purchases can be determined by multiplying the cost portion of the initial markup percent by the retail purchases planned for each month.

10. The total column can now be completed making the merchandise plan available for the buyer's use.

The student should note that the merchandise plan represents a guide to the purchasing technique of the retail organization rather than a hard and fast rule devoid of flexibility. Sound judgment on the part of the buyer and merchandise manager still plays a significant role in the firm's overall strategy. In addition, the student will readily recognize that the advances in computer technology have made this planning function even more meaningful in guiding the merchant. Despite the technology, the buyer-merchant still requires a thorough understanding of the relationship existing among the terms being planned.

EXAMPLE 1: Preparing a Merchandise Plan

Last year's figures and this year's planned stock turnover and percentages have been entered on the following merchandise plan. In addition, the divisional merchandise manager and the buyer have agreed upon a 10% increase in sales for the spring-summer season. The seasonal distribution of sales is expected to be similar to last year's, except for the months of March and April due to a change in the date of Easter.

Month	Sales		Reductions	
	Last Year	This Year	Last Year	This Year
February	13%	13%	12%	13%
March	24%	22%	5%	6%
April	20%	23%	18%	32%
May	17%	16%	24%	30%
June	16%	16%	22%	10%
July	10%	10%	19%	9%

As an assistant buyer, you are asked to complete the merchandise plan that follows.

Solution:

Insert the figures for each of the calculations on the merchandise plan as these figures are determined.

(1) The first step in preparing the merchandise plan will be to determine the initial markup, the maintained markup, and the gross margin for the department from the figures given in the left-hand section of the plan:

(a) Determining initial markup percent from the formula developed in a previous chapter,

$$\text{Initial Markup \%} = \frac{\text{Expenses + Profit + Alteration Expenses}\ -\ \text{Cash Discounts + Reductions}}{\text{Sales + Reductions}}$$

$$\text{Initial Markup \%} = \frac{31.0\% + 3.5\% + 1.0\% - 2.0\% + 8.0\%}{100\% + 8.0\%}$$

$$= \frac{41.5\%}{108.0\%} \times 100\%$$

$$= 38.4\%$$

SIX-MONTH MERCHANDISE PLAN

DEPARTMENT _Ladies Sportswear_

DEPARTMENT NO. _622_

FROM _February 1_ 19___

TO _July 31_ 19___

Department Control Data

	L.Y.	T.Y.
% Initial Markup	39.2	
% Reductions	11.0	8.0
% Maintained Markup	32.5	1.0
% Alteration Expense	1.0	2.0
% Cash Discount	2.0	
% Gross Margin	33.5	31.0
% Operating Expence	31.0	3.5
% Net Profit	2.5	2.5
Season Turnover	2.0	
Control Period		

Planning and Authorization

Buyer _Y. Edwards_

Merchandise Controller _Al Paul_

Date Prepared _Nov. 15_

Date Authorized _Nov. 25_

		Spring / Fall	Feb. / Aug.	Mar. / Sept.	Apr. / Oct.	May / Nov.	June / Dec.	July / Jan.	Total
Sales	Last Year		$27,300	$56,400	$42,000	$35,700	$33,600	$21,000	$210,000
	Plan								
	Actual								
+ Retail E.O.M.	Last Year		120,400	112,000	105,700	103,600	91,000	105,000	637,700
	Plan								
	Actual								
+ Reductions	Last Year		2,772	1,155	4,158	5,544	5,082	4,389	23,100
	Plan								
	Actual								
− Retail B.O.M.	Last Year		97,300	120,400	112,000	105,700	103,600	91,000	630,000
	Plan								
	Actual								
= Retail Purchases	Last Year		53,172	43,155	39,858	39,144	26,082	39,389	240,800
	Plan								
	Actual								
Cost Purchases	Last Year		32,329	26,238	24,234	23,800	15,858	23,949	146,408
	Plan								
	Actual								

(b) Determining maintained markup percent,

Maintained Markup = Initial Markup (100% + Reductions) - Reductions

Therefore,

$$\text{Maintained Markup} = 38.4 (100\% + 8.0\%) - 8.0\%$$
$$= 41.5\% - 8.0\%$$
$$= 33.5\%$$

(c) Determining gross margin percent,

$$\text{Gross Margin} = \text{Maintained Markup} + \text{Cash Discount} - \text{Alteration Expenses}$$
$$= 33.5\% + 2.0\% - 1.0\%$$
$$= 34.5\%$$

(2) The second step in the preparation of the plan is to determine the total sales planned for the season on the basis that the department is expected to show an increase of 10% over last year's sales. Therefore,

$$\text{Planned Sales This Season} = \$210,000 + (10\% \times \$210,000)$$
$$= \$231,000$$

and since the planned stock turnover for the season is 2.5,

$$\text{Average Stock} = \frac{\$231,000}{2.5} = \$92,400$$

and

$$\text{Average Monthly Sales} = \frac{\$231,000}{6} = \$38,500$$

(3) Determine the method to be employed in the calculation of the B.O.M. stock. Since the stock turnover is planned at 2.5 per season, this indicates that the basic stock method of planning stock should be used:

$$\text{Basic Stock} = \text{Average Stock} - \text{Average Monthly Sales}$$
$$= \$92,400 - \$38,500$$
$$= \$53,900$$

(4) On the basis of the seasonal distribution of sales planned, determine the planned sales for each month:

$$\text{February Sales} = 13\% \times \$231,000 = \$30,030$$
$$\text{March Sales} = 22\% \times \$231,000 = \$50,820$$
$$\text{April Sales} = 23\% \times \$231,000 = \$53,130$$
$$\text{May Sales} = 16\% \times \$231,000 = \$36,960$$
$$\text{June Sales} = 16\% \times \$231,000 = \$36,960$$
$$\text{July Sales} = 10\% \times \$231,000 = \$23,100$$
$$\text{Total Planned Sales} = \underline{\$231,000}$$

(5) On the basis of the seasonal distribution of sales and the addition of the basic stock, determine the B.O.M. stock for each of the months in the season. Since the basic stock has been determined at \$53,900 and the B.O.M. stock equals sales for the month plus basic stock,

$$\text{February B.O.M.} = \$30,030 + \$53,900 = \$83,930$$
$$\text{March B.O.M.} = \$50,820 + \$53,900 = \$104,720$$
$$\text{April B.O.M.} = \$53,130 + \$53,900 = \$107,030$$
$$\text{May B.O.M.} = \$36,960 + \$53,900 = \$90,860$$
$$\text{June B.O.M.} = \$36,960 + \$53,900 = \$90,860$$
$$\text{July B.O.M.} = \$23,100 + \$53,900 = \$77,000$$

(6) On the basis of this information, it is now possible to enter the E.O.M. stocks for each of the months in the season since the E.O.M. stock for each month is the same as the B.O.M. stock for the following month:

February E.O.M.	\$104,720
March E.O.M.	107,030
April E.O.M.	90,860
May E.O.M.	90,860
June E.O.M.	77,000

However, since we do not know what the B.O.M. stock for August is to be, we are unable to enter the E.O.M. for July. From the calculation that follows, it can be shown that the E.O.M. stock for July or the last month will be determined by applying the average stock:

$$\text{Average Stock for Season} = \frac{\text{Total of B.O.M. Stocks} + \text{July E.O.M.}}{7}$$
$$= \frac{\$554,400 + X}{7}$$

But the average stock has already been determined as \$92,400. Therefore, solving the equation for X,

$$\$92,400 = \frac{\$554,400 + X}{7}$$

or

$$\$646,800 = \$554,400 + X$$

Therefore,

$$X = \$92,400$$

and

$$\text{E.O.M. for July} = \$92,400$$

Students will note that in this example the E.O.M. for the month of July is the same as the average stock for the season. However, it is possible for the E.O.M. stock for the last month of the season to be greater or less than the average stock for the season, since the average stock for the season is the average of the stock to be carried over the seven time periods. The seven time periods are represented by the B.O.M. stocks for each of the 6 months in the season plus the E.O.M. for the last month.

(7) Since the reductions have been planned at 8% of sales for the coming season, the total reductions to be taken for the spring-summer season will be 8% of the planned sales of $231,000, or a total reduction of $18,480.

It is then necessary to break down the total reductions on the basis of the planned seasonal distribution, as outlined in the problem:

$$February\ Reductions = 13\% \times \$18,480 = \$2,402$$
$$March\ Reductions = 6\% \times \$18,480 = \$1,109$$
$$April\ Reductions = 32\% \times \$18,480 = \$5,914$$
$$May\ Reductions = 30\% \times \$18,480 = \$5,544$$
$$June\ Reductions = 10\% \times \$18,480 = \$1,848$$
$$July\ Reductions = 9\% \times \$18,480 = \$1,663$$

Students should note that it is not correct to determine the reductions in dollars by taking the reduction percentage as in seasonal distribution and multiplying these by the sales for that month. The reduction percentage is based on total sales, and the seasonal distribution is based on total reductions.

(8) From the information now available, it is possible to determine the amount of purchases at retail:

	Merchandise Needed		Planned Sales
		+	Planned Reductions
		+	Planned Retail E.O.M.
−	Merchandise Available	−	Planned Retail B.O.M.
		=	Retail Purchases

Therefore, the planned retail purchases for each of the months in the season will be as follows:

$$February\ Planned\ Purchases = \$30,030 + \$104,720 + \$2,402 - \$83,930$$
$$= \$53,222$$

$$March\ Planned\ Purchases = \$50,820 + \$107,030 + \$1,109 - \$104,720$$
$$= \$54,239$$

$$April\ Planned\ Purchases = \$53,130 + \$90,860 + \$5,914 - \$107,030$$
$$= \$42,874$$

$$May\ Planned\ Purchases = \$36,960 + \$90,860 + \$5,544 - \$90,860$$
$$= \$42,504$$

$$June\ Planned\ Purchases = \$36,960 + \$77,000 + \$1,848 - \$90,860$$
$$= \$24,948$$

$$July\ Planned\ Purchases = \$23,100 + \$92,400 + \$1,663 - \$77,000$$
$$= \$40,163$$

(9) With the initial markup percentage calculated as 38.4%, it is now possible to determine the planned purchases at cost. Since the markup is based on retail, retail is then 100%, and the cost will be 61.6% of the retail value of the planned purchases:

February Planned Cost Purchases = $53,522 × .616 = $32,785
March Planned Cost Purchases = $54,239 × .616 = $33,411
April Planned Cost Purchases = $42,874 × .616 = $26,410
May Planned Cost Purchases = $42,504 × .616 = $26,183
June Planned Cost Purchases = $24,948 × .616 = $15,368
July Planned Cost Purchases = $40,163 × .616 = $24,740

Therefore, the merchandise plan for the department for the spring-summer season is now complete. The completed plan follows on page 216.

SIX-MONTH MERCHANDISE PLAN

DEPARTMENT _Ladies Sportswear_

DEPARTMENT NO. _622_

FROM _February 1_ 19___

TO _July 31_ 19___

Department Control Data

	L.Y.	T.Y.
% Initial Markup	39.2	38.4
% Reductions	11.0	8.0
% Maintained Markup	32.5	33.5
% Alteration Expense	1.0	1.0
% Cash Discount	2.0	2.0
% Gross Margin	33.5	34.5
% Operating Expense	31.0	31.0
% Net Profit	2.5	3.5
Season Turnover	2.0	2.5
Control Period		

Planning and Authorization

Buyer _Y. Edwards_

Merchandise Controller _Al Paul_

Date Prepared _Nov. 15_

Date Authorized _Nov. 25_

Merchandise Plan

		Spring / Fall: Feb. / Aug.	Mar. / Sept.	Apr. / Oct.	May / Nov.	June / Dec.	July / Jan.	Total
Sales	Last Year	$27,300	$50,400	$42,000	$35,700	$33,600	$21,000	$210,000
Sales	Plan	30,030	50,820	53,130	36,960	36,960	23,100	231,000
Sales	Actual							
+ Retail E.O.M.	Last Year	120,400	112,000	105,700	103,600	91,000	105,000	637,700
+ Retail E.O.M.	Plan	104,720	107,030	90,860	90,860	77,000	92,400	562,870
+ Retail E.O.M.	Actual							
+ Reductions	Last Year	2,772	1,155	4,158	5,544	5,082	4,389	23,100
+ Reductions	Plan	2,402	1,109	5,914	5,544	1,848	1,663	18,480
+ Reductions	Actual							
− Retail B.O.M.	Last Year	97,300	120,400	112,000	105,700	103,600	91,000	630,000
− Retail B.O.M.	Plan	83,930	104,720	107,030	90,860	90,860	77,000	554,400
− Retail B.O.M.	Actual							
= Retail Purchases	Last Year	53,172	43,155	39,858	39,144	26,082	39,389	240,800
= Retail Purchases	Plan	53,222	54,239	42,874	42,504	24,948	40,163	257,950
= Retail Purchases	Actual							
Cost Purchases	Last Year	32,329	26,238	24,234	23,800	15,858	23,949	146,402
Cost Purchases	Plan	32,785	33,411	26,410	26,182	15,368	24,740	158,896
Cost Purchases	Actual							

PROBLEM 1: Katherine Browne, the buyer of a home fashions department, has the following information for the spring-summer season.

Average Sale for the Season	$15.00
Initial Markup	40%
Stock Turnover, Season	2

The planned sales for the season and the average sale by month are as follows:

Month	Planned Sales	Average Sale
February	$30,000	$10.00
March	40,000	16.00
April	50,000	20.00
May	50,000	20.00
June	40,000	16.00
July	30,000	10.00

The department has planned the reductions by months to be as follows:

Month	Planned Reductions
February	$3,600
March	3,800
April	5,000
May	5,000
June	3,800
July	3,600

Calculate the purchases at cost and retail for Miss Browne by completing the merchandise plan on page 218.

SIX-MONTH MERCHANDISE PLAN

DEPARTMENT _____

DEPARTMENT NO. _____

FROM _____ 19____

TO _____ 19____

Department Control Data

	L.Y.	T.Y.
% Initial Markup		40.0
% Reductions		
% Maintained Markup		
% Alteration Expense		
% Cash Discount		
% Gross Margin		
% Operating Expence		
% Net Profit		2.0
Season Turnover		
Control Period		

Planning and Authorization

Buyer *Katherine Browne*

Merchandise Controller *Maura Michael*

Date Prepared 10/15

Date Authorized 10/20

		Spring / Fall	Feb. / Aug.	Mar. / Sept.	Apr. / Oct.	May / Nov.	June / Dec.	July / Jan.	Total
Sales		Last Year							
		Plan							
		Actual							
+ E.O.M. Retail		Last Year							
		Plan							
		Actual							
+ Reductions		Last Year							
		Plan							
		Actual							
– B.O.M. Retail		Last Year							
		Plan							
		Actual							
= Retail Purchases		Last Year							
		Plan							
		Actual							
Cost Purchases		Last Year							
		Plan							
		Actual							

1. As a buyer of men's furnishings, Daniel Albert planned sales of $400,000 for the fall-winter season. The buyer has also decided to plan for a stock turnover of $2\frac{2}{3}$ for the season. In addition, he has already entered the important control figures for his department on the accompanying merchandise plan. On the basis of the information following and that given on the plan, complete the merchandise plan for the men's furnishings department.

Month	Portion of Total Sales	Portion of Total Reductions	B.O.M. Stock-Sales Ratios
August	10%	10%	2.0
September	10	10	2.5
October	20	15	2.5
November	30	15	2.0
December	20	15	2.0
January	10	35	3.0

SIX-MONTH MERCHANDISE PLAN

DEPARTMENT _Men's Furnishings_

DEPARTMENT NO. _615_

FROM _August 1_, 19__

TO _January 31_, 19__

Department Control Data

	L.Y.	T.Y.
% Initial Markup		9.0
% Reductions		
% Maintained Markup		1.0
% Alteration Expense		2.0
% Cash Discount		
% Gross Margin		32.0
% Operating Expence		4.0
% Net Profit		2 2/3
Season Turnover		
Control Period		

Planning and Authorization

Buyer _Daniel Albert_

Merchandise Controller _D. Scarrow_

Date Prepared _Sept. 5_

Date Authorized _Sept. 15_

		Spring / Fall	Feb. / Aug.	Mar. / Sept.	Apr. / Oct.	May / Nov.	June / Dec.	July / Jan.	Total
Retail	Sales	Last Year							
		Plan							
		Actual							
Retail	+ E.O.M.	Last Year							
		Plan							
		Actual							
	+ Reductions	Last Year							
		Plan							
		Actual							
Retail	− B.O.M.	Last Year							
		Plan							
		Actual							
Retail	= Purchases	Last Year							
		Plan							
		Actual							
Cost	Purchases	Last Year							
		Plan							
		Actual							

2. A department is expected to have a sales volume of $390,000 for the fall-winter season with with the following planned figures for this period:

Operating Expenses	31%
Net Profit	3%
Markdowns, Net	7%
Stock Shortages	1%
Alteration Expenses, Net	2%
Cash Discounts	2%
Stock Turnover, Season	5

The seasonal distribution of sales and reductions have been planned as follows for this season:

Months	Sales Distribution	Reductions, Distribution
August	11%	15%
September	17	5
October	23	10
November	19	15
December	21	20
January	9	35

As a management trainee in the department, you have been asked to complete the merchandise plan for Morgan Brooke, the buyer, by inserting the planned estimates for the fall-winter season.

SIX-MONTH MERCHANDISE PLAN

DEPARTMENT _____

DEPARTMENT NO. _____

FROM _____ 19 ___

TO _____ 19 ___

Department Control Data

	L.Y.	T.Y.
% Initial Markup		
% Reductions		
% Maintained Markup		
% Alteration Expense		
% Cash Discount		
% Gross Margin		
% Operating Expence		
% Net Profit		
Season Turnover		
Control Period		

Planning and Authorization

Buyer _Morgan Brooke_

Merchandise Controller _Michelle Cizmar_

Date Prepared _May 2_

Date Authorized _May 9_

		Spring / Fall	Feb. / Aug.	Mar. / Sept.	Apr. / Oct.	May / Nov.	June / Dec.	July / Jan.	Total
Sales		Last Year							
		Plan							
		Actual							
+ E.O.M. Retail		Last Year							
		Plan							
		Actual							
+ Reductions Retail		Last Year							
		Plan							
		Actual							
− B.O.M. Retail		Last Year							
		Plan							
		Actual							
= Purchases Retail		Last Year							
		Plan							
		Actual							
Purchases Cost		Last Year							
		Plan							
		Actual							

3. Kate Alexus, the buyer of the following department, has planned for the spring-summer season with the data listed:

Planned Season Sales	$295,000
Planned Operating Expenses	32.0%
Planned Alteration Expenses, Net	1.0%
Planned Cash Discounts	2.0%
Planned Net Profit	3.0%
Planned Reductions	10.0%
Planned Seasonal Turnover	2
Planned Control Period (weeks)	4-5

In addition, she has provided the following information:

Month	Proportion of Season Sales	Proportion of Season Reductions
February	15%	15%
March	15	10
April	25	15
May	15	20
June	20	15
July	10	25

Prepare the accompanying plan for the department, determining the purchases at cost and retail for the buyer and completing all control data in the left-hand margin. April and July have been designated as 5-week control periods, while the remaining months have 4-week control periods.

SIX-MONTH MERCHANDISE PLAN

DEPARTMENT _____

DEPARTMENT NO. _____

FROM _____ 19____

TO _____ 19____

		Spring / Fall	Feb. Aug.	Mar. Sept.	Apr. Oct.	May Nov.	June Dec.	July Jan.	Total
Sales	Last Year								
	Plan								
	Actual								
Retail E.O.M. +	Last Year								
	Plan								
	Actual								
Reductions +	Last Year								
	Plan								
	Actual								
Retail B.O.M. −	Last Year								
	Plan								
	Actual								
Retail Purchases =	Last Year								
	Plan								
	Actual								
Cost Purchases									

Department Control Data

	L.Y.	T.Y.
% Initial Markup		
% Reductions		
% Maintained Markup		
% Alteration Expense		
% Cash Discount		
% Gross Margin		
% Operating Expence		
% Net Profit		
Season Turnover		
Control Period		

Planning and Authorization

Buyer _Kate Alegna_

Merchandise Controller _Susan Lyn_

Date Prepared _October 25_

Date Authorized _November 14_

4. The men's furnishings department has planned an increase in sales of 20% over last year. As an assistant buyer, you have been asked to determine the planned purchases at retail and at cost for the fall-winter season. The buyer has provided you with last year's figures and the planned figures for this year as indicated on the accompanying merchandise plan.

The buyer has also informed you that the sales distribution is expected to be the same as last year. The total reductions of markdowns and stock shortages will increase this year, as indicated on the plan, but the seasonal distribution will be similar to that of last year. Again, the department will be operating with 4-week control periods for August, September, November, and December, and with 5-week control periods for the remaining two months.

Month	Sales Distribution	Reductions Distribution
August	10%	15%
September	15	15
October	15	10
November	25	10
December	20	15
January	15	35
Total	100%	100%

SIX-MONTH MERCHANDISE PLAN

DEPARTMENT _Men's Furnishings_

DEPARTMENT NO. _725_

FROM _____ 19 ___

TO _____ 19 ___

		Spring / Fall	Feb. / Aug.	Mar. / Sept.	Apr. / Oct.	May / Nov.	June / Dec.	July / Jan.	Total
Sales	Last Year		$26,000	$39,000	$39,000	$65,000	$52,000	$39,000	$260,000
	Plan								
	Actual								
+ Retail E.O.M.	Last Year		103,000	103,000	129,000	116,000	103,000	104,000	658,000
	Plan								
	Actual								
+ Reductions	Last Year		3,510	3,510	2,340	2,340	3,510	8,190	23,400
	Plan								
	Actual								
− Retail B.O.M.	Last Year		90,000	103,000	103,000	129,000	116,000	103,600	644,000
	Plan								
	Actual								
= Retail Purchases	Last Year		42,510	42,510	67,340	54,340	42,510	46,190	295,400
	Plan								
	Actual								
Cost Purchases	Last Year		24,953	24,953	39,529	31,888	24,953	27,114	173,390
	Plan								
	Actual								

Department Control Data

	L.Y.	T.Y.
% Initial Markup	41.3	
% Reductions	9.0	11.0
% Maintained Markup	36.0	
% Alteration Expense	3.0	3.0
% Cash Discount	1.0	1.0
% Gross Margin	34.0	
% Operating Expence	31.0	32.0
% Net Profit	3.0	3.0
Season Turnover	2.5	2.5
Control Period	4–5	4–5

Planning and Authorization

Buyer _A.R. DiThomas_

Merchandise Controller _S. Marotta_

Date Prepared _April 10_

Date Authorized _April 20_

## chapter 13

Planning Open-to-Buy Controls

In the previous chapter, the student was informed of the procedure involved in determining the dollar amount of purchases at retail and at cost for each month of a 6-month season. These planned purchase figures, determined in the merchandise plan, represent the amount of stock the buyer may plan to purchase as of the beginning of the month and for the duration of the month. In other words, the retail and cost purchase figures represent the buying limit for merchandise to be received into stock for the month indicated.

To ensure that actual purchasing is done according to the plan, retailers maintain what is known as an open-to-buy (O.T.B.) control. This control represents a system of charging off the committed orders against the buying limits of the planned purchase to determine what additional merchandise may be purchased. The control system is established to inform the buyer of situations where excess stock is brought into inventory. Orders that the retailer has placed with the supplier but that have not yet been delivered or received into stock are referred to as outstanding orders (O.O.) or on-order merchandise. The dollar open-to-buy figure is then determined by subtracting these outstanding orders from the planned purchase figure:

	Planned Sales
+	Planned E.O.M.
+	Planned Reductions
=	Total Merchandise Needed
−	Planned B.O.M.
=	Planned Retail Purchases
−	Outstanding Orders
=	Planned Open-to-Buy

As a result of the impact of the outstanding orders on the open-to-buy, a careful control of all committed orders is required by the retail firm. It is this control of outstanding orders that is applied to the purchase figures determined in the merchandise plan. It should now be obvious to the student that the merchandise plan represents the primary planning tool for the retailer, whereas the open-to-buy provides the controlling technique.

The need for understanding open-to-buy is explained when the student realizes that the retailer does not normally purchase inventory at the beginning of the month but elects to purchase goods at various times during the month. To merchandise successfully, it is necessary for the buyer to be able to purchase merchandise throughout the season or month for the following reasons:

1. To take advantage of new merchandise lines or new items that appear during the month or the season to generate continued interest in the merchandise assortment by both customers and sales personnel.

2. To take advantage of special promotions or special prices offered by suppliers during the season or month, thus increasing the promotional activity or markup or both.

3. To assure a complete assortment of merchandise in some lines that will require periodic refills to the stock.

Consequently, it is preferable for the retail buyer to attempt always to have a certain amount of open-to-buy dollars available.

In addition, the buyer must be able to determine, as of a specific date during the month or season, the amount of merchandise that he or she may purchase for the balance of the month. The buyer who continues to buy without regard for a planned purchase figure normally ends up with an overbought situation in which he or she has purchased more goods than are called for in the plan. As a result, the buyer runs the risk of increasing markdowns, decreasing maintained markup, and decreasing the open-to-buy in the following months.

The open-to-buy is initially calculated on a dollar basis as a follow-up to the merchandise plan, which is also based on dollar amounts. These dollar open-to-buy figures may then be broken down into units. In the remainder of this chapter, we will be concerned with the problems and techniques employed in calculating a store's open-to-buy in both dollars and units.

CALCULATING DOLLAR OPEN-TO-BUY

In a manner similar to the calculation of planned purchases in the merchandise plan, the dollar open-to-buy is a relatively simple calculation expressed by the following:

Open-to-Buy = Merchandise Needed – Merchandise Available

As noted earlier, it is important for the buyer to be able to determine the open-to-buy as of a specific date during the month. As a result, the determination of merchandise needed and merchandise available will refer to those amounts at a specific date, whether the first of the month or sometime during the month.

As noted at the beginning of this chapter, it will be recognized that the merchandise needed for a particular period is composed of the sum of the planned sales for the period, the planned reductions for the period, and the planned stock that is to be on hand at the end of the period. Therefore, the buyer must plan purchases so that he or she will have sufficient stock to cover sales, reductions, and an ending inventory. On the other hand, the merchandise that the buyer has available during a specific period will be the opening inventory for the period (B.O.M.) or the stock on hand (O.H.) as at a specific date during the period.

Consequently, in situations where the buyer is attempting to determine the open-to-buy at the beginning of the month, then the B.O.M. stock becomes the total merchandise available:

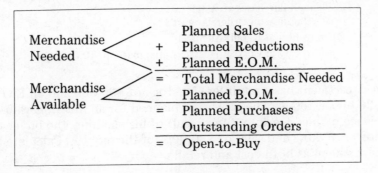

In situations where the buyer wishes to determine the open-to-buy figure during the middle of the month, such as November 14, the buyer is required to determine the stock on hand in the store on that date. The total merchandise available in the calculation will now become the O.H. position at November 14 rather than the B.O.M. for November 1.

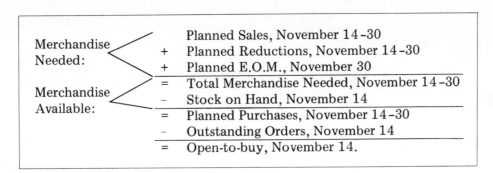

The student will note that the stock on hand must be determined at the specific date for which the buyer seeks to determine the open-to-buy dollar figure to arrive at the figure for merchandise available. In addition, we should note that the outstanding orders are, in fact, a portion of the merchandise available but are treated differently to control the buyer's open-to-buy from the planned purchases.

EXAMPLE 1: Finding O.T.B. as of the Beginning of the Month

The planned initial markup in a department as indicated on the merchandise plan, is 40%. In addition, the planned sales for the month of August are $35,000 with markdowns of 8%. The merchandise plan also indicates that the planned B.O.M. stock for the month is $31,000 and the planned E.O.M. stock is $34,000. As of August 1, the buyer has merchandise on order of $6,000 at retail to be delivered during the month. Calculate the buyer's O.T.B. at retail and at cost as of August 1.

Solution:

Merchandise Needed		
Planned Sales, August 1–31	$35,000	
Planned Markdowns, August 1–31	2,800	
Planned E.O.M. Stock, August 31	34,000	
Total Merchandise Needed, August 1–31		$71,800

Merchandise Available		
Planned B.O.M. Stock, August 1	$31,000	
Total Merchandise Available		$31,000
Planned Purchases at Retail		$40,800
− Merchandise on Order, August 1		6,000
Open-to-Buy at Retail, August 1		$34,800
Open-to-Buy at Cost, August 1 (initial markup, 40%)		$20,880

PROBLEM 1: A department has a retail B.O.M. stock of $30,000 and an E.O.M. stock of $26,000 at retail. The buyer has planned for an initial markup of 37.5% to realize his maintained markup. As a result of his planning, the buyer anticipates markdowns of 8.0% and sales of $30,000 for the month. Calculate the O.T.B. for the department at both cost and retail.

EXAMPLE 2: Finding O.T.B. During the Month Given Stock on Hand

As a result of the merchandise plan and the open-to-buy control, a department shows the following figures and wishes to determine its open-to-buy at retail as of June 18.

Planned Sales, June 1–30	$20,250
Actual Sales, June 1–18	$15,900
Planned Markdowns, June 1–30	$ 900
Actual Markdowns, June 1–18	$ 600
Stock on Hand, June 18	$36,750
Planned E.O.M. stock, June 30	$43,350
Outstanding Orders, June 18	$ 5,850

Solution:

Merchandise Needed, June 18–30:		
Planned E.O.M., June 30		$43,350
Planned Sales, June 1–30	$20,250	
Actual Sales, June 1–18	15,900	
Planned Sales, June 18–30		4,350
Planned Markdowns, June 1–30	$ 900	
Actual Markdowns, June 1–18	600	
Markdowns, June 18–30		300
Total Merchandise Needed, June 18–30		$48,000
Merchandise Available, June 18–30		
Stock on Hand, June 18		36,750
Planned Retail Purchases, June 18		$11,250
Outstanding Orders, June 18		5,850
Open-to-Buy, June 18		$ 5,400

PROBLEM 2: During the spring-summer season, a buyer shows the following information and has requested that you determine her open-to-buy as of April 20 at both cost and retail.

Planned Sales, April 1–30	$ 40,000
Actual Sales, April 1–20	$ 38,000
Planned Markdowns, April 1–30	$ 4,400
Actual Markdowns, April 1–20	$ 3,600
Planned Stock at Retail, May 1	$124,000
Stock on Hand at Retail, April 20	$100,000
Outstanding Orders at Cost, April 20	$ 7,800
Initial Markup	40%

EXAMPLE 3: Finding O.T.B. During the Month Given B.O.M. and Activity Data

NOTE: In this problem, you are to determine the O.T.B. during the month without knowing the stock on hand at the specific date during the month.

The buyer of a department has asked that you determine his O.T.B. of November 11 based on the following information:

B.O.M., November 1	$45,000
Purchases Received at Retail, November 1–11	$ 2,250
Merchandise on Order at Retail, November 1–11	$12,000
Planned Sales, November 1–30	$12,000
Actual Sales, November 1–11	$ 6,750
Planned Markdowns, November 1–30	$ 2,250
Actual Markdowns, November 1–11	$ 1,125
Planned E.O.M. Stock at Retail	$49,500

Solution:

Merchandise Needed, November 11–30:		
Planned E.O.M. Stock		$49,500
Planned Sales, November 1–30	$12,000	
Actual Sales, November 1–11	6,750	
Planned Sales, November 11–30		5,250
Planned Markdowns, November 1–30	$ 2,250	
Actual Markdowns, November 1–11	1,125	
Planned Markdowns, November 11–30		1,125
Total Merchandise Needed, November 11–30		$55,875

Merchandise Available, November 11-30:

B.O.M. Stock, November 1		$45,000
Purchases Received, November 1-11		2,250
Merchandise Handled, November 1-11		$47,250
Sales to Date, November 1-11	$ 6,750	
Markdowns to Date, November 1-11	1,125	
Reductions in Inventory, November 1-11		7,875
Stock on Hand, November 11		39,375
Planned Purchases, November 11-30		$16,500
On Order, November 11		12,000
Open-to-Buy, November 11		$ 4,500

PROBLEM 3: If Richard Joseph, a buyer in sporting goods, has the following information available, calculate his open-to-buy as of March 8 at retail.

Planned E.O.M. Stock at Retail, March 31	$110,000
Planned B.O.M. Stock at Retail, March 1	$ 90,000
Planned Sales for March	$ 36,000
Actual Sales, March 1-8	$ 18,000
Planned Markdowns for March	$ 6,000
Actual Markdowns, March 1-8	$ 3,000
Purchases Received at Retail, March 1-8	$ 7,000
Outstanding Orders, March	$ 25,000

CALCULATING UNIT OPEN-TO-BUY

In the previous section, an analysis of the dollar open-to-buy was undertaken. The means by which this dollar open-to-buy is subdivided into the desired number of items to be purchased is known as the unit open-to-buy. The calculation of the number of units to be purchased may be applied to both fashion and staple merchandise, as will become evident in this discussion.

The calculation of the unit open-to-buy is based on the following important elements that constitute the fundamental factors in the basic equation.

COMPONENTS OF UNIT OPEN-TO-BUY

Reserve (R). The reserve represents a safety factor for the retail store in the event that sales exceed expectations. Consequently, this factor is a contingency for unforeseen increases in volume. The reserve can be expressed in terms of weeks' supply of merchandise needed or as a specific quantity in units.

Delivery Period (DP). The delivery period represents the time that will elapse between the date on which the merchandise is ordered and the date it is received into stock. Because of unpredictable delivery schedules, retailers generally set this time period somewhat longer than normal delivery time. The delivery period is normally expressed in weeks.

Reorder Period (RP). The reorder period represents the frequency with which the particular item will be reordered from the supplier and will consequently affect the amount of merchandise to be kept on hand. The reorder period is, also, normally expressed in terms of weeks.

Rate of Sale (S). The rate of sale is the quantity of the item that the buyer anticipates will sell during a particular period of time. The rate of sale is normally expressed as the volume of units sold on a weekly basis. Consequently, it is possible to convert the delivery period expressed in weeks to units by multiplying the number of weeks by the weekly rate of sale. For example, if DP = 3 weeks and S = 20, then delivery period, is, in fact, expressed as 60 units to cover this time frame.

Minimum Stock (MIN). This indicates that a specific number of units are to be on hand at all times so as to avoid out-of-stock conditions before delivery can be made. In essence, the minimum stock is the stock that will be on hand at the moment the reorder is placed. It is calculated by determining the reserve (R) and the number of items to be sold before delivery of additional items can be effected. Depending on whether the merchant expressed the reserve and delivery periods in units or weeks, the unit minimum stock may be calculated in units or weeks:

Minimum Stock (MIN) in Weeks = Reserve (weeks) + Delivery Period (weeks)

Minimum Stock (MIN) in Units = (Weeks of Reserve + Weeks of Delivery Period)
$\times$ Rate of Sale

Maximum Stock (MAX). The maximum stock is equal to the minimum stock available at all times plus the amount of stock that might be sold during the period of time elapsing before the next reorder point. In fact, after the minimum stock has been determined, the buyer must decide upon the frequency of reorder. The maximum stock may also be expressed in terms of units or in terms of weeks as is the case with the minimum stock:

Maximum Stock (MAX) in Weeks = Minimum Stock (weeks) + Reorder Period (weeks)
or
Maximum Stock (MAX) in Weeks = R (weeks) + DP (weeks) + RP (weeks)
or
Maximum Stock (MAX) in Units = (Weeks of Reserve + Weeks of Delivery Period
+ Weeks of Reorder Period) $\times$ Rate of Sale

Open-to-Buy (O.T.B.). If the maximum stock, by definition, represents the merchandise needed for the period and the merchandise that is on hand and on order for delivery during the period represents merchandise available, it is then possible to determine open-to-buy in units as follows:

O.T.B. (units) = MAX (units) − (Stock on Hand + Stock on Order)

Average Stock.   The amount of stock on hand fluctuates between the "low" of the reserve before the reorder comes in and a "high" of the reserve plus the reorder amount. The midpoint between no reorder and full reorder is considered to be the average stock. However, it must be remember that by definition, a provision must always be made for a reserve or safety factor. The average stock is then expressed in an equation as

$$\text{Average Stock} = \text{Reserve} + \tfrac{1}{2} \text{ Reorder Period}$$

Therefore, we can summarize the equations that will be useful in determining the unit open-to-buy for a department or a store.

$$\text{MIN (weeks)} = R + DP$$
$$\text{MIN (units)} = (R + DP) \times S$$
$$\text{MAX (weeks)} = R + DP + RP$$
$$\text{MAX (units)} = (R + DP + RP) \times S$$
$$\text{O.T.B. (unit)} = \text{MAX} - (\text{O.H.} + \text{O.O.})$$
$$\text{Average Stock} = R + \tfrac{1}{2} RP$$

EXAMPLE 4:   Finding Unit O.T.B. for a Price Line

The buyer has the following information available for her department and wishes to determine the unit open-to-buy and unit annual stock turnover for a $19.95 item.

Rate of Sale	20 per week
Reserve	3 weeks
Delivery Period	3 weeks
Reorder Period	5 weeks
Stock on Hand	6 dozen
Stock on Order	2 dozen

Solution:

(a) Determining the unit open-to-buy, since

$$\text{O.T.B.} = \text{MAX} - (\text{O.H.} + \text{O.O.})$$

and

$$\text{MAX} = (R + DP + RP) \times S$$
$$= (3 + 3 + 5) \times 20$$
$$= 220 \text{ units}$$

therefore,

$$\text{O.T.B.} = 220 - (72 + 74)$$
$$= 220 - 96$$
$$= 124$$

(b) Determining unit annual stock turnover, since

$$\text{Stock Turnover} = \frac{\text{Sales}}{\text{Average Stock}}$$

and

$$\text{Sales for Year} = 52 \text{ weeks} \times 20 \text{ per week}$$
$$= 1,040 \text{ per year}$$

therefore,

$$\text{Average Stock} = R + \tfrac{1}{2} RP$$
$$= 3 + \tfrac{1}{2}(5)$$
$$= 5\tfrac{1}{2} \text{ weeks}$$

To convert average stock in weeks, multiply by the weekly rate of sale. Therefore,

$$5\tfrac{1}{2} \times 20 = 110$$

and

$$\text{Unit Annual Stock Turnover} = \frac{1,040}{110} = 9.45$$

PROBLEM 4: The rate of sale of a tie is estimated at 50 per week by Ed George, the buyer. He wishes to maintain a reserve of 6 dozen ties and plans to reorder stock every 2 weeks. On the basis of past experience, Mr. George estimates that delivery will take 2 weeks after the order is placed. If there are 100 ties in stock and another 36 on order, calculate the unit open-to-buy and the planned annual stock turnover for the tie.

EXAMPLE 5: Finding Unit O.T.B. Based on Weekly Sales Percentages

A buyer estimates that a maximum stock representing 4 weeks' supply is to be kept on hand and on order for a line of hammers. During the first 4 weeks of the period, the department sold 234 items, and at the end of this period there were 150 hammers on hand and another 75 on order. Calculate the unit open-to-buy at the end of the fourth week if the weekly distribution of sales is as follows.

Week of Season	Weekly Distribution Percentage of Season Sales
1	2
2	4
3	3
4	4
5	5
6	7
7	6
8	5
9	6

Solution:

Based on the weekly distribution of season sales, it can be calculated that the first 4 weeks of the season accounted for 13% of the season's sales. But during the first 4 weeks, 234 hammers were sold. Therefore,

$$13\% = 234$$

and

$$1\% = \frac{234}{13} = 18 \text{ hammers}$$

And, since the buyer wishes to keep 4 weeks' supply on hand and on order, his maximum stock must be 4 weeks' supply and is represented at the end of the fourth week by the next 4 weeks—that is, weeks 5, 6, 7, and 8:

Since the sales for these 4 weeks are expected to represent 23% of the season's sales,

$$23\% = 23 \times \text{value of } 1\%$$
$$= 23 \times 18 = 414$$

and since

$$\text{Unit O.T.B.} = \text{MAX} - (\text{O.H.} + \text{O.O.})$$

then

$$\text{Unit O.T.B. in hammers} = 414 - (150 + 75)$$
$$= 189$$

for the fourth week.

PROBLEM 5: Ronald Kimaid, a buyer of men's furnishings, has estimated that a 4-week supply of an undershirt is to be kept on hand and on order as his maximum stock. During the first 3 weeks of the season, he has discovered that 180 shirts have been sold and that he has 200 on hand and another 4 dozen on order. As Mr. Kimaid's assistant, you are required to determine the unit open-to-buy for the fourth week of the undershirts based on the following weekly distribution of sales.

Week of Season	Cumulative Percentage Weekly Distribution of Season's Sales
1	4%
2	7
3	12
4	16
5	22
6	27
7	32
8	38
9	42

SUMMARY PROBLEMS

1. On the basis of the following information, the buyer of a hardware department has asked that you determine her open-to-buy at cost and retail as of December 15.

Planned Sales, December 1–31	$42,000
Actual Sales, December 1–15	$27,000
Planned Markdowns, December 1–31	$ 2,000
Actual Markdowns, December 1–15	$ 1,100
Stock on Hand, December 15	$70,000
Planned E.O.M. Stock, December 15	$80,000
Outstanding Orders, December 15	$ 9,000
Initial Markup	40%

2. On August 1, Andrew John, a drapery buyer, had a retail inventory of $72,000 and a planned inventory at retail for September 1 of $68,000. On August 10, his sales totaled $21,000 and his markdowns were $2,100. His markdowns for the month were expected to be 10% of his total planned monthly sales of $27,000. From August 1 to 10, Mr. John received purchases valued at $12,000 at retail and on August 10 had stock on order of $13,200. Determine the O.T.B. for the department as of August 10.

3. Ruth Murray, a buyer of staple merchandise, has established that her merchandise must maintain a maximum of a 3-week supply at all times. During the first 4 weeks of the period, Miss Murray reports that she has sold 273 items and that there are 90 items on hand and another 30 on order. Based on the figures provided, calculate the unit open-to-buy for the fifth week.

Week of Season	Cumulative Percentage Weekly Distribution of Season's Sales
1	3%
2	6
3	10
4	13
5	18
6	24
7	29
8	34
9	37

4. The gift department of a major department store provides you with the following information to calculate the dollar open-to-buy for the department as of November 14.

Planned Sales, November	$45,000
Planned Sales, December	$45,000
Markdowns, November 1–30	$ 4,000
Actual Sales, November 1–14	$20,000
Actual Markdowns, November 1–14	$ 1,600
Purchases Received, November 1–14	$ 9,000
Outstanding Orders, November 14	$ 2,400
B.O.M. Stock-Sales Ratio, November	3.0
B.O.M. Stock-Sales Ratio, December	2.5

5. Sharon Weir, the buyer of stationery, has provided you with the following details and has requested that you calculate the open-to-buy for the department as of April 6 at both cost and retail.

Planned Sales, April	$25,000
Actual Sales, April 1–6	$ 8,000
Planned Markdowns, April	$ 2,000
Actual Markdowns, April 1–6	$ 650
Purchases Received at Cost, April 1–6	$ 9,000
Outstanding Orders at Cost, April 6	$ 6,000
B.O.M., April 1, at Retail	$60,000
Planned Stock at Retail, May 1	$65,000
Initial Markup	$33\frac{1}{3}\%$

6. Robert Kimaid, the buyer of men's furnishings, has established a reserve of 10 dozen for a line of men's dress shirts. Mr. Kimaid plans to reorder the shirts every 3 weeks and, after consultation with his supplier, estimates that delivery will take 2 weeks after the order is placed. At the present time there are 250 shirts on hand and another 6 dozen on order. Mr. Kimaid has estimated that the shirts will sell at the rate of 90 per week; calculate his open-to-buy in units and the unit annual stock turnover for this line of shirts.

7. Christopher Cizmar, a hardware department buyer, has asked you to calculate the department's O.T.B. at both cost and retail as of May 18 based on the following information:

B.O.M., May 1	$44,000
E.O.M., May 31	$38,000
Planned Sales, May 1–31	$24,000
Planned Markdowns, May 1–31	$ 4,800
Actual Sales, May 1–18	$13,500
Actual Markdowns, May 1–18	$ 1,300
Purchases Received, at Retail, May 1–18	$ 6,400
Outstanding Orders, at Retail, May 18	$ 3,600
Initial Markup	$33\frac{1}{3}\%$

8. A buyer has planned reserve stock of 12 items in his $5.95 price line. The buyer plans to reorder stock every 3 weeks and has established a 2-week delivery period. If the item will sell at 10 per week and there are $1\frac{1}{2}$ dozen in stock and 1 dozen on order, determine the unit open-to-buy and annual stock turnover.

9. On March 1 a buyer had a retail inventory of $40,000 and a planned inventory of $36,000 for April 1. On March 17 his sales totaled $12,000 and his markdowns to date reached $500. His markdowns for the month of March were expected to be 8% of his planned sales of $19,000 for the month. From March 1 to March 17, the buyer received merchandise valued at $5,000 at retail and at March 17 had stock on order of $4,000 of retail. If the initial markup planned for the department is 37.5%, determine the dollar open-to-buy at cost and retail for the department.

10. The buyer of a staple item has calculated that a 3-week supply will have to be kept on hand and on order in an effort to capitalize on all sales opportunities. During the first 3 weeks of the season, the buyer reported that 486 items were sold and at the end of the third week she had 100 items on hand and another 30 on order. As an assistant buyer, you are asked to calculate the unit open-to-buy for the fourth week, assuming the same weekly rate of sale.

11. Calculate the dollar open-to-buy at cost in a department if the buyer has reported the following figures as of June 17.

Purchases Received at Cost, June 1–17	$12,000
Outstanding Orders at Cost, June 17	$ 5,000
Planned Sales, June 1–30	$28,000
Actual Sales, June 1–17	$15,000
Planned Markdowns, June 1–30	8%
Actual Markdowns, June 1–17	6%
Initial Markup	40%
Stock on Hand at Retail, June 1	$27,000
Planned Stock on Hand at Retail, July 1	$33,000

12. On March 12 John Romeo, a buyer of leather goods, reports the following information to you. In addition, he has asked that you determine the dollar open-to-buy for the department as of March 12.

B.O.M. Stock, March 1	$76,000
Purchases Received at Retail, March 1–12	$12,000
Outstanding Orders at Retail, March 12	$10,000
Actual Sales to Date as Percent of Monthly Sales	10%
Planned E.O.M. Stock, March 31	$64,000
Planned Markdowns for March	$ 3,800
Actual Markdowns, March 1–12	$ 1,200
Planned Annual Stock Turnover	9

13. In purchasing staple items for her department, Sandra DiThomas plans her purchasing on the basis of the seasonal distribution of sales per week. She anticipates that the items will sell in the following manner:

Week of Season	Cumulative Percentage Weekly Distribution Season's Sales
1	4%
2	7
3	12
4	17
5	20
6	26
7	31
8	38
9	42

Miss DiThomas reports that sales for the first 2 weeks totaled 210 items and that at the end of the second week there were 10 dozen on hand and 1 gross on order. The buyer considers a maximum of a 4-week supply should be kept on hand and on order. Calculate the unit open-to-buy for Miss DiThomas.

14. George Arjane, the buyer for men's furnishings, has discovered that a short-sleeve dress shirt sells at the rate of 6 dozen per week during the spring-summer season. The buyer plans to keep a reserve of 4 dozen in stock. To control his inventory, the buyer has decided to reorder his stock every 2 weeks, and it will take 2 weeks for delivery after the order is placed. Calculate the unit open-to-buy for Mr. Arjane in dozens and the unit seasonal turnover on these shirts, if he has 3 dozen on hand and 4 dozen on order.

15. As the buyer of men's hats, Maurice Mattar has established a reserve of 5 dozen in one price line. Mr. Mattar plans to reorder these hats every 3 weeks and after consultation with his supplier discovers that it will take 2 weeks for delivery after the order is placed. At the present time, there are 20 hats in stock and 24 on order. If the buyer estimates that the hats sell on an average of 10 per week, calculate the unit open-to-buy and the annual stock turnover for the hats.

chapter 14

Planning Model Stocks

Although the merchandise plan discussed earlier implies the planning tool of the retailer, it was discovered that the open-to-buy calculations provided the control factor for the merchant. In this chapter, it is our intention to analyze and determine the mechanics of building a model stock plan, which is the breakdown of the open-to-buy into the assortment plan desired by a retailer.

A model stock plan is a plan on paper of a unit assortment of merchandise, kept with dollar control limits, that is distributed in a way that best satisfies customer demand at the store for a specified period of time. In other words, the model stock plan is a quantitative picture of the merchandise assortment at a specified time. Therefore, the model stock plan becomes a breakdown of the units established through the open-to-buy control according to the various selection factors of color, size, material, style, pattern, and so on. Model stock plans are used for fashion merchandise when certain selection factors remain relatively stable from one year to the next. For example, a buyer may discover that the sale of certain basic styles or colors is relatively the same proportion of total sales in each spring-summer season.

The model stock becomes the balancing of merchandise assortment with regard to the selection of the merchandise in relation to customer demands. The obvious purpose of the model stock must be to obtain maximum sales and profits from the investment in merchandise inventory. A unit control system will provide the necessary stock and sales information for the building of a model stock plan. It should be noted, however, that current trends must be considered along with past experience in planning the model stock assortment. Further, it is not advisable to keep stock in direct proportion to sales, since some stocks may require a larger percentage of merchandise than others. It is also anticipated that the turnover in the larger classification should be somewhat greater than that in the smaller classification. As a result, the stock percentages will vary from the sales percentages with a greater percentage of stock in the classification that contributes a smaller percentage of total sales, and vice versa. For example, if ties in a men's furnishings store account only for 1% of the sales, it is obvious the merchant will have to provide for more than 1% of the stock in ties to achieve his or her sales volume. On the other hand, if men's slacks account for 20% of the sales, the retailer will be able to provide the customer with a large enough assortment and selection if he or she carries less than 20% of stock in slacks.

The planning of the merchandise assortment in terms of its breadth and depth may be accomplished by a retailer in one of two ways, depending on the type and classification of merchandise:

1. *Basic stock list.* This type of planning involves the provision of an assortment of merchandise that is to be kept on hand for a certain period of time. Obviously, its use is found primarily in staple merchandise.

2. *Model stock planning.* This type of planning is used primarily for merchandise that is classified as shopping goods.

In addition to these two methods of merchandise assortment planning, a retailer may elect to establish an "always-in-stock" list. In such a list, the retailer ensures that he or she always has a representative assortment of best-sellers or key items in stock to satisfy customer demand. For example, if a retailer establishes that the best-selling size in men's dress shirts is a size $15\frac{1}{2}$ neck with a 33-inch sleeve, he or she will then establish this as an always-in-stock item. In fact, he or she will always have a representative assortment of this size in men's shirts.

Retail organizations have found it particularly useful and profitable to use the concept of model stock planning for the various selection factors represented with the following items:

Bedding	Gifts	Lamps	Shoes
Boys' Apparel	Gloves	Linens	Towels
Costume Jewelry	Handbags	Men's Clothing	Umbrellas
Draperies	Handkerchiefs	Neckwear	Underwear
Furniture	Infants' Apparel	Pictures	Women's Apparel

As noted earlier, the breakdown of units for a model stock plan will result from the establishment of the degree of stability among the various selection factors for each classification of merchandise. As can be readily noticed from the list, the items are essentially shopping goods for which the customer will shop around comparing features of styles, color, price, material, and so on.

In contrast to the many shopping goods items, there are many items that are characterized by a greater degree of stability in the selection factors. Such merchandise is normally prepared on a basic stock list and represents merchandise that should be maintained in inventory for some period of time. The basic stock list pinpoints the exact selection factors of each item that are to be carried in stock, while the depth of the stock may be left up to the department or store manager, depending on the organization of the buying function. The following is a representative list of merchandise that is normally indicated on a basic stock list:

Appliances	Dinnerware	Hardware	Notions
Art Supplies	Domestics	Hosiery	Radio and Television
Books	Drugs	Housewares	Silverware
Cameras	Glassware	Luggage	Sporting Goods
Confectionary	Groceries	Needlework	Toiletries

In this chapter, we will analyze and determine the mechanics involved in determining the model stock plan for shopping goods such as fashion merchandise. In addition, it is necessary to determine the mechanics involved in the preparation of a basic stock list by the periodic reordering of staple merchandise to provide for the assortment established. Therefore, the chapter is divided into the following two sections:

1. Periodic Fill-ins for Staple Stock: Basic Stock List
2. Model Stock Planning for Fashion Merchandise: Model Stock Planning

PERIODIC FILL-INS FOR STAPLE STOCK: BASIC STOCK LIST

The basic stock list for staple merchandise is based upon the maximum stock required for a particular period of time. The buyer of such staple items is, therefore, required periodically to fill in the merchandise to the maximum level for the item. The buyer of such merchandise is constantly building his or her merchandising assortment to the maximum level. The periodic reordering of staples is then best accomplished by a series of periodic inventory counts rather than by attempting to record and analyze every unit of sale.

Since the periodic fill-in of staple stock is the process of building to a maximum stock, the student is asked to recall the elements of the maximum stock that were discussed in the previous chapter. It was noted that

> Maximum Stock = (Weeks of Reserve + Weeks of Delivery Period
> + Weeks of Reorder Period) $\times$ Rate of Sale
> $= (R + DP + RP) \times S$

To facilitate the planning of periodic fill-ins of staple stock, retailers have found it to their advantage to utilize a basic reorder form illustrating the item's maximum stock and the merchandise commitments. A sample reorder form appears in Exhibit 2 on page 248.

EXAMPLE 1: Calculating Periodic Fill-ins of Staple Stock

The buyer of a ladies' hosiery department uses a system of periodic reordering for her $2.49 line of ladies' pantyhose. As her assistant, you have been asked to complete the plan for the three weeks of June that follows.

	Short	Medium	Long	Extra Long
Rate of Sale	24	40	30	12
Delivery Period (weeks)	1	1	1	1
Reorder Period (weeks)	2	2	2	2
Reserve (weeks)	1	1	1	1

Solution:

(a) To determine the weekly maximum stock, since

$$MAX = (R + DP + RP) \times S$$

EXHIBIT 2

PERIODIC REORDER FORM

PERIODIC REORDER FORM

DEPARTMENT: _____ LINE: _____

DEPARTMENT NO.: _____ ITEM: _____

BUYER: _____ PRICE: _____ UNIT: _____

COLOR	SIZE	MAXIMUM STOCK	DATE _____			DATE _____			DATE _____			DATE _____		
			OH	OO	S	OH	OO	S	OH	OO	S	OH	OO	S

PERIODIC REORDER FORM

DEPARTMENT: HOSIERY
DEPARTMENT NO.: 422
BUYER: S. Cizmar

LINE: PANTI-HOSE
ITEM: PERFECT-FIT
PRICE: $2.49
UNIT: PAIR

COLOR	SIZE	MAXIMUM STOCK	DATE June 6			DATE June 13			DATE June 20			DATE June 27		
			OH	OO	S	OH	OO	S	OH	OO	S	OH	OO	S
MICHELLE	SHORT		32		21			36			30			
	MEDIUM		46		36			48			40			
	LONG		38		24			40			35			
	X-LONG		18		12			18			15			

then

$$
\begin{aligned}
\text{Short} \quad &(\text{MAX}) = (1 + 1 + 2) \times 24 = 96 \\
\text{Medium} \quad &(\text{MAX}) = (1 + 1 + 2) \times 40 = 160 \\
\text{Long} \quad &(\text{MAX}) = (1 + 1 + 2) \times 30 = 120 \\
\text{Extra Long} \quad &(\text{MAX}) = (1 + 1 + 2) \times 12 = 48
\end{aligned}
$$

(b) To determine the unit open-to-buy as of June 6 in order to fill in the on-order (O.O.) column, since

$$
\text{O.T.B.} = \text{MAX} - (\text{O.H.} + \text{O.O.})
$$

then

$$
\begin{aligned}
\text{Short} \quad &(\text{O.T.B.}) = 96 - 32 = 64 \\
\text{Medium} \quad &(\text{O.T.B.}) = 160 - 46 = 114 \\
\text{Long} \quad &(\text{O.T.B.}) = 120 - 38 = 82 \\
\text{Extra Long} \quad &(\text{O.T.B.}) = 48 - 18 = 30
\end{aligned}
$$

(c) To determine the stock on hand as of June 13,

$$
\frac{\text{Stock on Hand}}{\text{June 13}} = \frac{\text{On Hand}}{\text{June 6}} + \frac{\text{On Order}}{\text{June 6}} - \frac{\text{Sales}}{\text{June 6}}
$$

NOTE: Since delivery is one week, it is assumed that stock on order during the week of June 6 has arrived.

Therefore, the stock on hand (O.H.) for June 13 in each size is

$$
\begin{aligned}
\text{Short} \quad &(\text{O.H.}) = 32 + 64 - 21 = 75 \\
\text{Medium} \quad &(\text{O.H.}) = 46 + 114 - 36 = 124 \\
\text{Long} \quad &(\text{O.H.}) = 38 + 82 - 24 = 96 \\
\text{Extra Long} \quad &(\text{O.H.}) = 18 + 30 - 12 = 36
\end{aligned}
$$

(d) To determine the unit O.T.B. as of June 13,

$$
\begin{aligned}
\text{Short} \quad &(\text{O.T.B.}) = 96 - 75 = 21 \\
\text{Medium} \quad &(\text{O.T.B.}) = 160 - 124 = 36 \\
\text{Long} \quad &(\text{O.T.B.}) = 120 - 96 = 24 \\
\text{Extra Long} \quad &(\text{O.T.B.}) = 48 - 36 = 12
\end{aligned}
$$

(e) To determine the stock on hand (O.H.) as of June 20,

$$
\begin{aligned}
\text{Short} \quad &(\text{O.H.}) = 75 + 21 - 36 = 60 \\
\text{Medium} \quad &(\text{O.H.}) = 124 + 36 - 48 = 112 \\
\text{Long} \quad &(\text{O.H.}) = 96 + 24 - 40 = 80 \\
\text{Extra Long} \quad &(\text{O.H.}) = 36 + 12 - 18 = 30
\end{aligned}
$$

PERIODIC REORDER FORM

DEPARTMENT: HOSIERY
DEPARTMENT NO.: 422
BUYER: S. Cizmar

LINE: PANTI-HOSE
ITEM: PERFECT-FIT
PRICE: $2.49
UNIT: PAIR

COLOR	SIZE	MAXIMUM STOCK	DATE June 6			DATE June 13			DATE June 20			DATE June 27		
			OH	OO	S	OH	OO	S	OH	OO	S	OH	OO	S
MICHELLE	SHORT	96	32	64	21	75	21	36	60	36	30			
	MEDIUM	160	46	114	36	124	36	48	112	48	40			
	LONG	120	38	82	24	96	24	40	80	40	35			
	X-LONG	48	18	30	12	36	12	18	30	18	15			

(f) To determine the unit O.T.B. as of June 20,

Short	(O.T.B.) =	96 –	60 =	36
Medium	(O.T.B.) =	160 –	112 =	48
Long	(O.T.B.) =	120 –	80 =	40
Extra Long	(O.T.B.) =	48 –	30 =	18

The completed stock plan for the $2.49 pantyhose in the Michelle color is presented on page 251.

PROBLEM 1: The buyer of crystal and glassware maintains a basic stock list for stemware. On the basis of the information given for a line of goblets, complete the plan on page 253 for her $5.95 line of stemware for the 3 weeks of May that are indicated.

	Cocktail	*Wine*	*Sherbert*	*Water*	*Juice*
Rate of Sale	8	10	6	12	9
Delivery Period (weeks)	1	1	1	1	1
Reorder Period (weeks)	4	4	4	4	4
Reserve (weeks)	2	2	2	2	2

MODEL STOCK PLANNING FOR FASHION MERCHANDISE

As pointed out earlier in this chapter, the sale of fashion merchandise is much more volatile than is the sale of staples. The unpredictability of the fashion cycle demands constant supervision of the merchandise assortment by the buyer and the merchant. Therefore, it is necessary to make some estimate of the likely sales by the various selection factors long before the season starts. Once a selling season has begun, fashion "runners" may be reordered by periodic checking such as in staple merchandise. However, delivery of fashion goods is generally too slow to allow delay in ordering until the fashion "runners" can be determined. It is virtually impossible for a successful merchant to buy fashion merchandise on a hand-to-mouth basis. As a result, buyers of fashion merchandise are required to prepare a model stock plan to determine their merchandise assortment for the season. These plans are normally made for the opening of the season, but they have a built-in flexibility that allows adjustment in the merchandise assortment. As the term indicates, the model stock plan is a guide and not an absolute plan in much the same way as the 6-month merchandise plan.

There are three basic steps in the preparation of a model stock plan for fashion merchandise for the opening of a season:

1. Deciding on the selection factors that must be provided for the merchandise assortment: classifications, prices, colors, sizes, styles, fabric, and so on.

2. Deciding on the important dates in the season for which the model stock plan must be constructed: Christmas, Easter, Mother's Day, or similar focal dates in the season.

3. Planning sales in units for the months preceding and following the date for which the model stock is to be set and translating the total into dollars to check against the dollar merchandise plan.

PERIODIC REORDER FORM

DEPARTMENT:	CRYSTAL AND GLASSWARE	LINE: _STEMWARE_
DEPARTMENT NO.:	440	ITEM: _"FIRST-LOVE"_
BUYER:	J. Marie	PRICE: _$5.95_ UNIT: _EACH_

COLOR	SIZE	MAXIMUM STOCK	DATE May 2 OH	OO	S	DATE May 9 OH	OO	S	DATE May 16 OH	OO	S	DATE OH	OO	S
FIRST-LOVE	COCKTAIL		12		9			12			8			
STEMWARE	WINE		16		12			15			10			
	SHERBERT		9		8			10			6			
	WATER		18		14			18			12			
	JUICE		12		10			14			9			

The actual planning of the model involves making decisions on the number of items to have on hand in the major breakdowns such as price lines, basic styles, and classification types. It is advisable to establish a model stock plan for fashion merchandise according to a price line in each classification. The unit open-to-buy for each price line may then be calculated.

The importance of model stock planning becomes evident when the selection problem of the buyer is fully realized. Since the buyer must choose from an ever-increasing number of colors, patterns, styles, fabrics, price lines, and brands, the model stock plan allows the buyer to reduce the risk of an overbought or out-of-stock situation. The model stock forces the buyer into planning the merchandise assortment for the season.

A model stock plan that is used in planning the merchandise assortment is illustrated in Exhibit 3.

EXAMPLE 2: Taylor Dean, a buyer in the men's clothing department of a major department store, has forecasted sales of his two-piece suits at $270,000 for the coming fall-winter season. His department carries two price lines of men's two-piece suits at $175 and $225. The former price line accounts for 70% of the season sales; the latter accounts for the remaining 30%. Both price lines of suits come in three basic styles: two-button suits account for 25% of the sales in both price lines, the three-button suits account for 50% of the volume in the $175 price line and 60% in the $225 price line, and the double-breasted suits account for 25% in the $175 price line and 15% in the $225 price line.

After a thorough analysis of the past history of the two piece suits, Mr. Dean has entered the expected percentages needed in each size and color on the accompanying model stock plans for each price line. As an assistant buyer in the department, you have been asked to complete the model stock plan for the two price lines of suits for the fall-winter season.

Solution: The buyer has planned for a total sales volume of $270,000 for the fall-winter season in two-piece suits that are divided as follows:

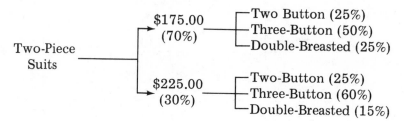

Consequently, we begin to breakdown the figures as follows:

$$\begin{array}{lll} \$175.00 \text{ Suits} = 70\% \text{ of } \$270,000 = & \$189,000.00 \\ \$225.00 \text{ Suits} = \underline{30\%} \text{ of } \$270,000 = & \underline{81,000.00} \\ \qquad \text{Total} \qquad = \underline{100\%} & = \underline{\$270,000.00} \end{array}$$

(a) Model Stock Plan I—Men's Two-Piece Suits, $175.00

Consequently, the buyer anticipates a sales volume of $189,000 in the $175.00 suits based on the calculation above. The breakdown by style is then calculated as follows:

Two-Button	25% = 25% of $189,000 =	$ 47,250
Three-Button	50% = 50% of $189,000 =	94,500
Double-Breasted	25% = 25% of $189,000 =	47,250
Total	100%	$189,000

MODEL STOCK PLAN

MODEL STOCK PLAN

Department: _____

Dept. No.: _____

Item: _____

Retail Price: _____

Buyer: _____

Season: Fall-Winter _____

Spring-Summer _____

CLASSIFICATION	SIZE	QUANTITY FOR MODEL STOCK		COLOR SELECTIONS															
		%	#	%	#	%	#	%	#	%	#	%	#	%	#	%	#	%	#
_____																			
% _____																			
# _____																			
TOTAL																			
_____																			
% _____																			
# _____																			
TOTAL																			
_____																			
% _____																			
# _____																			
TOTAL																			
PLANNED GRAND TOTAL																			

Since these figures represent sales in each style for the 6-month season, it is then necessary to determine the sales in each style for the average month in the season to provide for a representative assortment. Consequently, we will provide for our opening assortment to be a 1-month supply and hence divide the foregoing figures by 6 months:

Two-Button	$47,250/6 months	$ 7,875.00
Three-Button	$94,500/6 months	15,750.00
Double-Breasted	$47,250/6 months	7,875.00
Total		$31,500.00

Therefore, a representative assortment of the $175.00 suits for the merchant would be valued at $31,500 at retail, the average monthly sales in all styles.

The next step in the plan is to divide the dollar amounts of each style into units. Since the suits retail for $175.00, we can divide the average monthly sales for each style by $175.00 to determine the required units:

Two-Button	$ 7,875/$175.00	45 suits
Three-Button	$15,750/$175.00	90 suits
Double-Breasted	$ 7,875/$175.00	45 suits
Total		180 suits

These 180 suits at $175.00 are then subdivided into units according to various colors and sizes as indicated on the following model stock plan. The students should note that the "Total" columns in the plan must balance with each other. For example, the total of the sizes, the total of the colors, and the total of the three styles must equal the 180 suits.

NOTE: All figures are to be rounded to the nearest whole number, since it is not possible to purchase a fraction of an item. Students should also note in dividing items that a certain amount of judgment is involved in deciding which selection factor will received the extra unit. The goal is to obtain a balanced assortment with relation to customer demand. This is especially true when the assortment is not extremely large and the store will not be stocked in all colors and sizes.

(b) Model Stock Plan II—Men's Two-Piece Suits, $225.00

The same procedure is followed in planning the assortment of $225.00 suits as was just used in the preparation of Model Stock Plan I. Since $225.00 suits account for 30% of the season's sales, the volume of these suits will be $81,000.

The breakdown of the three styles of suits will be

Two-Button	25% = 25% of $81,000 =	$20,250
Three-Button	60 = 60% of $81,000 =	48,600
Double-Breasted	15 = 15% of $81,000 =	12,150
Total	100%	$81,000

The breakdown of sales in each style for the average monthly sales would be

Two-Button	$20,250/6 months	$ 3,375.00
Three-Button	$48,600/6 months	8,100.00
Double-Breasted	$12,150/6 months	2,025.00
Total		$13,500.00

MODEL STOCK PLAN I

Department: __Men's Clothing__ Item: __2-Piece Suits__
Dept. No.: __644__ Retail Price: __$175.00__
Season: Fall-Winter __✓__ Spring-Summer ____ Buyer: __Taylor Dean__

COLOR SELECTIONS

CLASSIFICATION	SIZE	QUANTITY FOR MODEL STOCK %	#	#36 Plains %	#	#41 Stripes %	#	#48 Checks %	#	%	#	%	#	%	#	%	#
2-Button	36	5		1/3		1/3		1/3									
	38	15		1/3		1/3		1/3									
% 25	40	25		1/4		1/2		1/4									
	42	30		1/4		1/2		1/4									
	44	20		1/2		1/4		1/4									
#	46	5		1/2		1/4		1/4									
TOTAL		100%															
3-Button	36	5		1/3		1/3		1/3									
	38	15		1/3		1/3		1/3									
% 50	40	25		1/3		1/3		1/3									
	42	30		1/2		1/4		1/4									
	44	20		1/4		1/2		1/4									
#	46	5		1/2		1/4		1/4									
TOTAL		100%															
Double Breasted	36	10		1/3		1/3		1/3									
	38	15		1/5		2/5		2/5									
% 25	40	30		1/5		2/5		2/5									
	42	25		1/3		1/3		1/3									
	44	15		1/5		2/5		2/5									
#	46	5		1/3		1/3		1/3									
TOTAL		100%															
PLANNED GRAND TOTAL																	

MODEL STOCK PLAN II

Department: __Men's Clothing__
Dept. No.: __644__
Season: Fall-Winter __✓__ Spring-Summer _____

Item: __2-Piece Suits__
Retail Price: __$225.00__
Buyer: __Taylor Dean__

CLASSIFICATION	SIZE	QUANTITY FOR MODEL STOCK		COLOR SELECTIONS																
		%	#	#36 Plains %	#	#41 Stripes %	#	#48 Checks %	#	%	#	%	#	%	#	%	#	%	#	
2-Button	36	5		1/3		1/3		1/3												
	38	10		1/4		1/2		1/4												
% __25__	40	30		1/3		1/3		1/3												
	42	30		1/3		1/3		1/3												
	44	15		1/2		1/4		1/4												
# _____	46	10		1/2		1/4		1/4												
TOTAL		100%																		
3-Button	36	5		1/3		1/3		1/3												
	38	10		1/3		1/3		1/3												
% __60__	40	25		1/4		1/2		1/4												
	42	30		2/5		2/5		1/5												
	44	20		1/3		1/3		1/3												
# _____	46	10		2/5		2/5		1/5												
TOTAL		100%																		
Double Breasted	36	10		1/5		2/5		2/5												
	38	15		1/3		1/3		1/3												
% __15__	40	30		1/5		2/5		2/5												
	42	25		1/3		1/3		1/3												
	44	15		1/3		1/3		1/3												
# _____	46	5		2/5		2/5		1/5												
TOTAL		100%																		
PLANNED GRAND TOTAL																				

And the number of units of each style on these average monthly sales would then be determined by dividing by the retail price line of the suit of $225.00:

Two-Button	$3,375.00/$225.00	15 suits
Three-Button	$8,100.00/$225.00	36 suits
Double-Breasted	$2,025.00/$225.00	9 suits
Total		60 suits

These 60 suits in the $225.00 price line are then subdivided according to style on the basis of the proportion of colors and sizes indicated on the accompanying model stock plan.

The completed model stock plans for the $175.00 and $225.00 suits are shown on pages 260 and 261.

MODEL STOCK PLAN I

Department: **Men's Clothing**
Dept. No.: **644**
Season: Fall-Winter **✓** Spring-Summer ____
Item: **2-Piece Suits**
Retail Price: **$175.00**
Buyer: **Taylor Dean**

COLOR SELECTIONS

CLASSIFICATION	SIZE	Qty for Model Stock %	Qty for Model Stock #	#36 Plains %	#36 Plains #	#41 Stripes %	#41 Stripes #	#48 Checks %	#48 Checks #
2-Button	36	5	2	1/3	3	1/3	1	1/3	1
% 25	38	15	7	1/3	3	1/3	2	1/3	2
	40	25	11	1/4	3	1/3	5	1/4	3
# 45	42	30	14	1/4	4	1/2	7	1/4	4
	44	20	9	1/2	1	1/4	2	1/4	3
	46	5	2	1/2		1/4	1	1/4	
TOTAL		100%	45		14		18		13
3-Button	36	5	4	1/3	1	1/3	2	1/3	1
% 50	38	15	14	1/3	4	1/3	5	1/3	5
	40	25	23	1/3	8	1/3	8	1/3	7
# 90	42	30	27	1/2	13	1/4	7	1/4	7
	44	20	18	1/4	4	1/2	9	1/4	5
	46	5	4	1/2	2	1/4	1	1/4	1
TOTAL		100%	90		32		32		26
Double Breasted	36	10	5	1/3	2	1/3	2	1/3	1
% 25	38	15	7	1/5	1	2/5	3	2/5	3
	40	30	13	1/5	3	2/5	5	2/5	5
# 45	42	25	11	1/3	4	1/3	4	1/3	3
	44	15	7	1/5	1	2/5	3	2/5	3
	46	5	2	1/3	1	1/3	1	1/3	
TOTAL		100%	45		12		18		15
PLANNED GRAND TOTAL			180		58		68		54

MODEL STOCK PLAN II

Department: **Men's Clothing**
Dept. No.: **644**
Season: Fall-Winter **✓**　　Spring-Summer

Item: **2-Piece Suits**
Retail Price: **$225.00**
Buyer: **Taylor Dean**

COLOR SELECTIONS

CLASSIFICATION	SIZE	QTY FOR MODEL STOCK %	#	#36 Plains %	#	#41 Stripes %	#	#48 Checks %	#	%	#	%	#	%	#	%	#
2-Button %__25__ #__15__	36	5	1	1/3	1	1/3	-	1/3	1								
	38	10	2	1/4	-	1/2	1	1/4	-								
	40	30	4	1/3	2	1/3	-	1/3	-								
	42	30	4	1/3	1	1/3	1	1/3	2								
	44	15	2	1/2	1	1/4	-	1/4	-								
	46	10	2	1/2	1	1/4	1	1/4	1								
TOTAL		100%	15		6		4		5								
3-Button %__60__ #__36__	36	5	2	1/3	1	1/3	1	1/3	1								
	38	10	3	1/3	1	1/3	1	1/3	1								
	40	25	9	1/4	3	1/2	4	1/4	2								
	42	30	11	2/5	4	2/5	4	1/5	3								
	44	20	7	1/3	2	1/3	2	1/3	3								
	46	10	4	2/5	1	2/5	2	1/5	1								
TOTAL		100%	36		12		14		10								
Double Breasted %__15__ #__9__	36	10	1	1/5	1	2/5	1	2/5	1								
	38	15	1	1/3	-	1/3	-	1/3	-								
	40	30	3	1/5	1	2/5	1	2/5	1								
	42	25	2	1/3	-	1/3	1	1/3	1								
	44	15	1	1/3	-	1/3	-	1/3	-								
	46	5	1	2/5	1	2/5	1	2/5	-								
TOTAL		100%	9		3		4		2								
PLANNED GRAND TOTAL			60		21		22		17								

PROBLEM 2: Michael Browne is responsible for buying and controlling the sleepwear section of the men's furnishings department. Mr. Browne anticipates that the pajama section will account for 10% of the department's sales, which have been set at $675,000 for the fall-winter season, including sleepwear. Mr. Browne anticipates that 75% of the men's pajama sales will come from the regular line and 25% from the shortie line. In the regular line, the buyer offers an assortment that will retail at $20.00 and one that will retail at $30.00 per pair. If 60% of the regular line comes from the $20.00 price point and 40% is generated by the $30.00 price line, prepare a model stock plan for Mr. Browne based on the information given. The percentage breakdown of colors and sizes is planned to be the same in each price line of pajamas.

Sizes	Percentage of Sales	Color Distribution		
		#10 Plain	#15 Patterns	#17 Wild
Small	10%	50%	20%	30%
Medium	30	40	30	30
Large	40	40	40	20
Extra Large	20	50	30	20

MODEL STOCK PLAN

Department: _Men's Furnishings_

Dept. No.: _725_

Season: Fall-Winter _✓_   Spring-Summer _____

Item: _Pajamas - Regular_

Retail Price: _$ 20.00_

Buyer: _Michael Broome_

CLASSIFICATION	SIZE	QUANTITY FOR MODEL STOCK		COLOR SELECTIONS															
		%	#	%	#	%	#	%	#	%	#	%	#	%	#	%	#	%	#
_____																			
% _____																			
# _____																			
TOTAL																			
_____																			
% _____																			
# _____																			
TOTAL																			
_____																			
% _____																			
# _____																			
TOTAL																			
PLANNED GRAND TOTAL																			

MODEL STOCK PLAN

Department: Men's Furnishings

Dept. No.: 725

Season: Fall-Winter ✓ Spring-Summer

Item: Pajamas - Regular

Retail Price: $30.00

Buyer: Michael Browne

CLASSIFICATION	SIZE	QUANTITY FOR MODEL STOCK		COLOR SELECTIONS															
		%	#	%	#	%	#	%	#	%	#	%	#	%	#	%	#	%	#
___ % ___ #																			
TOTAL																			
___ % ___ #																			
TOTAL																			
___ % ___ #																			
TOTAL																			
PLANNED GRAND TOTAL																			

1. Allan Root is the main buyer of the dinnerware section of the china and gift department. To control his inventory effectively, Mr. Root has established a system of periodic reordering to bring his stock up to a maximum level. On the basis of the information provided, determine Mr. Root's open-to-buy in units for each of the 3 weeks indicated.

BONE CHINA PATTERNS—5-PIECE SETTINGS

	Rondeau	Debutante	Beverly	Shangri-la
Rate of Sale	7	5	4	8
Delivery Period	1	1	1	1
Reserve Period	2	2	2	2
Reorder Period	2	2	2	2

	Belvedere	Trillium	Blossom	Tiara
Rate of Sale	4	6	5	3
Delivery Period	1	1	1	1
Reserve Period	2	2	2	2
Reorder Period	2	2	2	2

Complete the plan that follows.

PERIODIC REORDER FORM

DEPARTMENT: China and Gifts   LINE: Dinnerware

DEPARTMENT NO.: 207   ITEM: English Bone China

BUYER: A. H. Root   PRICE: $55.00   UNIT: 5-pce.

PATTERN	MAXIMUM STOCK	DATE April 20			DATE April 27			DATE May 4			DATE May 11		
		OH	OO	S	OH	OO	S	OH	OO	S	OH	OO	S
Rondeau		24		7			10			8			
Debutante		18		5			7			6			
Beverly		15		6			5			4			
Shangri-La		25		10			11			9			
Belvedere		15		5			6			4			
Trillium		22		10			8			8			
Blossom		18		7			6			8			
Tiara		12		5			7			3			

5-Piece Settings

2. Daniel Scarrow, the buyer of ladies' sportswear, had planned sales of $350,000 in the sweater section of the department for the coming fall-winter season. The buyer estimates that 60% of his volume will come from ladies' cardigans and the balance will be generated by long- and short-sleeve pullovers. Based upon last year's sales and the buyer's anticipation for this season, Mr. Scarrow estimates that 40% of the cardigan sales will come from the $40 price line and 20% will come at the $60.00 price point. The remainder will be generated by other price lines carried in the department.

In the $40.00 price line, approximately 40% will be obtained from wool sweaters, 20% from acrylic, and 40% from blended fabrics. In the $60.00 price line, 60% will come from wool, 10% from acrylic, and the balance from blended fabrics.

The sales distribution by size and color is planned as follows for both price lines:

Size Distribution	Colors	
	Basic Shades[a]	High Shades[b]
32 = 5%	50%	50%
34 = 10%	40	60
36 = 20%	40	60
38 = 30%	40	60
40 = 20%	40	60
42 = 10%	50	50
44 = 5%	60	40

[a] Basic shades for the fall season include black and white and the basic fall colors of brown, wine, navy, and dark green.
[b] High shades vary with each season and represent shades that are in fashion during the season. The high shades are normally the new shades and hues that are introduced before the season begins.

On the model stock plans that follow, prepare and complete the plans for ladies' cardigans, at $40.00 and at $60.00.

MODEL STOCK PLAN

Department: _____

Dept. No.: _____

Season: Fall-Winter _____

Spring-Summer _____

Item: _____

Retail Price: _____

Buyer: _____

CLASSIFICATION	SIZE	QUANTITY FOR MODEL STOCK		COLOR SELECTIONS													
		%	#	%	#	%	#	%	#	%	#	%	#	%	#	%	#
_____ % _____ #																	
TOTAL																	
_____ % _____ #																	
TOTAL																	
_____ % _____ #																	
TOTAL																	
PLANNED GRAND TOTAL																	

MODEL STOCK PLAN

Department: _____

Dept. No.: _____

Season: Fall-Winter _____

Spring-Summer _____

Item: _____

Retail Price: _____

Buyer: _____

CLASSIFICATION	SIZE	QUANTITY FOR MODEL STOCK		COLOR SELECTIONS																	
		%	#	%	#	%	#	%	#	%	#	%	#	%	#	%	#	%	#		
___ ___ ___ % #																					
TOTAL																					
___ ___ ___ % #																					
TOTAL																					
___ ___ ___ % #																					
TOTAL																					
PLANNED GRAND TOTAL																					

3. The buyer of men's furnishings maintains a basic stock list for men's hosiery. On this basis, the buyer has provided you with the following information on a line of executive hosiery, which retails at $5.00 per pair. With the information given and on the accompanying chart, indicate the basic stock plan in its completion for the 4 weeks in March.

	Small	Medium	Large	Extra Large
Average Rate of Sale	8	12	12	6
Delivery Period (weeks)	1	1	1	1
Reorder Period (weeks)	3	3	3	3
Reserve (weeks)	2	2	2	2

4. Raymond Aleppo, the buyer of ladies' coats and suits, has planned sales of $550,000 for the season in ladies' coats. The buyer estimates that 20% of this volume will come from suede and leather jackets and 30% will be derived from the sale of full-length suede and leather coats. In both coats and jackets the buyer estimates that 40% of the sales will be in suede and 60% will be in leather.

The jackets in suede and leather will retail at $150 and are expected to be distributed among sizes and colors as follows:

	Size		Deep Tones	Colors Neutral	High Shades
Suede Jackets $150	8	10%	$\frac{1}{3}$	$\frac{1}{3}$	$\frac{1}{3}$
	10	10	$\frac{1}{5}$	$\frac{2}{5}$	$\frac{2}{5}$
	12	15	$\frac{2}{5}$	$\frac{1}{5}$	$\frac{2}{5}$
	14	15	$\frac{1}{3}$	$\frac{1}{3}$	$\frac{1}{3}$
	16	20	$\frac{2}{5}$	$\frac{1}{5}$	$\frac{2}{5}$
	18	15	$\frac{3}{5}$	$\frac{1}{5}$	$\frac{1}{5}$
	20	15	$\frac{3}{5}$	$\frac{1}{5}$	$\frac{1}{5}$
Leather Jackets $150	8	10	$\frac{1}{3}$	$\frac{1}{3}$	$\frac{1}{3}$
	10	10	$\frac{1}{5}$	$\frac{2}{5}$	$\frac{2}{5}$
	12	20	$\frac{2}{5}$	$\frac{1}{5}$	$\frac{2}{5}$
	14	15	$\frac{1}{3}$	$\frac{1}{3}$	$\frac{1}{3}$
	16	15	$\frac{2}{5}$	$\frac{2}{5}$	$\frac{1}{5}$
	18	15	$\frac{2}{5}$	$\frac{2}{5}$	$\frac{1}{5}$
	20	15	$\frac{3}{5}$	$\frac{1}{5}$	$\frac{1}{5}$

PERIODIC REORDER FORM

DEPARTMENT: Men's Furnishings
DEPARTMENT NO.: 308
BUYER: T. J. Desanti

LINE: Men's Hosiery
ITEM: "Executive"
PRICE: $5.00 UNIT: Pair

	SIZE	MAXIMUM STOCK	DATE March 2			DATE March 9			DATE March 16			DATE March 23		
			OH	OO	S	OH	OO	S	OH	OO	S	OH	OO	S
"Executive" Hosiery	Small		40		10			8			12			6
	Medium		60		15			12			18			9
	Large		72		12			12			20			8
	X-Large		36		9			6			10			6

The suede and leather coats will retail at \$250 and are expected to be distributed among sizes and colors as follows:

	Size		Deep Tones	Colors Neutral	High Shades
Leather Coats					
\$250	8	5%	$\frac{1}{3}$	$\frac{1}{3}$	$\frac{1}{3}$
	10	10	$\frac{1}{5}$	$\frac{1}{5}$	$\frac{3}{5}$
	12	15	$\frac{2}{5}$	$\frac{1}{5}$	$\frac{2}{5}$
	14	15	$\frac{1}{3}$	$\frac{1}{3}$	$\frac{1}{3}$
	16	15	$\frac{2}{5}$	$\frac{1}{5}$	$\frac{2}{5}$
	18	20	$\frac{2}{5}$	$\frac{1}{5}$	$\frac{2}{5}$
	20	20	$\frac{2}{5}$	$\frac{2}{5}$	$\frac{1}{5}$
Suede Coats					
\$250	8	5%	$\frac{1}{3}$	$\frac{1}{3}$	$\frac{1}{3}$
	10	10	$\frac{1}{5}$	$\frac{2}{5}$	$\frac{2}{5}$
	12	15	$\frac{1}{5}$	$\frac{2}{5}$	$\frac{2}{5}$
	14	15	$\frac{2}{5}$	$\frac{2}{5}$	$\frac{1}{5}$
	16	20	$\frac{1}{3}$	$\frac{1}{3}$	$\frac{1}{3}$
	18	20	$\frac{2}{5}$	$\frac{1}{5}$	$\frac{2}{5}$
	20	15	$\frac{3}{5}$	$\frac{1}{5}$	$\frac{1}{5}$

Complete the model stock plans for the buyer for the beginning of the fall-winter season. Use one plan for coats and one for jackets.

PROBLEM 4 WORKSHEET

MODEL STOCK PLAN

Department: __LADIES COATS AND SUITS__

Dept. No.: __667__

Season: Fall-Winter _____

Spring-Summer __✓__

Item: __SUEDE AND LEATHER JACKETS__

Retail Price: __$150__

Buyer: __Raymond Aleppo__

CLASSIFICATION	SIZE	QUANTITY FOR MODEL STOCK		COLOR SELECTIONS															
		%	#	%	#	%	#	%	#	%	#	%	#	%	#	%	#	%	#
_____																			
% _____																			
# _____																			
TOTAL																			
_____																			
% _____																			
# _____																			
TOTAL																			
_____																			
% _____																			
# _____																			
TOTAL																			
PLANNED GRAND TOTAL																			

MODEL STOCK PLAN

Department: LADIES COATS AND SUITS

Dept. No.: 667

Season: Fall-Winter ___ Spring-Summer ✓

Item: SUEDE AND LEATHER COATS

Retail Price: $250

Buyer: Raymond Aleppo

CLASSIFICATION	SIZE	QUANTITY FOR MODEL STOCK		COLOR SELECTIONS																
		%	#	%	#	%	#	%	#	%	#	%	#	%	#	%	#	%	#	
_____																				
%																				
#																				
TOTAL																				
_____																				
%																				
#																				
TOTAL																				
_____																				
%																				
#																				
TOTAL																				
PLANNED GRAND TOTAL																				

Review Problems for Chapters 9, 10, 11, 12, 13, and 14

To ensure an understanding of the concepts presented, solve the problems that follow without referring back to the previous chapters. The workspace for each question has purposely been eliminated so that you may review the problems without the solutions being readily available.

1. A ladies' sweater department has an opening inventory of $86,000 for October. The planned B.O.M. stock-sales ratio for October is 2.5. On the basis of this information, calculate the planned sales in ladies' sweaters for October.

2. A gift boutique had sales last year during June of $38,000 with 25 selling days. The buyer anticipates that there will be a 12% increase this year over last year. If June of this year will have 26 selling days, determine the planned sales for the month.

3. A sleepwear department has a planned B.O.M. stock-sales ratio of 2.5 for February. Determine the B.O.M. stock for March for the department if the planned February sales are $30,000 and the planned stock turnover for February is .5.

4. Calculate the stock that should be on hand on December 1 in a department that has the following planned figures:

Planned Season Sales	$320,000
Planned Sales, December	$ 75,000
Planned Average Sale, December	$ 20
Planned Average Sale, Season	$ 10
Planned Stock Turnover, Season	2
Planned Control Period (weeks)	5

5. If Joseph's Bath Boutique has the following information, calculate the open-to-buy as of March 22.

Planned E.O.M. Stock-Sales, Ratio, March	1.5
Planned B.O.M. Stock, March 1	$40,000
Planned Sales, March 1–31	$30,000
Actual Sales, March 1–22	$21,000
Planned Markdowns, March 1–31	10%
Actual Markdowns, March 1–22	$ 1,800
Purchases Received at Retail, March 1–22	$ 8,200
Outstanding Orders at Retail, March 22	$12,600

6. The buyer of Antoine's Men's and Boys' apparel has calculated that a staple item had sold at the rate of 286 after the first 4 weeks of the season. The buyer also informs you that at the end of the fourth week there are 75 items on hand and another 20 on order. If the buyer

anticipates that a 3-week supply will be kept on hand and on order, calculate the open-to-buy for the item based on the same rate of sale.

7. Tracy DiThomas wishes to determine the amount of stock that should be on hand on October 1 in her department given the following information:

Planned Sales, Fall-Winter	$220,000
Planned October Sales	$ 40,000
Average Sale, Fall-Winter	$ 8
Average Sale, October	$ 12
Control Period (weeks)	4
Stock Turnover, Season	5

8. A shirt department has planned sales of $160,000 for the season with a planned stock turnover of 2. If the typical markup for the department is 37.5%, calculate the department's capital turnover.

9. Calculate the B.O.M. stock for June for a department that has the following information for the spring-summer season:

Number of Transactions, Season, Last Year	21,000
Number of Transactions, This Year/Last Year, Season	+10%
Average Sale, Season, Last Year	$15.00
Average Sale, This Year/Last Year, Season	+8%
Planned June Transactions, This Year	3,300
Planned June Average Sale, This Year	$18.00
Control Period, June (weeks)	4
Stock Turnover, Season	2

10. A ladies' dress department has its sales influenced by the date of Easter. Jeannette Suzanne, the buyer, has anticipated a 10% increase in sales this year over last year. During March of last year, sales were $48,000 and April sales were $34,000. However, this year Easter falls on April 21. The last time Easter fell on this date the department realized sales of $16,000 in March and $26,000 in April. Determine the planned sales for March and April for the dress department for the coming season.

11. A buyer is planning a 12% increase in sales this year over last year and has planned a stock turnover of 6 for the 6-month period. On the basis of the data given for last year, determine the stock that should be carried for the next few weeks.

Week of Period	Sales Last Year	Sales This Year
1	$ 6,000	$7,000
2	7,000	7,560
3	10,000	
4	12,400	
5	15,600	
6	14,000	
7	13,000	
8	14,000	
9	14,400	

12. A department is expected to have a sales volume increase of 12% this year over last year's sales of $250,000. The department also has planned for the following operating data for the coming season.

Operating Expenses	30%
Net Profit	4%
Markdowns, Net	6%
Stock Shortages	1%
Alteration Expenses, Net	2%
Cash Discounts	2%
Employee Discounts	1.5%
Stock Turnover, Season	5

The seasonal distribution and sales and reductions for the department has been planned as follows.

Month	Planned Sales Distribution	Planned Reductions Distribution
August	11%	15%
September	17%	5
October	23	10
November	19	15
December	21	20
January	9	35

As a management trainee in the department, you have been asked to prepare the merchandise plan on page 278 by inserting the planned estimate for the buyer, Bill O'Hara, for the fall-winter season.

13. The buyer of a department has established a reserve of 20 dozen for a staple item. The item is to be ordered every 3 weeks and the source indicates that delivery will take 4 weeks. At the present time, there are 450 items on hand and another 20 dozen on order. If the buyer estimates that the units will sell at the rate of 150 per week, calculate the unit open-to-buy and the unit annual stock turnover for the item.

SIX-MONTH MERCHANDISE PLAN

DEPARTMENT _____

DEPARTMENT NO. _____

FROM _____ 19 ___

TO _____ 19 ___

Department Control Data

	L.Y.	T.Y.
% Initial Markup		
% Reductions		
% Maintained Markup		
% Alteration Expense		
% Cash Discount		
% Gross Margin		
% Operating Expence		
% Net Profit		
Season Turnover		
Control Period		

Planning and Authorization

Buyer ___ *Bill O'Hara*

Merchandise Controller ___ *Al Alberts*

Date Prepared ___ *March 24*

Date Authorized ___ *March 30*

	Spring / Fall	Feb. / Aug.	Mar. / Sept.	Apr. / Oct.	May / Nov.	June / Dec.	July / Jan.	Total
Sales	Last Year							
	Plan							
	Actual							
Retail E.O.M.	Last Year							
	Plan							
	Actual							
Reductions	Last Year							
	Plan							
	Actual							
Retail B.O.M.	Last Year							
	Plan							
	Actual							
Retail Purchases	Last Year							
	Plan							
	Actual							
Cost Purchases	Last Year							
	Plan							
	Actual							

Sales + E.O.M. + Reductions − B.O.M. = Retail Purchases

14. A department has net sales of $200,000 and carries an average retail stock of $50,000 with a markup of 40%. Another department has sales of $120,000 with an average retail stock of $40,000 and a markup of 35%. Determine the stock turnover and capital turnover ratios for each department.

15. The men's shoe department has planned sales for the spring-summer season of $490,000. On the basis of past experience, the buyer estimates that his line of loafer slip-ons will account for 40% of the planned sales volume of the department. The buyer plans to carry three price lines in loafers at $40.00, $60.00, and $90.00. A further analysis of departmental records shows that 30% of the loafer sales will come from the $40.00 price line, 50% will come from the $60.00 line, and the remaining 20% will be generated by the $90.00 price line.

The unit control system of the department reveals the following size and width breakdown of men's loafers. On the basis of this information, you have been asked to prepare a model stock plan for the $40.00 and $60.00 price lines of men's loafers. The buyer has informed you that he will subsequently prepare a breakdown of the unit by color selection since the shoes will only be offered in black and brown.

MEN'S LOAFERS

Size Distribution		Widths				
		A	B	C	D	E
8	= 5%	10%	10%	30%	40%	10%
$8\frac{1}{2}$ =	5%	10	10	30	40	10
9	= 20%	5	10	30	40	15
$9\frac{1}{2}$ =	25%	5	5	30	40	20
10	= 15%	5	5	30	45	15
$10\frac{1}{2}$ =	10%	5	5	25	45	20
11	= 10%	5	5	15	50	25
$11\frac{1}{2}$ =	5%	5	5	15	50	25
12	= 5%	5	5	15	50	25

16. Calculate the open-to-buy at cost and retail as of June 10 in a department that has the following information:

Planned Sales, June	$ 50,000
Actual Sales, June 1–10	$ 16,000
Planned Markdowns, June	5%
Actual Markdowns, June 1–10	4%
Purchases Received at Cost, June 1–10	$ 18,000
Outstanding Orders at Cost, June 10	$ 12,000
B.O.M. June 1	$120,000
Planned Stock at Retail, July 1	$130,000
Initial Markup	37.5%

17. A ladies' fashion department has an annual stock turnover rate of 4 with planned annual sales $285,000. For the months of October, November, and December, the sales are planned at $18,000, $23,000, and $32,000, respectively. Determine the dollar value of the stocks that should be planned for the beginning of each of these months. What B.O.M. stock-sales ratios would result from these plans?

MODEL STOCK PLAN

Department: Men's Shoes
Dept. No.: 615
Season: Fall-Winter ___ Spring-Summer ✓

Item: Men's Loafers
Retail Price: $40.00
Buyer: A. Edwards

CLASSIFICATION	SIZE	QUANTITY FOR MODEL STOCK		COLOR SELECTIONS																	
		%	#	%	#	%	#	%	#	%	#	%	#	%	#	%	#	%	#		
___																					
% ___																					
# ___																					
TOTAL																					
___																					
% ___																					
# ___																					
TOTAL																					
___																					
% ___																					
# ___																					
TOTAL																					
PLANNED GRAND TOTAL																					

MODEL STOCK PLAN

Department: _Men's Shoes_
Dept. No.: _615_
Season: Fall-Winter _____
Spring-Summer __✓__

Item: _Men's Loafers_
Retail Price: _$60.00_
Buyer: _A. Edwards_

CLASSIFICATION	SIZE	QUANTITY FOR MODEL STOCK		COLOR SELECTIONS															
		%	#	%	#	%	#	%	#	%	#	%	#	%	#	%	#	%	#
_____																			
% _____																			
# _____																			
TOTAL																			
_____																			
% _____																			
# _____																			
TOTAL																			
_____																			
% _____																			
# _____																			
TOTAL																			
PLANNED GRAND TOTAL																			

18. A department buyer planned sales at $66,000 for a month, markdowns of $2,400, and stock shortages of $1,200. At the beginning of the month, the stock was $60,000 at retail and was to be reduced to $48,000 by the end of the month. The value of the goods on order for delivery in the month amounted to $15,000 at retail. Determine the purchases that should have been planned for the month and the dollar open-to-buy.

19. The average sale in a department is expected to increase by 12% and the number of transactions are expected to decrease 4% over last year as a result of the inflationary pressures of the economy. Sales last year for the month of June were $42,000 with 25 selling days and for July were $49,500 with 24 selling days. This year June will have 24 selling days and July will have 25 selling days. Calculate the planned sales for June and July of this year.

20. Housewares department maintains a basic stock list of stainless steel flatware. On the basis of the information given, complete the periodic reorder plan for the 3 weeks indicated.

	Dinner Knife	Dinner Fork	Salad Fork	Teaspoon	Tablespoon
Rate of Sale	24	24	12	24	12
Delivery Period (weeks)	1	1	1	1	1
Reorder Period (weeks)	3	3	3	3	3
Reserve (weeks)	2	2	2	2	2

PERIODIC REORDER FORM

DEPARTMENT: HOUSEWARES
DEPARTMENT NO.: 319
BUYER: M. Sutcliffe

LINE: FLATWARE
ITEM: STAINLESS STEEL -- CORONET
PRICE: $ 6.95 **UNIT:** EACH

COLOR	SIZE	MAXIMUM STOCK	DATE APRIL 5			DATE APRIL 12			DATE APRIL 19			DATE		
			OH	OO	S	OH	OO	S	OH	OO	S	OH	OO	S
CORONET -- S/S	DINNER KNIFE		48		22			26			28			
	DINNER FORK		36		20			25			27			
	SALAD FORK		40		16			12			14			
	TEASPOON		54		26			24			28			
	TABLE-SPOON		38		8			14			10			

APPENDICES

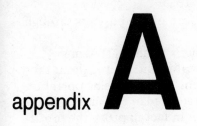

appendix **A**

The Operating Statement

In a free enterprise system, profits are the reward for the successful management of business risks. In essence, profits represent the dollars that remain after the payment of all merchandise acquisition costs, operating expenses, and taxes. For the retail establishment to survive and progress in the environment in which it operates, long-term profit goals must be established for the enterprise. The ultimate step in achieving these goals will be dependent upon the retailer's ability to understand the interaction of the various factors of the business that affect profitability. It is incorrect to assume that the retailer who is able to increase sales volume will automatically increase the profit ratio. The summary of those factors that affect the retailer's profit picture are presented in what the retailer designates as the operating statement.

Throughout, we have been concerned with understanding the various types of markups and planning involved in a retail operation. It is at this point that the moment of truth comes for the retailer in determining whether he or she has been successful in planning the merchandising function. Just as the unit and dollar open-to-buy systems in a retail operation represent a control tool for the retailer, so does the analysis and interpretation of the store's operating statement.

It should be obvious to every student of retailing that the merchant's primary financial objective in establishing and operating a retail store is to satisfy the firm's long-term profit objective. It becomes imperative that every merchandising function performed in the establishment be measured in terms of its overall effect on profit. Immediate profit may be sacrificed for increased sales volume and market share, but growth over the long run requires profit for reinvestment. Consequently, it becomes the responsibility of every merchant to seek effective ways in which to increase sales volume and profits.

Profit is said to be the excess of business income over the costs and expenses incurred in generating that income. It is essentially in this process of planning profits for a retail operation that we have undertaken a study of the mathematics of retail merchandising.

The relationship that exists among sales, costs, operating expenses, and profits helps us to explain the merchandising strategy that will allow the merchant to reach a predetermined profit objective. The profits become essential to a business since they provide a return to the owner for capital invested in the firm and at the same time provide for expansion of the business through inventory, equipment, and space.

The fundamental elements of profit are expressed in the retailer's financial statement, known as an income and expense statement or the profit and loss statement. Throughout the book, we have been concerned with the effect that each aspect of the merchandising operation has on the profitability of the firm. Retailers are, therefore, required to plan the various functions of the business so that the implementation of the strategy will in fact improve the profit objective of the firm.

BASIC PROFIT ELEMENTS

The three basic factors that enter directly into the operating profit of the retail store are sales volume, the cost of the merchandise generating this sales volume, and the store's operating expenses. Consequently, the fundamental format of the store's income and expense statement expresses the relationship that exists among these factors.

BASIC FORMAT OF INCOME AND EXPENSE STATEMENT

	Net Sales	$400,000
−	Cost of Merchandise Sold	240,000
=	Gross Margin	$160,000
−	Operating Expenses	140,000
=	Net Operating Profit	$ 20,000

Students should note that we make reference to profit here as the "net operating profit" rather than simply "net profit," since we are concerned with the profit that is generated by the merchandising operation. Retailers may have additional income and expenses generated from partial rental of the premises, or from investments, or from other nonmerchandising functions. This would then appear on the foregoing statement as "other income" and "other expenses" following the calculation of net operating profit:

	Net Operating Profit		$20,000
+	Net Other Income		
	Other Income	$15,000	
−	Other Expenses	10,000	5,000
=	Net Profit Before Taxes		$25,000

Some merchants tend to believe that they have more control over their gross margin than they do over the cost of the merchandise sold. But through more effective buying and systematic inventory control, the merchant is able to monitor the cost of merchandise sold that ultimately will improve the store's gross margin. It is essentially in this area of the merchandising operation that this book addresses itself. The ability to plan and control inventory in a retail store generally separates the successful merchant from those continuing the struggle for survival. Since the merchandise inventory is one of the largest assets on the balance sheet of the retailer, it is not surprising to note that merchants spend much of their time watching, counting, and worrying about the merchandise on hand and on order. Careful planning of all aspects of buying and inventory control consequently affect the profitability of the firm.

It should be noted at this point that profit should not simply be defined as the residual or "left-over" amount between the net sales and merchandise costs but, rather, an amount that retailers have carefully planned to ensure the survival of the firm.

Since the basic profit elements are composed of the three factors of sales, merchandise costs, and operating expenses, then we must be concerned with the planning of those variables that affect the planning of each of these. Consequently, we observe the following relationship between the elements and the variables:

Profit Elements		Profit Variables
Sales	=	Unit Price × Unit Volume Sold
Cost of Merchandise Sold	=	Unit Cost × Unit Volume Sold
Operating Expenses	=	Variable Expenses + Fixed Expenses

On the basis of these relationships, the profit and loss statement illustrated earlier might be constituted from the following variables:

	Net Sales (80,000 units × $5.00)		$400,000
−	Cost of Merchandise Sold (80,000 × $3.00)		240,000
=	Gross Margin (80,000 × $2.00)		$160,000
−	Operating Expenses		
	Variable Expenses	$95,000	
	Fixed Expenses	45,000	140,000
=	Net Operating Profit		$ 20,000

This profit and loss statement when further expanded is a summary of the operations of a retail store or department for a period of time that may be 1 month, a season, or an entire year. Although the statement may be prepared for any length of time desirable, it is usually prepared for a uniform length of time to facilitate comparison and analysis with other stores or other departments within the same organization.

The operating statement is prepared for owners, executives, and other store personnel in the retail establishment who might have limited knowledge of the various accounting methods. However, it is the analysis of the statement that leads to proper decision making at all levels within the organization. The analysis of the operating statement requires the inidividual to be aware of the factors that constitute income and those that constitute the costs for the retailer.

SALES AND REVENUES

The sales figure for a retail store will normally consist of revenue from the sale of merchandise as explained. However, some retail stores earn revenue by the sale of a service such as repairs, alterations, storage, installations, and so on. In this type of retail establishment, it is important to keep the two types of revenue separated for management to analyze the operations of the department or store on the same basis.

As noted, the sales figure is dependent upon the relationship of price to quantity. In other words, the retailer must decide to what extent an increase in price will affect sales as a result of a subsequent decrease in the number of transactions or units sold. This relationship between price and quantity on the retailer's gross margin is expressed as

(a) Initial pricing:

Sales (80,000 × $5.00)	$400,000
Cost of Goods Sold (80,000 × $3.00)	$240,000
Gross Margin	$160,000
Operating Expenses	140,000
Net Operating Profit	$ 20,000

(b) Assuming a price increase of 10% per unit without competitive retaliation, and all other things being equal;

Sales (80,000 × $5.50)	$440,000
Cost of Goods Sold (80,000 × $3.00)	240,000
Gross Margin	$200,000
Operating Expenses	140,000
Net Operating Profit	$ 60,000

Therefore, in this case, a 10% increase in the retail price results in a 200% increase in net operating profit, assuming that all other things remain constant.

(c) Assume a price decrease of 10% at retail that will result in a 50% increase in the number of transactions, while other things remain equal:

Sales (120,000 × $4.50)	$540,000
Cost of Goods Sold (120,000 × $3.00)	$360,000
Gross Margin	$180,000
Operating Expenses	140,000
Net Operating Profit	$ 40,000

Therefore, comparing this situation to our initial pricing, we find that a 10% decrease in price followed by a 50% increase in transactions will in fact double the retailer's profit, if all other things remain constant.

The foregoing examples are used to point out the relationship among price, volume, and profit. The student will observe quickly that other things do not remain constant and that retaliation can be expected from competitors or selling expenses could increase as volume increases. Management's decision, therefore, hinges on its ability to obtain the right mix of price and volume for profitability.

COST OF MERCHANDISE SOLD

This section of the store's operating statement is a summary of the store's merchandise costs. The mathematical determination of this figure is expressed in the following relationship:

Cost of Merchandise Available for Sale – Cost of Goods on Hand

Consequently, as we have seen earlier, it is necessary to determine the cost of the purchases received into inventory and subsequently added to the merchandise available for sale during the period in the form of the opening inventory. With the deduction of the cost of the inventory that is on hand at the end of the period, the merchant is able to calculate the cost of the merchandise that has been sold during the period. This became obvious in our calculations regarding the retail method of inventory.

Purchase costs are determined from the invoices submitted by vendors. The invoice may indicate list prices from which trade discounts are taken to determine the retailer's cost price. In situations where the retailer is required to pay for transportation of the goods to the store, transportation charges must also be considered as part of the cost of the goods purchased. The student will recall our handling of these items in earlier discussions.

Further, as we noted in a previous chapter, the determination of the value of the inventory at the beginning of the period or the ending inventory will depend on the method of valuation used. The two basic methods employed by retail organizations earlier noted were the cost and retail methods of inventory valuation.

The cost of merchandise sold section of the profit and loss statement would then be determined in the following manner:

Net Sales			$400,000
Cost of Merchandise Sold			
Opening Inventory		$220,000	
Purchases	$130,000		
Less: Purchase Returns	10,000		
Net Purchases	$120,000		
Transportation in	4,000	124,000	
Cost of Merchandise Available		$344,000	
Closing Inventory		104,000	240,000
Gross Margin			$160,000

OPERATING EXPENSES

The operating expenses of the retail store can be separated between those that are deemed to be fixed and those that fluctuate with sales volume or other operating incomes. They represent expenditures for services and supplies required for the operation of the business. Such expenses are normally divided into the following classifications for planning and control by the merchant: administrative, occupancy, buying, selling, and miscellaneous.

We noted earlier that the operating expenses are deducted from the gross margin dollars to determine the net operating profit available to the store for its merchandising activity during the period. The student should note that operating expenses account for a very significant portion of the store's gross margin, and consequently, management and control of these expense items play an important role in ensuring the profitability of the firm.

SUMMARY

The profit and loss statement of the retail organization tends to provide more information to the manager at the operating level of the firm than does the balance sheet. Consequently, buyers, department managers, and sales managers in retail operations tend to make much more extensive use of this financial statement. The operating manager's ability to contribute to the overall profitability of the firm and his or her performance level tends to be illustrated in the department's operating statement of profit and loss.

This section has been included simply to review the basic components of the store's operating statement because of their importance in the planning and control functions. We, obviously, have not set our objective to teach the details of accounting. To this end, we would ask the student to prepare an income and expense statement as outlined in the accompanying problem. This problem has been included to allow the student to review the basic concepts presented.

PROBLEM Determine the net profit for the Suedean Furniture Mart given the following information:

Gross Merchandise Sales	$500,000
Income from Repair Service	35,000
Expense for Operating Repair Service	40,000
Service Charges on Installment Sales, Received	350
Sales Returns	20,000
Sales Allowances	6,000

Inventory, Beginning of the Year	105,000
Inventory, End of the Year	120,000
Gross Merchandise Purchases	300,000
Cash Discounts Earned	6,000
Purchase Returns	4,000
Purchase Allowances	3,000
Transportation Charges in	7,000
Operating Expenses	75,000
Rents Received from Offices Above	7,200
Expenses for Offices Above	5,000
Interest on Government Bonds	1,000
Cumulative Quantity Discount Earned	6,000

appendix B

Arithmetic Review

Many of us have become so dependent upon the use of the electronic calculator that we have lost sight of the basic computations undertaken in addition, subtraction, division, and multiplication. Consequently, the following sets of problems are included as a means of reviewing the basic arithmetic calculations. Solve these problems without the assistance of your calculators to obtain the benefit anticipated in presenting this section.

CALCULATIONS WITH WHOLE NUMBER AND DECIMALS

1. Find the total for each of the following:

   (a) $1,250.68   (b)   6.0456   (c) 1.56 + 3.678 + 15.89 = _____
          306.46   .3956
          267.80   .2763   (d) 16.29 + 15.49 + 9.97 = _____
        1,450.91   1.4579
   +   8.95   .67   (e) 12.25 + 1.29 + .067 = _____
                         + 4.37858

2. Find the difference for each of the following:

   (a) $7,000.90   (b)   2.6798   (c) $295.95 minus $59.90 = _____
      -    645.50   -   .2365
                                        (d) $339.95 – $695.00   = _____

3. Multiply the following sets of numbers:

(a)   144
      ×$12

(b)   5,050
      ×1.267

(c) 35.3 × 12.75 = _____

(d) 30003 × 15.1 = _____

4. Determine the quotient by dividing the following:

(a) $24\overline{)120.12}$ (b) $7.5\overline{)1966.78}$ (c) $.019\overline{)369.90}$

5. Round off the following to the nearest dollar:

(a) $32,559.67 _____   (b) $19,999.89 _____   (c) $1,067.43 _____

6. Round off the following to the nearest whole number:

(a) 265 × 14.5 _____   (b) .176 × 5.76 _____   (c) 12.6 × 42 _____

7. Round off the following to the nearest tenth:

(a) 3,745.6758 _____   (b) 23,456.9090 _____

(c) 1.46372 _____   (d) 42.677 _____

CALCULATIONS WITH FRACTIONS

Answer the following questions in the space provided by performing the functions indicated by the signs:

8. 1/2 + 1/4 + 1/8   = _____

9. 1/3 + 1/9 + 1/12   = _____

10. 1/4 + 1/8 − 1/2 + 1 1/4 = _____

11. 1/6 × 1 1/3   = _____

12. 3/4 divided by 1 1/8   = _____

13. 21,000 divided by 3 1/2 = _____

14. 5/16 × 19.50   = _____

CALCULATIONS WITH PERCENTS, FRACTIONS, AND DECIMALS

15. Convert the following to both fractions and decimals from the percent given:

	Fraction	*Decimal*
(a) 25%	_____	_____

	Fraction	Decimal
(b) 42%	_____	_____
(c) 37.5%	_____	_____
(d) $33\frac{1}{3}$%	_____	_____
(e) 162.5%	_____	_____

16. Convert the following fractions and decimals to a percentage figure:

	Percent
(a) .625	_____
(b) .067	_____
(c) 1/6	_____
(d) 3/5	_____
(e) 1.467	_____

CALCULATING PERCENTS OF WHOLE NUMBERS

Answer the following questions in the space provided.

17. What percentage is $45.00 of $135.00?   _____

18. $895.00 is 42% of what dollar amount? (round to the
    nearest dollar)   _____

19. What is 37.5% of $240.00?   _____

20. If a ballplayer obtains 63 hits at 127 times at bat, what
    percentage is he hitting?   _____

21. Find 125% of $375.00.   _____

22. If hockey tickets increase from $10.00 each to $13.00 each,
    what is the percentage increase in price?   _____

23. Government statistics report that unemployment was reduced
    from 8.9% to 7.6%, what is the percentage decrease?   _____

24. If a retailer has reduced the price of a garment from $75.00 to
    $50.00, what percent reduction is this?   _____

25. The same retailer increased the price of an item by $320.00 or
    10% over last year's price, what did the merchant charge last
    year? What will this year's price be?   _____

26. If a merchant purchases an item at the manufacturer's price of $160.00 plus 12% federal sales tax, determine the retailer's total cost for the item.

_____

27. Divide 738.5 by $1.66\frac{2}{3}$.

_____

28. If the selling cost of a department is planned to be 12.6% of sales, how much need a salesperson being paid a weekly salary of $225.00 sell?

_____

29. A set of patio furniture originally retailed at $900.00 but was reduced to $730.00. What was the percentage by which the original retail price was reduced?

_____

30. This year a retail store achieved sales of $475,000 compared to a sales volume of $415,000 last year. What was the percentage increase in sales?

_____

31. A retail store offers its sales personnel a commission of 2.5% of sales over a weekly sales quota of $4,000. If a salesman sold $5,200 during the week, what compensation should he receive if his base salary is $250.00?

_____

32. If this year's sales are planned to decrease 8.5% over last year's sales of $145,000, what should the planned volume be?

_____

33. A fabric store has a bolt of all wool tweed that contains $46\frac{2}{3}$ yards of material. During the week, five sales were made as follows: $5\frac{1}{2}$ yards, $3\frac{1}{4}$ yards, $4\frac{3}{4}$ yards, $3\frac{1}{8}$ yards, and 6 yards. How much material was left on the bolt?

_____

34. If an employee for a retailer earns $5.15 per hour, works $7\frac{3}{4}$ hours per day, and works $5\frac{1}{2}$ days per week, what will be her weekly pay? If deductions from her pay total $63.45, what is her take home pay for the week?

_____

35. $62.50 is 25% of what amount?

_____

36. $16\frac{2}{3}$% is the equivalent of what fraction?

_____

37. If the rent expense for a merchant is 12% of net sales, and the annual rent paid is $30,000, what are the planned net sales?

_____

38. What percentage is 12 of $37\frac{1}{2}$?

_____

39. The sales tax on a new car is 7% of the selling price. A buyer has discovered that the sales tax on the car he wishes is $1,085. What is the selling price of the car?

_____

40. 4/10 + 19/20 - 5/6 + 1/3 + 8/3 - 1/2 =   ?

_____

41. If turkey is advertised at $1.29 per pound, and a bird is priced at $21.70, determine the weight of the turkey to the nearest tenth of a pound.

_____

42. If a car averages $30.00 for a tankful of gasoline that costs 42.3 cents per liter, determine the number of liters purchased on average.

_____

43. A retailer is offering a set of golf clubs reduced by 25% from the original selling price of $275.00. If the sales tax is 6%, determine what a customer must pay for this set including tax.

_____

44. If a hardware merchant sells electrical wire at 11 cents per foot and a customer requires 13.75 feet of this wire, determine the total price to be charged.

_____

45. If 4.67 gallons equals 1 liter of gasoline, and gasoline sells at 45 cents per liter, how much is gasoline selling per gallon?

_____

46. If a house sells for $135,000 and the land transfer tax is set at two-fifths of 1% on the first $45,000 and four-fifths of 1% on the balance, determine the amount of the transfer tax.

_____

47. A company has reduced its executive contingent by 20%. If the company had 125 executives at an average salary of $60,000, what would be the savings to the company of this reduction in employees?

_____

48. If a retail store sold the following items over the course of the day, determine the average sale that was experienced by the store: $15.60, $12.75, $29.95, $49.90, $110.00, $4.98, $69.75, $59.80, $156.90, $150.00.

_____

49. If a retail merchant is offered a deal from his supplier of 20 dozen caps at a cost of $1.80 each plus 10% federal sales tax, determine the price the retailer will be required to pay for this deal. If he is offered a 3% discount if he pays it in 10 days, what additional discount may he take?

_____

50. If a retail merchant has achieved a sales volume of $280,000 and shows a net profit of 4% of sales as a result of operating expenses of 32% of sales, determine the net profit and operating expenses in dollars.

_____

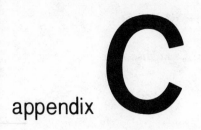

appendix C

Mathematical Formulas for Retailers

Average Stock $= \dfrac{\text{B.O.M.} + \text{E.O.M.}}{2}$ or   Reserve $+ \frac{1}{2}$ Reorder Period

Basic Stock $=$ Average Stock $-$ Average Monthly Sales

B.O.M. with Basic Stock $=$ Planned Sales for Month $+$ Basic Stock

B.O.M. with Percentage Variation $=$ Average Stock $\times \frac{1}{2}$ or $\left(1 + \dfrac{\text{Sales for Month}}{\text{Average Monthly Sales}}\right)$

B.O.M. with Stock Sales Ratio $=$ Planned Sales for Month $\times$ Stock-Sales Ratio for Month

Capital Turnover $= \dfrac{\text{Net Sales}}{\text{Average Inventory at Cost}}$

Gross Margin $= \dfrac{\text{Net Sales} - (\text{Gross Cost of Goods Sold}}{\;\;\; - \text{Cash Discount} + \text{Alteration Expense})}$

or $=$ Maintained Markup $+$ Cash Discount $-$ Alteration Expense

or $=$ Operating Expenses $+$ Net Profit

Initial Markup $= \dfrac{\text{Operating Expenses \% + Profit \% + Reductions \%}}{100\% + \text{Reductions \%}}$

or $= \dfrac{\$ \text{ Operating Expenses} + \$ \text{ Profit} + \$ \text{ Reductions} + \$ \text{ Alteration Expense} - \$ \text{ Cash Discount}}{\$ \text{ Net Sales} + \$ \text{ Reductions}}$

or $= \dfrac{\text{Maintained Markup} + \text{Reductions}}{\text{Net Sales} + \text{Reductions}}$

or $= \dfrac{\text{Gross Margin} + \text{Alteration Expenses} - \text{Cash Discounts} + \text{Reductions}}{\text{Net Sales} + \text{Reductions}}$

Lead Time $=$ Reorder Period $+$ Delivery Period

Maintained Markup	= Initial Markup (100% + Reductions) – Reductions
	or = Net Sales – Cost of Goods Sold
	or = Gross Margin + Alteration Expense – Cash Discount

Maintained Markup   = Initial Markup (100% + Reductions) – Reductions
                  or = Net Sales – Cost of Goods Sold
                  or = Gross Margin + Alteration Expense – Cash Discount

Markup $ = $ Retail – $ Cost

Markup % on Cost
$$= \frac{\$ \text{ Retail} - \$ \text{ Cost}}{\$ \text{ Cost}} \times 100\% = \frac{\$ \text{ Markup}}{\$ \text{ Cost}} \times 100\%$$

Markup % on Retail
$$= \frac{\$ \text{ Retail} - \$ \text{ Cost}}{\$ \text{ Retail}} \times 100\% = \frac{\$ \text{ Markup}}{\$ \text{ Retail}} \times 100\%$$

Maximum Stock = Reserve + Delivery Period + Reorder Period

Minimum Stock = Reserve + Delivery Period

Net Profit = Gross Margin – Operating Expenses

Open-to-Buy, Dollars = Planned Purchases – Merchandise On Order

Open-to-Buy, Units = Maximum Stock – (On Hand + On Order)

Planned Purchases = Merchandise Needed – Merchandise Available

Reductions
$$= \frac{\text{Initial Markup} - \text{Maintained Markup}}{1 - \text{Initial Markup}}$$

Stock Turnover, at Cost
$$= \frac{\text{Cost of Goods Sold}}{\text{Average Inventory at Cost}}$$

Stock Turnover, at Retail
$$= \frac{\text{Net Sales}}{\text{Average Inventory at Retail}}$$

Stock Turnover, in Units
$$= \frac{\text{Number of Units Sold}}{\text{Average Unit Stock}}$$

Stock-Sales Ratio, B.O.M.
$$= \frac{\text{B.O.M. Stock}}{\text{Planned Sales for the Month}}$$

Stock-Sales Ratio, E.O.M.
$$= \frac{\text{E.O.M. Stock}}{\text{Planned Sales for the Month}}$$

appendix D

Fractional Equivalents

The student will find a table of fractional equivalents on page 302. This table is designed to aid the student in computations dealing with percentages when such percentages can be quickly reduced to a fraction. Frequently, reducing the percentage to a fraction facilitates calculations. For example, it is much easier to deal with the fraction $\frac{2}{3}$ than it is to compute using the percentage of $66\frac{2}{3}\%$.

To determine the fractional equivalent of the percentage required, look down the columns labeled "Percent" and then move to the columns labeled "Fraction" for the fraction required. Percents and fractions not included in the table may be determined by reducing the percentage when expressed as the numerator over the denominator of 100%. Therefore, 35%, which is not included in the table, would be 35%/100% or $\frac{7}{20}$, as a fraction.

FRACTIONAL EQUIVALENTS TABLE

Percent	Fraction	Percent	Fraction	Percent	Fraction
$8\frac{1}{3}$	$\frac{1}{12}$	$36\frac{4}{11}$	$\frac{4}{11}$	70	$\frac{7}{10}$
$9\frac{1}{11}$	$\frac{1}{11}$	$37\frac{1}{2}$	$\frac{3}{8}$	$71\frac{3}{7}$	$\frac{5}{7}$
10	$\frac{1}{10}$	40	$\frac{2}{5}$	$72\frac{8}{11}$	$\frac{8}{11}$
$11\frac{1}{9}$	$\frac{1}{9}$	$41\frac{2}{3}$	$\frac{5}{12}$	75	$\frac{3}{4}$
$12\frac{1}{2}$	$\frac{1}{8}$	$42\frac{6}{7}$	$\frac{3}{7}$	$77\frac{7}{9}$	$\frac{7}{9}$
$14\frac{2}{7}$	$\frac{1}{7}$	$44\frac{4}{9}$	$\frac{4}{9}$	80	$\frac{4}{5}$
$16\frac{2}{3}$	$\frac{1}{6}$	$45\frac{5}{11}$	$\frac{5}{11}$	$81\frac{9}{11}$	$\frac{9}{11}$
$18\frac{2}{11}$	$\frac{2}{11}$	50	$\frac{1}{2}$	$83\frac{1}{3}$	$\frac{5}{6}$
20	$\frac{1}{5}$	$55\frac{5}{9}$	$\frac{5}{9}$	$85\frac{5}{7}$	$\frac{6}{7}$
$22\frac{2}{9}$	$\frac{2}{9}$	$57\frac{1}{7}$	$\frac{4}{7}$	$87\frac{1}{2}$	$\frac{7}{8}$
25	$\frac{1}{4}$	$58\frac{1}{3}$	$\frac{7}{12}$	$88\frac{8}{9}$	$\frac{8}{9}$
$27\frac{3}{11}$	$\frac{3}{11}$	60	$\frac{3}{5}$	90	$\frac{9}{10}$
$28\frac{4}{7}$	$\frac{2}{7}$	$62\frac{1}{2}$	$\frac{5}{8}$	$90\frac{10}{11}$	$\frac{10}{11}$
30	$\frac{3}{10}$	$63\frac{7}{11}$	$\frac{7}{11}$	$91\frac{2}{3}$	$\frac{11}{12}$
$33\frac{1}{3}$	$\frac{1}{3}$	$66\frac{2}{3}$	$\frac{2}{3}$	95	$\frac{19}{20}$

Answers to Problems

PART I—TERMS OF PURCHASE

CHAPTER 1—TRADE DISCOUNTS (pp. 3–11)

1. $50.00   2. $90.72   3. 46.8%   4. 50.4%   5. $1,448.79

Summary Problems

1. (a) $54.74 (b) 52.4%   2. $12.60   3. $1,500.00   4. (a) 47.6%   (b) 53.55%
5. $4,010.29   6. $2,592   7. (a) $241.92   (b) 49.6%   (c) 50.4%   8. $63.18
9. (a) 47.51%   (b) $629.88

CHAPTER 2—CASH DISCOUNTS AND DATING (pp. 13–22)

1. (a) If paid on or before January 25, pay $970.
   (b) If paid on or between January 26 and February 14, pay full amount $1,000, after which
        it can be subject to an interest charge.
2. (a) If paid on or before November 25, pay $485.
   (b) If paid on or between November 26 and December 15, pay full amount of $500, after
        which it can be subject to an interest charge.
3. (a) If paid on or before May 10, pay $2,646.
   (b) If paid on or between May 11 and May 30, pay full amount of $2,700, after which it can
        be subject to an interest charge.

4. (a) If paid on or before May 10, pay $1,455.
   (b) If paid on or between May 11 and May 30, pay full amount of $1,500, after which it could be subject to an interest charge.
5. (a) If paid on or before May 16, pay $582.
   (b) If paid on or between May 17 and June 5, pay the full amount of $600, after which it could be subject to an interest charge.
6. (a) If paid on or before September 21, pay $1,164.
   (b) If paid on or between September 22 and October 11, pay full amount of $1,200, after which it could be subject to an interest charge.
7. $481.14

Summary Problems

1. (a) If paid on or before May 31, pay $2,352.
   (b) If paid on or between June 1 and June 20, pay full amount of $2,400, after which it could be subject to an interest charge.
2. (a) If paid on or before July 16, pay $668.25.
   (b) If paid on or between July 17 and August 5, pay full amount of $675, after which it could be subject to an interest charge.
3. (a) If paid on or before November 10, pay $1,584.
   (b) If paid on or between November 11 and November 30, pay full amount of $1,600, after which it could be subject to an interest charge.
4. $1,653.68
5. (a) If paid on or before October 10, pay $2,254.
   (b) If paid on or between October 11 and October 30, pay full amount of $2,300, after which it could be subject to an interest charge.
6. $1,863.07   7. $2,675.82   8. $859.95

CHAPTER 3—SHIPPING TERMS   (pp. 23–32)

1. (a) Jenny's Fashions is payer and bearer of the charges of $79.90.
   (b) Highland Sportswear is owner and insured while in transit.
2. (a) Supplier is responsible for the freight charges of $68.
   (b) Retailer is responsible for filing the insurance claim for the loss.
3. (a) Retailer is responsible for the freight charges of $57.80.
   (b) Supplier is responsible for the insurance claim of loss.
4. (a) Frosty Luggage, Inc.
   (b) Frosty Luggage, Inc.
   (c) At point of origin of shipping
   (d) Rosemary Leather Goods, Inc.

Summary Problems

1. (a) Buying terms of 2/10, n/30 D.O.I.: 2% cash discount is allowed if invoice is paid within 10 days from the date of invoice and the net amount is due within 30 days from the date of invoice.
   (b) Shipping terms of F.O.B. origin, freight prepaid and charged back: the freight charges from Caistorville to Minden are to be paid by Spectrum Paints, Inc., but will be charged back to Jonathan Hardware. The retailer will have ownership and responsibility for insurance while in transit.

2. (a) Shipping terms imply Papp's Home Center will pay freight charges of $89.90 to the carrier and subsequently deduct this amount from the invoice from the supplier, Andrew's Building Supplies, Inc., which retains ownership and insurance responsibility while in transit.

   (b) The buyer terms indicate that a discount of 2% is allowed if the invoice is paid within 10 days from receipt of goods and the net amount is due within 30 days from the receipt of goods.

3. F.O.B. warehouse, freight prepaid.

4. (a) Samantha's Gifts will pay the transportation charges of $128 to the carrier and subsequently deduct this from the invoice amount with the supplier; Allison Gift Center is responsible for insurance and ownership in transit.

   (b) $1,988.80

REVIEW PROBLEMS

1. (a) If paid on or before May 10, pay $970.20.
   (b) If paid on or between May 11 and May 30, pay the full amount of $990, after which it could be subject to an interest charge.

2. (a) If paid on or before June 15, pay $869.12.
   (b) If paid on or between June 16 and July 5, pay full amount of $896, after which it could be subject to an interest charge.

3. $13,471.91

4. (a) $3,628.80   (b) 49.6%   (c) 50.4%
   (d) The supplier retains all responsibilities in shipping to destination.

5. $2,079.00

6. (a) If paid on or before January 10, pay $1,493.80.
   (b) If paid on or between January 11 and January 30, pay full amount of $1,540, after which it could be subject to an interest charge.

7. (a) If paid on or before May 8, pay $1,057.78.
   (b) If paid on or between May 9 and May 28, pay full amount less freight or $1,080.79, after which it could be subject to an interest charge.

8. (a) If paid on or before January 10, pay $415.55.
   (b) If paid on or between January 11 and January 30, pay full amount of $428.40, after which it could be subject to an interest charge.

9. (a) July 2, pay $980.00.
   (b) July 4, pay $980.00.
   (c) July 10, pay $980.00.
   (d) July 12, $967.92.

10. (a) July 4   (b) $4,539.60   (c) Retailer   (d) Supplier

11. Net price, $7,164.00
    (a) If paid on or before September 10, pay $7,020.72.
    (b) If paid on or between September 11 and September 30, pay the full amount of $7,164.00, after which it may be subject to an interest charge.

12. Net price, $971.02.
    (a) On July 10, pay $943.78.
    (b) On July 30, pay $948.99.

CHAPTER 4—CALCULATING INDIVIDUAL MARKUP   (pp. 35-50)

1. 43.75%   2. $10.00   3. $250.00   4. $165.00 $300.00   5. 71.4%
6. $75.63   7. $42.86   8. $37.50 $52.50   9. 60%   10. 31.03%

Summary Problems

1. $32.00   2. $81.8%   3. $40.00 $64.00 37.5%   4. $126.00
5. 69.2% 40.9%   6. $30.00 $48.00   7. $83\frac{1}{3}$% 45.45%   8. (a) 29.58%
(b) 60% (c) $54.00 (d) $6.75 $11.25 (e) $45.71   9. $2.89   10. $843.75
11. $27.20   12. 77.78% 43.75%   13. $11.60 $20.00   14. $22.06
15. $12.57

CHAPTER 5—CALCULATING AVERAGE MARKUP   (pp. 51-77)

1. 36.36%   2. 38.78%   3. 46.0%   4. 26.77%   5. $11,550 $21,000
6. $9,600 $16,000   7. 19 @ $7.00   6 @ $4.50   8. 24 dz @ $120   6 dz @ $96
9. 2 @ $7.25   3 @ $6.00   10. 28 dz @ $36   16 dz @ $25   11. $37\frac{1}{3}$%   12. 50%
13. 34.21%   14. 28.57%

Summary Problems

1. 200 @ $5.25   100 @ $7.50   2. 36.33%   3. $7,127.59 $13,448.28   4. 40%
5. 44.44%   6. 38.14%   7. $8,533.33 $13,333.33   8. 8 dz @ $29   12 dz @ $34
9. 28%   10. 36.67%   11. $32,662.50 $50,250.00   12. 133 @ $18   67 @ $24
13. 43.15%   14. 30 dz @ $11   5 dz @ $9.60   15. $9,280 $16,000   16. 27%
17. 2 @ 39%   1 @ 36%   18. 154 @ $13.60   206 @ $15.00   19. 36.59%
20. $9,360.00 $15,600.00   21. 38.41%   22. 5 dz @ $40   5 dz @ $60
23. $54,810 $94,500   24. 35.56%   25. $21,333.33 $33,333.33

CHAPTER 6—DETERMINATION OF MARKUP   (pp. 79-108)

1. 42.68%   2. 39.25%   3. 35.8%   4. 5.0%   5. $60,312.50   6. 27.2%
7. 8.0%   8. $24.24   9. 36.2% 37.7%   10. $5,240

Summary Problems

1. 38.89%   2. 10.91%   3. $65,980   4. 36.75%   5. 44.29%
6. 31.52% 32.52%   7. $7,672   8. $8.44   9. 10.17%   10. $9,504 4.32%
11. 43.27%   12. $18,066   13. 4.28%   14. $2,840   15. $90,000 $87,500
16. $5.24   17. $6,800 16.19%   18. $7.44   19. $28,020.50 23.35%
20. $5,421 4.17%   21. 39.29% 22. 41.41%   23. 36.78% 24. $2.62

REVIEW PROBLEMS

1. $16,312.50 $27,187.50   2. 69.77%   41.1%   3. 34.0%   4. 9.06%
5. 117 @ $26   63 @ $34   6. $91.93   7. 35.61%   31.13%   33.52%
8. $44,300   35.44%   9. 81.82% $263.64
10. $104,687.50   32.71% $100,687.50   31.46%   11. $7,816   12. 40.86%
13. 173 @ $108 dz   115 @ $126 dz   14. 38.44%   15. 7.6%   16. $17,240
17. $7,494   7.8%   18. 40.19%   19. $36,000 $60,000
20. 13 @ $1,250   23 @ $1,800   21. (a) 50 @ $65.90   100 @ $30.00
(b) 45.37%   40.0%   (c) 47.05%   22. 34.6%   36.6%   23. $28.61
24. 41.0%   33.8%   34.0%

PART III—INVENTORY VALUATION

CHAPTER 7—THE COST METHOD OF INVENTORY VALUATION (pp. 111-23)

1. $75,325   2. $138,420   3. $1,262.50   4. $1,055

Summary Problems

1. $37,282.70   2. $49,057.50   3. $1,666   4. $1,580   5. $41,714.80
6. $59,220

CHAPTER 8—THE RETAIL METHOD OF INVENTORY VALUATION (pp. 125-40)

1. $5,000   2. (a) $75,000   (b) ($3,000)   (c) $43,200   (d) $46,800   (e) $28,200
(f) $8,200   3. (a) $118,800   (b) ($3,800)   (c) $71,185   (d) $126,115   (e) $73,885
(f) $29,885   4. (a) $92,000   (b) $400   (c) $58,674   (d) $106,426   (e) $49,574
(f) $17,574

Summary Problems

1. $31,322   2. $48,300   3. (a) $46,000   (b) ($2,000)   (c) $29,348   (d) $61,752
(e) $28,748   (f) $6,748   4. (a) $97,500   (b) ($3,500)   (c) $51,982   (d) $133,118
(e) $91,882   (f) $25,882   5. $3,000 $13,600

REVIEW PROBLEMS

1. $9,512   2. $85,317.50   3. $40,040.00   4. (a) $52,500   (b) $30,651
(c) ($1,500)   (d) $82,249   (e) $37,751   31.5%   (f) $9,751   8.1%
5. (a) $71,000   (b) ($1,000)   (c) $45,504   (d) $37,496   (e) $22,904   37.9%
(f) ($8,096)   (13.4%)   6. (a) ($2,500)   (b) 84,685   33.9%   (c) $26,685   10.7%
7. $26,341.50   ($636.50)   8. (a) $1,737.50   (b) $1,740.00   9. $14,600
10. $156.00 $138.00

CHAPTER 9—PLANNING TURNOVER (pp. 143-61)

1. .5   2. 1.0   3. 3.88   4.08   4. $112,000   5. $80,000   6. $70,000
7. $16,666.67 $16\frac{2}{3}$%   8. $40,000   50%   9. 2.78   10. 2.46   11. 12.0
12. 3.9   13. 6.4   14. 5.1

Summary Problems

1. 3.43   2. $16\frac{2}{3}$%   3. 4.57   4.09   7.0   4. 20% $4,000   5. 5   6. 14.3%
7. 3.65   8. 8.0   9. .74   .748   10. 4.51   4.47   7.3   11. (a) $156,600
(b) $90,000   (c) $53,846.15   12. $25,600   15.4%   5.0   13. 12.5%   14. 1.9
15. .73   .74   1.14

CHAPTER 10—SALES PLANNING (pp. 163-78)

1. Dec., Jan.: +12%   2. Oct. $68,400   Nov. $79,200   Dec. $86,400   Jan. $36,000
3. $43,124.40   4. Mar. $27,297.90   Apr. $35,702.10   5. $164,160   +2.6%
6. 3.1%   7. +11.34%

Summary Problems

1. Oct. $96,800   Nov. $88,000   Dec. $105,600   Jan. $39,600   2. $35,616
3. Mar. $53,822.56   Apr. $39,457.44   4. +5.8%   5. +12.0%   6. +12.4%
7. $24,200   8. $34,875   9. Mar. $28,291.20   Apr. $38,908.80   10. $225,412
11. -2%   12. +15.8%   13. Oct. $96,000   Nov. $64,000   Dec. $48,000
Jan. $32,000   14. $42,187.50   15. Mar. $35,300   Apr. $70,400
16. Mar. $30,479.17   Apr. $33,105.60   17. +19.1%   18. +11.3%   19. +4.8%
20. $309,430

CHAPTER 11—STOCK PLANNING IN DOLLARS (pp. 179-206)

1. $111,000   2. $105,538.50   3. $122,772   4. $34,500   5. $74,210
6. $16,900   7. $37,537.50   8. B.O.M.:   2.5   4.0   2.33   1.75   1.6   3.0;
E.O.M.:   3.2   4.38   2.33   2.0   1.2   2.0   9. $54,000   10. $18,000
11. Nov. $100,000   Dec. $90,000   .42

Summary Problems

1. $143,076   2. $48,750   3. $24,000   4. $151,800   5. $64,000   6. $55,125
7. 156 dz   8. $38,920.35   9. $104,769.23   10. $131,923.08   11. $67,540
12. $64,687.50   13. $46,800   14. $20,592   15. $13,000   16. $49,000
17. $119,230   18. $45,500   19. 52 dz   20. $36,749   21. .32
22. B.O.M.:   3.75   3.4   1.68   2.0   1.4   2.5;
E.O.M.:   4.25   4.2   1.6   1.75   1.2   2.0   23. .364   24. $11,250

CHAPTER 12—PLANNING PURCHASES—THE MERCHANDISE PLAN (pp. 207-26)

Planned Purchases	Feb.	Mar.	April	May	June	July	Total
Retail	$75,600	$75,133	$55,000	$23,667	$1,800	$59,603	$290,803
Cost	45,360	45,080	33,000	14,200	1,080	35,762	174,482

Summary Problems

1. Initial Markup, 40.4%; Maintained Markup, 35.0%; Gross Margin, 36.0%

Planned Purchases	Aug.	Sept.	Oct.	Nov.	Dec.	Jan.	Total
Retail	$63,600	$143,600	$125,400	$45,400	$45,400	$82,600	$506,000
Cost	37,906	85,586	74,738	27,058	27,058	49,230	301,576

2. Initial Markup, 38.9%; Maintained Markup, 34.0%; Gross Margin, 34.0%

Planned Purchases	Aug.	Sept.	Oct.	Nov.	Dec.	Jan.	Total
Retail	$61,620	$81,900	$83,460	$83,460	$60,060	$63,960	$434,460
Cost	37,650	50,041	50,994	50,994	36,697	39,080	265,456

3. Initial Markup, 40%; Maintained Markup, 34%; Gross Margin, 35%

Planned Purchases	Feb.	Mar.	Apr.	May	June	July	Total
Retail	$48,675	$65,354	$60,021	$64,900	$22,579	$64,108	$325,637
Cost	29,205	39,212	36,013	38,940	13,547	38,465	195,382

4. Initial Markup, 43.2%; Maintained Markup, 37.0%; Gross Margin, 35.0%

Planned Purchases	Aug.	Sept.	Oct.	Nov.	Dec.	Jan.	Total
Retail	$51,948	$39,948	$93,342	$65,832	$39,948	$72,012	$363,120
Cost	29,506	22,690	53,069	37,393	22,690	40,903	206,251

CHAPTER 13—PLANNING OPEN-TO-BUY CONTROLS (pp. 227-44)

1. $17,750 $28,400   2. $8,280 $13,800   3. $30,000   4. 136   21.3
5. 52

Summary Problems

1. $10,140 $16,900   2. $500   3. 216   4. $15,100   5. $6,333 $9,500
6. 248   18.4   7. $8,533.33 $12,800   8. 32   19.3   9. $4,700 $7,520
10. 356   11. $4,744   12. $22,300   13. $25\frac{1}{2}$ dz (306)   14. 21 dz   15.6
15. 66   6.93

CHAPTER 14—PLANNING MODEL STOCKS (pp. 245-84)

1. Maximum stocks: cocktail, 56;   wine, 70;   sherbert, 42;   water, 84;   juice, 63
2. Model stock for opening the 6-month season: $20.00 regular pyjamas, 253 pairs; $30.00 regular pyjamas, 113 pairs

Summary Problems

1. Maximum stocks: Rondeau, 35;   Debutante, 25;   Beverly, 20;   Shangri-la, 40; Belvedere, 20;   Trillium, 30;   Blossom, 25;   Tiara, 15
2. Model stock for opening the 6-month season: $40.00 cardigans, 350 sweaters; $60.00 cardigans, 117 sweaters
3. Maximum stocks: small, 48;   medium, 72;   large, 72;   X-large, 36
4. Model stock for opening the 6-month season: $150.00 jackets—suede, 49, leather, 73; $250.00 coats—suede, 44, leather, 66

REVIEW PROBLEMS

1. $34,400   2. $44,262.40   3. $45,000   4. $271,920   5. $17,200   6. 120
7. $58,998.58   8. 3.2   9. $203,328   10. Mar. $34,366.20   Apr. $55,833.80
11. $63,093   12. Cost purchases: Aug. $27,026   Sept. $35,793   Oct. $36,451
Nov. $36,625   Dec. $26,387   Jan. $28,283   Total $190,565   13. 600   16.8
14. 4.0   6.67;   3.0   4.6   15. $40.00 loafers, 245 pairs; $60.00 loafers, 272 pairs
16. $9,062.50 $14,500.00   17. Oct. $65,000, 3.64   Nov. $70,500, 3.07
Dec. $79,500, 2.48   18. $57,600 $42,600   19. June $43,352.06   July $55,440.00
20. Maximum stocks: dinner knife, 144;   dinner fork, 144;   salad fork, 72;   teaspoon, 144; tablespoon, 72

APPENDIX A (pp. 287-92)

$124,550

APPENDIX B (pp. 293-97)

1. (a) 3,284.80   (b) 13.22398   (c) 21.128   (d) 41.75   (e) 13.607   2. (a) $6,355.40
(b) 2.4433   (c) $236.05   (d) - $355.05   3. (a) $1,728   (b) 6,398.35   (c) 450.075
(d) 453,045.3   4. (a) 5.005   (b) 262.237   (c) 19,468.421   5. (a) $32,560
(b) $20,000   (c) $1,067   6. (a) 3.843   (b) 1   (c) 529   7. (a) 3,745.7   (b) 23,457
(c) 1.5   (d) 42.7   8. $\frac{7}{8}$ 9. $\frac{19}{36}$ 10. $1\frac{1}{8}$ 11. $\frac{4}{18}$ 12. $\frac{2}{3}$ 13. 6.000
14. 6.09375   15. (a) $\frac{1}{4}$, .25   (b) $\frac{21}{50}$, .4   (c) $\frac{3}{8}$, .375   (d) $\frac{1}{3}$, .333   (e) $1\frac{5}{8}$, 1.625
16. (a) 62.5%   (b) 6.7%   (c) $16\frac{2}{3}$%   (d) 60%   (e) 146.7%   17. $33\frac{1}{3}$%
18. $2,130.952   19. $90   20. 49.6%   21. $468.75   22. 30%   23. 14.61%
24. $33\frac{1}{3}$%   25. $3,200, $3,520   26. $179.20   27. 443.01   28. $1,785.71

29. 18.89%   30. 14.46%   31. $280   32. $132,675   33. 24\frac{1}{24}$

34. $219.52, $156.07   35. $250   36. $\frac{1}{6}$ 37. $250,000   38. 32%

39. $15,500   40. $3\frac{1}{60}$ 41. 16.8 lb   42. 70.9 liters   43. $218.63   44. $1.51

45. $2.10   46. $900   47. $1,500,000   48. $65.96   49. $475.20, $14.26

50. $11,200, $89,600